Read This Please Volume Two

Editions 7 - 12

Edited by Sheila Cano and Donna Lewis

Contributing Writers: *Steven Bird, Sheila Cano, Jac, B G Lewis, Adrienne S Moody, Bruce Reisner, Casimirr Rexregys, Sarah Scott, M Dawn Thacker, Trularin, and Gaboo. Special thanks to Steve Bryson and Donna Lewis for their technical and organizational skills making this happen.*

Cover image by Sarah Scott.
Back cover image by M Dawn Thacker.

 sage press

Vancouver, Canada

Read This Please
Volume Two / 2012
Copyright © 2012 ReadThisPlease.com

Published by Sage Press, Vancouver, Canada

Read This Please Volume One / ReadThisPlease.com

ISBN: 978-0-9809201-8-5
Literary Collections/General. Format: Paperback book, text
Release: 20120701

Cover art: ReadThisPlease.com

Read This Please

Volume Two

Table of Contents

Volume 2 Edition 10 – Ticket To Ride 177

Read This Please

Volume 2 Edition 7 – All About the Love

February 14, 2011

Welcome to Read This Please Volume 2, the print version of our online periodical highlighting short stories, anecdotes and verse. Edition 7 is all about the love---shall we get a little intimate? Perhaps reveal some inner yearnings that pull us all toward bonding? For you, we've dipped this edition in invisible chocolate and draped it in sweet stuff for your reading pleasure---amore!

Chancing a Dance

by Sarah Scott

Decisions. Procrastinations. Transformations.

Life, a dance. Our thoughts, the music. Our choices the rhythm, our bodies move to it. We spin, twirl, pause, begin again. We dance. Some better than others, some standing still. We choose our dances, or perhaps they choose us.

Today I will dance in flounced skirt, silk blouse, with my hair done up, wearing oxfords. Spin me round, whisper in my ear. Sing me a song. My heart flutters, catches, hammers out a tune. My voice lifts, a melody to celestial skies. My eyes dart around the room, seeking a partner, link arm and arm, share life together.

Dance with me. Your feet in step with mine, sideways glances beckoning each other. Calling, closer together, distinct in ourselves, united in common theme. We dance. Your arms encircle me, guide me this way and that, my skirt floating on our breaths, extended in air, in motion, in time. Your heart beating against mine. We dance through joy. Sing through sorrow. Tomorrow we will dance some more, each day connected to the day before. An endless circle.

Dare to live the dance, to take the chances. Life is short, time fleeting. All we have in life is perpetual motion. Doors open to new doors, close to old ones. Walk through, move forward, begin again. Live. Breathe. Experience. Move. Dance. Dance in ballrooms, on staircases, in bedrooms, on air. Dance in hallways, in silence, in darkness, in pairs. Dance in sadness, each mournful song carrying body across emotion. Dance in joy, boisterous drum and guitar filling rooms. Dance solo or duet. Live the dance. Share a moment, connect with time, bond your heart with mine.

Dear Steven

by Steven Bird

Dear Steven,

I almost mistook your email for spam I'm on so many meds these days I can't see straight. And you're writing? Cool. You always were a big liar. Ha ha. I figured you'd eventually choose something that'd lead to poverty or suicide. But, as you know, I really am a sucker for storytellers. I lived up your way with Harold for awhile. Boyfriend. He was the best storyteller though. I would have followed him anywhere. He convinced me that Kila, a small town outside of Kalispell, was in the banana belt of Montana. There were no other women who weren't married. He stayed drunk all the time while I cooked on a wood stove with no electricity or running water. One day I decided to surprise him and run through the cabin in my garter belt and black stockings. Tiny little bra. I was coming down the steps and my stocking feet slipped on the stair. I grabbed the hot stovepipe in a panic, the only thing there to grab, and it came down on my leg causing serious second-degree burns. Harold thought I was being a wimp, but I was concerned about the water we had as the cows were pooping in it. I had to drive myself to the ER room and they wanted to hospitalize me but I didn't agree and took off back to the cabin, where Harold kept calling me a "city girl wimp". Good thing I had packed some vicodan in case something went wrong. He left me home the night that Spinks took Ali. I was livid that he didn't take me to town – leaving me five miles from the main road in a wilderness. When he came home, I was a little drunk, and I had the shotgun. I made him sleep in the teepee that night and I left the next day. He ended up living in Spokane with another woman. I don't miss his smelly socks all that much. But he sure

11

could tell a story. I loved the cabin, but I would have liked to have electricity and some music. He hooked up the car battery to a radio that played Michael Jackson nonstop. Not what I had in mind when I said I wanted music. It was a long time ago. I cut down a tree for the stove. He refused to gather wood for winter. I guess you could say the writing was on the wall.

Love Always, Elizabeth

Carnal Chevy

by Bruce Reisner

cans behind a wedding car
an Impala with a stern four banger
rust spread across the doors and chassis
black smoke out the exhaust pipe with smear of lipstick
they got it off a suicide's granny
the speed of their union roaring
gaseous flame from the heart-like carburetor
bumpers fit to clear a death-wish cow
valve action rising and falling like young huge breasts
three hundred eighty seven horses inside the randy groom
soon they will engage like the clutch
drive into one another with the same steel doom
steering wheel mounted shift being taken from park
jack boot down on the gas pedal
they speed to brutal love

Sound of Breaking Glass

by Adrienne S Moody

Tobias and Paige moved into the second level a year ago. They appeared to be in their 30's; he was a good looking man with deep blue eyes. She was petite with thick brown hair, always pulled back in a pony tail. They made an attractive couple. Shane and I were both very busy and rarely saw them, but we occasionally glimpsed into their lives.

Three Weeks Ago

"I was doing my laundry, Adrienne and I could hear them having sex like I was in the same room with them," Shane, my roommate, said to me while he ate his dinner and I was doing dishes.

"If only they knew, Shane. Next time you see Tobias, rib him about it," I laughed.

"Are you kidding? Have you seen the size of that guy?"

Shane noticed things like that. I guess being into the body building and personal training he had a sensitivity to it. Tobias must be close to six feet tall; Shane is powerfully built, but about the same height as me which is five feet seven inches.

Two Weeks Ago

"I left for work this morning at five and I saw Tobias sitting in the driver's seat of his SUV with the driver's door open, his arm and leg hanging out. He was passed out," Shane told me one evening last week; he demonstrated sitting on the kitchen chair.

"Somebody didn't quite make it home?"

"Yeah, no kidding. Somebody has a drinking problem."

"Aren't you glad those days are behind you, Shane?"

"I am."

One Week Ago

I was on the lower level where my washer and dryer are and as I was loading dirty clothes into the machine, I stopped suddenly. I could hear Paige sobbing. She became more agitated and the crying grew louder and then I heard Tobias laughing, a mocking sinister sound.

I turned the dial of the washer and started it. The sound of water filling the tub drowned her cries, but his laughter rose above. I climbed the stairs passing their open door and cleared my throat hoping to break up the fight.

The door slammed shut.

Last Night

"I couldn't sleep last night, Adrienne, so I got up at 2 am and slept outside on the swing. I nearly fell asleep and then I heard Tobias banging on the door downstairs. He was yelling, obviously drunk, 'let me in you bitch!'"

Four Months Ago

I remember hearing them for the first time. It was after a long weekend when they were arriving home after being away for three days. It was late at night. I was in bed with my window open.

I heard him say something to her in this soft, endearing voice. I couldn't make out all the words, but I heard him call her babe. She responded in a teasing voice and the sound of her laughter made me smile.

The Hogger

by N Ratched

I don't often consort with the patients; I am much better at monitoring, punishing, setting rules, and watchdogging that they are followed to the LETTER. But at the mention of trains, I slip into romance. I will share a bit of myself, your superior. This is a part of me you may not suspect is in my makeup. This story is about Lloyd.

Lloyd was a railway man. He was called 'The Hogger'. He is the main man engineering the train. I would never lift my skirt for anyone less than the main man. I was a babe in the woods so to speak. I just celebrated my 20th birthday when I saw Lloyd passing by me at the crossroads of Main and Bathurst. He raised his cute little engineering hat to me and winked. He had a cigarette in the corner of his narrow lips and when I giggled, his eyes twinkled and he pulled his cigarette into his mouth. I gasped at this dangerous trick. Just as he chugged slowly by, he opened his mouth and pushed the still lit cigarette out. At that precise moment, I knew I belonged to him.

I was engaged to Jon who was rising quickly in the ranks at our one and only banking institution. His family owned everything in our town. I was betrothed to him at the sensitive age of 16. They forced me into a medical examination to make sure I was pure. Of course I was. Or at least until I set my eyes on Lloyd. From that moment on, I knew my fate. Lloyd had my heart on the tracks.

The following day I could not stop myself from returning to that very same spot at exactly the same time. I knew trains were timely and I could count on seeing my new love again there. I dressed in all my finery, my favorite gingham dress with the lace trim and the

17

rose coloured bonnet with the silk ribbon and yes, a suitcase. I waited.

In the distance I could hear the train's whistle and my heart thumped in my chest and beads of sweat broke out on my powdered forehead. I stood on the tracks facing the mighty beast. I could tell as it approached, huffing and puffing, that Lloyd was slowing the engine down.

Prairie Storms and Crinolines

by Adrienne S Moody

I would have been around ten years old when I first saw my parents kissing. Sitting on the curb in front of our house I listened to Kathy Wilson, a girl who lived across the street, explain to me what crinolines can do to make a skirt look pretty. She lifted her red cotton skirt up enough to expose this crinkly fabric.

"It makes your skirt flare out," she explained. A few years older than I made her the experienced one, wiser than me to worldly, womanly ways, which included makeup, nylons held up with garters, and the opposite sex.

It was August and the temperature soared near the 90 degree mark. The prairies are reputed to have the -30 in the winter, but in the summer the heat scorched bare feet on the pavement. The sprinklers waved and furry fat bumblebees huddled over dandelions. I held my hand to my eyes shielding the sun so I could see my sophisticated friend strut and pirouette.

"Oh look!" she stopped suddenly and pointed towards my house.

I turned and could see my mother and father embraced and kissing in front of the living room window in plain view. I felt my face flush red hot with embarrassment. I looked down at my dirty bare feet to see a June bug bigger than the size of my big toe. It clicked its wings. I picked up a stick and stuck him down the middle with it.

"You're really gross, Adrienne. Boys are never going to like you if you don't grow up. Look at your knee! Why is it all red and puffed out like that?"

"I fell off my bike is why."

"And look at that bulge above your knees. Your legs are so muscular and boys hate that. You still do that track and field?"

"Yeah I do."

I loved to run cross-country and placed third in the provincials that spring.

"Don't you ever manicure your nails?"

I held my dirty hands in front of me. She had a point there. My nails were black from digging in the dirt earlier in the day. My best friend Colleen Clayton and I buried a dead gopher in the baseball field behind third base. We planned on using it for an initiation rite to our new secret club. Any ideas we had needed to have some disgusting deterrent to keep my younger sister out. She trailed behind us daily, with her pathetic desire to be part of our activities.

Prairie storms happen suddenly and with great force. While we discussed matters of growing up and my failures in becoming a young woman, dark, menacing thunderclouds appeared at the top of the hill, the entrance to our block. Dagger shaped lightening touched down, followed by ear-numbing thunder. I stood abruptly. I could hear the raindrops getting closer and closer. They hit the road as big as a golf balls. The musty smell of the earth rose and filled the air.

"Run!" Kathy ordered as she ran across the street, her fine clothing matted to her girlish frame.

I bolted into the house and slammed the screen door. My parents were at their usual stations, Mom at the stove stirring a pot and Dad sat in his recliner, newspaper in his hands. He peered at me over the top, cleared his throat, then resumed his reading. I stood at the open door and watched the storm and vowed to always, no matter what, remember that day.

The storm passed overheard leaving grumblings of thunder in the distance. As I passed by my parents' bedroom, I felt the urge to enter. The room smelled of lemon oil and traces of my mother's perfume, Chanel # 5. At her dressing table mirror, I examined my boyish frame. There weren't any curves yet to see. I inherited my mother's freckles which I hated, but at least I didn't have them on my arms as she did.

I picked up a lipstick and read the name, 'Candy Apple Red,' and opened my mouth into an 'O' like I saw her do so many times. I wasn't any good at colouring between the lines and I could see that painting my mouth would be a challenge too. I pressed my lips together; what I saw looking back at me appeared hideous.

About to wipe it off with the back of my hand, I felt someone watching. My Mother stared back at me in the mirror with a smile on her face. She stood in the doorway holding a dish in one hand and a red and white checked towel in the other. Our eyes held.

"Be a little girl as long as you can, Adrienne. Don't be in such a rush to grow up."

Pawn Shop Love

by M Dawn Thacker

We don't do "new." I'm not sure whether it's born in us or if it's leaned behavior, but we don't know how to go into a Big-Box store and buy something with dangle tags or peel off stickers. No unopened box with Styrofoam protected item for us. We're on a treasure hunt. Our cars, clothes, tools, and furniture are all second, third or fourth hand. Today we go in search of a chain saw at the pawn shop.

"The pawn shop?" I ask. Pawn shops sell used guitars, bongo drums, stereo systems, used wedding band sets and wicked looking knives in leather sheaths. Going to look for a chain saw in the pawn shop sounds to me like going to look for a set of gourmet pots and pans, or high thread count sheets in a hardware store---a wasted trip.

"I called the shop," Bruce says. "It's a used Stihl, five hundred dollars, worth a drive for a look."

"I might ride with you," I say. I haven't been to a pawn shop since we stopped at one on a whim coming back home from the beach.

"OK," Bruce says. "Ben's going. He said he'd drive." Ben's looking for a deal on some electronic gadget I'm sure. He has the buy-used gene too.

When we leave, it's sunny outside, but cold. I wish I had wrapped a scarf around my neck. All four of us squeeze into Ben's Explorer. At ten o'clock on a Saturday morning, Ryan is usually immersed in dreamland under a quilt, but he's in the back seat, leaned against the

22

car door, face covered to the nose by his hoodie. I'm not sure of his motivation, but know he has one.

Bruce is a no-nonsense shopper. He pulls his cap down, focuses his attention straight ahead, ignores all flashy bargain signs, and trudges to the item of interest. The rest of us browse.

I look into the glass jewelry case at the rows of engagement and wedding rings, sad symbols of lost love. Someone working in the shop has shined the tarnish off. The gold circles and diamonds sparkle. "Who would buy those, Mom?" Ryan asks, then lowers his voice an octave to simulate a man. "Come on Honey, let's go down to the pawn shop to buy some divorced couple's rings, see if we can make them work a second time around."

Farther down the case is an assortment of belt buckles. Two especially gaudy ones are six inches across and four inches tall, proclaiming "ELVIS" in silver letters. "You know, it was Elvis' birthday last month," Ben says, always a font of historical facts and trivia. "Maybe we should buy them to wear in tribute."

Both boys walk around looking at bicycles, scooters, a motorcycle that Ben swears he could resell for four thousand dollars at school. Everything wears price tags higher than we are willing to pay.

Ryan wanders off to a case in the back of the store. There's a young man next to him in a wheelchair. The two of them are surveying the contents of the case. They are pointing and talking. Ben and I wander over to Bruce as he barters for the chainsaw.

"It doesn't even have a chain break," Bruce says.

"A chainsaw just like this one's selling on eBay for four hundred-fifty dollars, with three days to go," the salesman says.

"When I left home, it was listed for four-thirty, and it has a chain break," Bruce says.

"You can buy a chain break," the salesman says.

"Yeah, but that adds another fifty dollars to the cost."

"Let me go check my books," the salesman says, slipping around us and heading to the back of the store.

Bruce looks at me and shakes his head. "It's older than I want and doesn't have a chain break."

The man returns. "I can't go lower than four seventy-five."

"Thanks for your time," Bruce says shaking the man's hand.

"Here let me give you my card in case you change your mind," the man offers.

"Thanks," Bruce says putting the man's number in his pocket. Ben and I follow him out the door.

Halfway down the block, Bruce turns around. "Where's Ryan?"

"I thought he was behind us," I say.

"I'll go back and get him," Ben says.

Bruce and I stand together, huddled, backs to the cold wind and wait for the boys. "I've decided I don't like pawn shops," I say.

"Why? I've found some good deals in pawn shops over the years," he says.

"It's sad," I say. "people taking their belongings into the place to trade for some small amount of money." I look down at my wedding and engagement rings.

"You know, a long time ago, I got those..." he starts.

Our attention is drawn to the the boys as they hurry toward us. Ryan is waving a bag. "Hey look what I got," he says, pulling a video game from the bag. "Half the price you pay at Best Buy."

"You got what at the pawn shop years ago?" I ask Bruce.

"Never mind," he says, putting his arm around me as we walk to the car.

Disheveled

by M Dawn Thacker

My kid got dumped today. When my cousin called to tell me that Ben was listed as "single" on Facebook, I felt like I did when the bully in Kindergarten called my child a 'retard'. I clenched my fists and teeth. Immediately, I wanted to cradle his six foot, six inch frame in my lap and croon to him. His heart is too big and kind to be broken by a four foot, eleven inch, red haired girl.

I called him to make sure he was alright. He answered the phone on the eighth ring. His sluggish voice said, "Hello."

"Hey, whatcha up to?"

"Um, sleeping, what's up?"

"Just calling to check on you, make sure you're alright."

"I'm good Mom…darn, I've got to get up, got class in 20 minutes."

"Becky called and told me you're single."

"Yeah, I'll call you later."

"Are you sure you're alright?"

"I'm fine, really," he said with a sigh, like he wished I'd found out later. " I'll call you after class and we'll talk, OK?."

"Sure Baby, I love you."

"Love you too, Mom."

He sounded OK, disheveled, with his hair sticking up and his arm over his eyes kind of OK, but OK. I felt better having talked to him.

My mother called me at work. It was three o'clock.

"Hello."

"Hi Sweetheart, are you OK?"

"Yeah Mama, I'm fine, how are you?"

"Oh I'm alright, just talked to Becky and heard about Ben. Have you talked to him? Is he OK?"

"Yeah, I talked to him. He's OK. He said he'd call later after class."

"How are you doing?"

"I'm alright, just feel bad for him and mad at her. Wish he was home. Wish she was in Kalamazoo."

"I know, I remember wanting to strangle a boy one time when you were about sixteen."

We laugh, remembering. "Thanks Mama, I love you."

"Love you too baby. It'll be alright. He'll be fine."

"I know. I'll give you a call when I hear from him."

"OK, tell him I love him."

"I will."

The Kiss

by Jac

Almost every culture has a form of celebration, commemorating love and affection between intimate companions. Many are far older than any Christian martyrs.

To be honest, I have always been a follower of "antivalentinism". I didn't know that word existed until two minutes ago, but the criticisms listed on Wikipedia that refer to the word, are also my objections.

Like most inherently decent traditions, consumerism has gotten hold of it and turned it into a way for someone to make a profit.

We shouldn't need a day to remind us of our loves or to exclaim to the rest of humanity that we do love.

Simpler days of cakes and cookies decorated with home-made pink frosting, crayons and construction paper decorated with joy, are what I yearn for.

That is, if we have to share any materialistic thing with our intimate companions.

Thoughts and actions do a far better job of expressing how we feel…

The Kiss

light touch on my arm and shoulder
warm bright smiling face
sensation glides to my neck
then shivers under my ear
fingers combed through my roots
tenderly supporting my head
eyes held for moments
please never end
faces move closer
"I love you" echoes inside me
our lips touch

- *Jac*

Love Is

by Gaboo

Love is the joy of like.

Death By Choking

by Adrienne S Moody

Divorce was unheard of when I was growing up. The parents stuck it out regardless of how ill-suited they were, regardless of insults flung at each other or the deafening silence at dinnertime. Parents stayed together. In the small town I grew up in large families were the norm. I thought it was like that, well, everywhere, but I've come to know now that it isn't so. The majority of the population was Catholic and the nationality was French. Add to the fact that during this time the Pope forbade birth-control and families of six plus became commonplace. On our block alone there were 100 children; I know that because my brother announced it at dinner one night.

There was never a lack of something to do after dinner, before the street lights flickered on. Baseball, football, hide-and-go-seek were played daily until one by one we'd be called in. Domestic violence was evident on our block. Across from our place, at the Martel house, home to eight children and an alcoholic father, we knew she, the mother, was a victim of it. She didn't bother covering up her black eyes and one morning we stood out on the road looking up at their broken bedroom window.

"My mom and dad got into it last night," Kelly, the eldest offspring announced to us. "My dad said this morning that mom has to pay for the window because it was her head that broke it."

So when it was rumoured that Karen Hebert's parents were divorcing, it was shocking news to us. We were in the seventh grade when this happened and it caused a stir. She suddenly looked different to me. Karen was a cheerleader and in the yearbook, there was a photograph of her with her mouth wide open and her arms straight up revealing sweat marks. In grade seven that was difficult to live down.

She was double-jointed and would demonstrate how she could move her legs in such a way that her knee caps would be flush with her thighs. She spoke with a slight lisp and her nose needed constant wiping. She looked different to me after this news circulated. Something in her eyes, like she would stare into mine a little longer than what felt comfortable.

She was quite popular with the cheerleading crowd, but after this news you could see her standing alone, between cheers, with those pom-poms on either side of her, eyes down and looking out of place with the other bouncing young girls.

And then the news that her mother died spread like a cold virus. I heard it from Cathy Tourneur and I immediately searched for Karen at lunch. She wasn't to be found. Authorities said that she died eating a doughnut at the local coffee shop. Apparently, she choked on a piece of it and died right there, head down on the table.

In the school washroom Leonie Moreau, the girl everyone admired, the one for whom all the boys tripped over their own feet to get her attention, stated with authority, as she backcombed her impossibly cute, curly, black hair, "It's obvious she died of a broken heart."

I believed that. Maybe she didn't chew that piece of doughnut on purpose and let it lodge in her throat. Maybe she was choking back tears as it was heading down and it stuck there.

I remember thinking that having a parent die was probably the worst thing that could ever happen, especially a mom, who looks after everything for you. She's the one who forgives you even if you've done something unforgivable. She has the lap to climb onto and the arms to hold you when you think your world is unbearable.

A couple days after this tragic news, Karen showed up on our street just before the streetlights flickered on. She didn't live on our block and she was a long ways from home. She wasn't dressed with a sweater or a jacket like we all were. Her eyes darted around like she was looking for something. I avoided her; I felt afraid of her, like she had something contagious.

The Mating Game

by Sheila Cano

A Short Discourse on Variations in the Animal Kingdom

The lioness is a hunter who lives for the thrill of the chase. Expert at out-maneuvering her prey, she will often feign vulnerability in order to lure her potential mate. Nothing strokes the manly lion ego more than a submissive female. However, lions beware, this huntress has all the angles covered. She will hide in the tall grass until a prospect comes along, then leap out and playfully pounce upon him.

Once engaged in the game, each one takes a turn chasing the other until they are out of breath and have to lay down awhile in the shade. The lioness waits impatiently for the male to get up. If he languishes too long under the tree, she will poke him to get his attention. If he ignores her, she will prowl around him, looking for an opening to tug at his tail or nip his ear. Should this fail, the lioness grows bored and peevish. At this point she is likely to emit a warning growl, just before sinking her fangs into his nape. If he is smaller than she is, she will take him by the scruff of the neck and give him a good shake. When she lets go, nine times out of ten the humiliated lion will streak away, putting as much distance as possible between him and the Queen of Beasts. She quickly regroups and goes off into the tall grass to look for another feckless feline.

By contrast, the female bear has little to do with the male except during mating season. She prefers to lounge on the mountainside, nibbling blueberries and the occasional squirrel. In the fall, the aroma of rotting flesh entices her to the riverbank for an easy meal of spawning salmon. It is during this time that her usual indifference to the male falters, and if one should approach, she might entertain a liaison for a few days. To the observer, these encounters may appear more akin to rough play than romance. A lot of rolling and tumbling and occasional thumping and huffing accompanies the bear mating rituals.

Once she has had enough, the she-bear will turn on her mate, baring her fangs, and snarl loudly to snap him out of his sensual trance. If he doesn't heed this cue, she will lunge and swat the daylights out of his furry head. A bear who is well-seasoned at the game will take the hint and get the hell out of there. The she-bear then retires to her den, pushing a big boulder towards the entrance to seal herself off for the winter. Somewhere during the long night of hibernation, she gives birth to a couple of little handfuls of squirming nakedness which will grow into terminally cute cubs. In the spring they will venture outside the den to find roots and shoots, to cavort until the berries are ripe once more. Should a male come anywhere near this happy little family, she will box his ears so he won't forget his manners, until they meet again in the fall.

Dirty Feet & The Moaning If Onlys

by Gaboo & B G Lewis

Well, when I get asked to sing a ditty, most likely people are less interested in what's goin' on stage than what's goin' on sittin' next to them. But isn't that the way? Band's always just decoration on the evening. The real hoopla's catchin' fire somewhere in a booth, or at a table, or on the floor, somewhere between that first giggle and a heartbreak—isn't that where all the good Westerns start? Someone does someone wrong, with no cards to play, and then it's… hit the high prairie in search a what yer made of. Most of my thumb waggin's been in search of company—a lonely road—with little more to do than kick gravel and pick flatbed slivers outta my backside. Here's just one a those songs…

//Slow strum…
Been up and down
From town to town
Never made much sense
This old guitar
Has served me well
Held me up when I had no friends
//1,2,3,4 drums…
Now here I stand
A suitcase in my hand
Wanna find you, wanna hold you
Wanna help you understand
//Pause
That– I– will
//Big beat chorus…
Try a little harder

Run a little farther
Call a little louder
Into the wind
//Bring it down low now...
The smile on the face
On picture in my wallet
Holds a place
That is dear
To my heart
//gasp
If given half a chance
I would dedicate this dance
And sing a song
That ends
With a brand, new start
So– I–
//Kick it...
Try a little harder
Run a little farther
Call a little louder
Into the wind
I will search a little deeper
All through the night
I will find my way
And lie down
By your side

//Slide guitar, repeat chorus, big wind up, tada!

//1,2,3,4—double time...
Hey, Hey, Momma git you head outta bed
See what's goin' in our front yard
Hey brutha Bill, get yer specs of the sill
See what's goin' in our front yard

Neighbor, Neighbor, do me a favor
Take a picture of my front yard
There's a circus goin by
And writin' in the sky
And a love who won my heart
//Roll out the big sound, light it up!
How did I know?
You'd be the one
Ta turn my head around!
How did I know?
You'd be the one
Ta turn my head around!
//Train's movin' now—fast shuffle…
Well, well, this is how we like to travel… gettin' up past fiffy-five.
Put some two step inta those ponies!
//Big back beat rumble comin' off the drums…

Lemme tell ya bout my baby
She got feathas in er hair
And lotsa leatha patches
On the Lee-vize that she wears
She go runnin' thru the forest
she go runnin' thru the town
tho many men have tried
not one has tied her down
Dirty Feet—
My sweet—Princess
(Now ya know)
Her daddy waz the sheriff
Ya know he'd raise her right
Taught her how ta stand her ground
Taught her how ta fight
Taught her how ta teach a man
Who didn't treat her right

Ta dread the day he did her wrong
And wish he died that night
Dirty Feet—
Gotta treat her—Right!
Now I seen her little footprints
Lying in the sand
Out among the waves
Where the water kisses land—
Tracked her in the winter
Just as far as I could go
But no man or beast can catch her
When she's barefoot in the snow
Dirty Feet—
Where did you—go?
//Double the speed, double the fun—floor it! Hey, an give us a once
around! Twang out that solo…
(On– the–)
Day she said we'd marry
Caught her readin' magazines
She combed out her feathers
And she peeled off her jeans
Her long legs and stockin's
Left me sweatin' where I stood
I swear I fell down cryin'
Cause my Dirty Feet looked good!
Dirty Feet—
You look so—good!
Well, now I sit an worry
Waitin' thru the night
My Dirty Feet go runnin'
Til the mornin' light—
I know my baby's love is true
But how can I be sure?
When those dirty feet come back to me

A little dirtier than before
Dirty Feet—
I love you—more
//Now the band…
Dirty Feet—
We love you—more and more!
//Solo that puppy one more time!
//Big wind up, bim bam boom, kadashabash,
skirrrrrrrittttllllllllleDeee BA! Bwaangggggg

And that's a set, everybody. Go check on your pony, get all lovee
duvee with your someone special, an we'll see ya'll back here ta test
the gas gauge on yer dancin' boots!
//Big beat splash! Then the harmonica—wawa waaaaaaaa

Memories of First Love

A Collaborative

Ever challenging, Adrienne S Moody has coaxed Gaboo and M Dawn to recreate scenes of curious trepidation, to remember a time of purity when love was a glance, or just hanging out, or the act of holding hands. They agreed and submitted stories of embarrassment and heart palpitation. Journey with us through memories of first love… and teenage angst.

Lovely Lorelei by Gaboo

I could write about Lorelei, lovely Lorelei, aah the beaus all lined up for Lorelei . She was pretty, thick brown curly hair, lithe, smart, she was an advocate in class, a free thinker. The crew scrutinized, despite her formal elocution and high class upbringing (daddy owned a drug factory and they lived in one of the uppity hillside mansions.) I hadn't really noticed her until everyone else had. Lorelei this, Lorelei that, they all were talking about Lorelei. So I started watching her. She was soft to look at and independent. She sat at the front of the class and wanted to answer questions. Not because she was a suck, but because she didn't care what anyone thought and dove into debate. She was hard to handle and couldn't be pegged. Neither nerd nor jock, she was cool, funky Lorelei.

So the big school ski trip came up. We all boarded the bus and left to a day of snow frolic. Lorelei was up at the front of the bus with her posse of girlfriends and the boys hung back. They were jousting among each other to see who would win the right to go up the chairlift with Lorelei. (She was looking pretty fine in her powder

42

blue powder suit, too!) Well, I didn't get the fuss. Call me naive, but I walked up and sat behind Lorelei and Paulette Caldern, joked for a few minutes and then asked her point blank if she wanted to ski with me—a few runs down the hill. She said yes. I returned to the back of the bus for my beating.

After the rental outfitters, we all trooped to the bunny hill and did a few runs. Lorelei, the preening brunette bombshell was a disaster. It took her 40 minutes to travel the length of a football field. She broke down, cried, swore, and looked like a total feeb. Despite her reputation as a catch around school, she lost it all on the ski hill. She sucked.

Whatever, I waited. See, I was smart. I had it all planned out. For a month prior, in the early rock season, I had talked my aunt into taking skiing lessons with me. She drove to the hill and I blew the paper route cash and learned the basics with a crazed group of seniors who wanted to learn the fine art of break neck boards on the guppy hill. They did not slow me down and I forced myself to learn parallel, skidding stops, and primary bump jumping without tumbling. Was I unfairly prepared in the game of love---or adaptive? While the competition was hurtling down the hill, like first timers do, I was perched effortlessly on my skis and facing the nubile Lorelei lying helpless in the snow. yaha.

So we got her confidence up and coaxed her on to the chairlift, me and the patient pro shop crew. On board, her fear of heights kicked in. She grimaced, looked ill, and clung to me like a grimacing, ill, schoolgirl. I feared for my own personal safety. Arriving at the top, the lower side chair lift operator had telephoned up to the top operator and advised him to slow down the lift when the spasmodic pedestrian in the powder blue bunny suit made it to the crest. This was highly embarrassing, as was her dismount and backslide into low firs that line the off ramp. I suggested we try the 'Granny Run' round the mountain's gentler slope. After ten minutes of moderately

43

controlled sliding, we ended off a side trail and plunked into a snow drift in the bent pines. We could see the hill sprawl ahead of us and watched the other students bop and bumble below. There was nothing to talk about. We didn't know each other. The anti-climax of the death defying chairlift ride kicked in. She didn't like skiing much, but we did have a good laugh. So we looked at each other, puffing and red cheeked in the crisp air of the alpine, and it just seemed obvious—we were both there to neck. So we did.

It was great. We practiced all sorts of face plant maneuvers, whispered passions to each other, pledged our boyfriend/girlfriendness, and then slowly peeled ourselves off, all sweaty ripstop nylon hormones. I refused to stand immediately because I discovered that much front end facial activity had a direct effect on the elongation of specific otherwise unnoticed recreational equipment. This dilemma seemed embarrassing at the time and I made excuses and adjustments while she called to finish our run. We had kissed. I felt elated and became spelled by Lorelei.

The next week we were an item: cooing and gooing at breaks during school; hand holding from the front door to her daddy's limo. I was even invited for dinner at the mansion. They were polite but unmemorable. I realized that going steady with Lorelei was boring.

The next week I dumped her. No explanation, no excuses. There was a party on or something and I just said I'd rather play football with friends than get involved seriously with someone. We split. Now I feel a little bad; I should have been more forward, more professionally prepared, maybe offered a reasonable let down. Heck, I was in grade seven. She was one great kisser, though, Lorelei. Wow!

Backseat Strike Out by Adrienne S Moody

Arlene and I were best friends throughout Junior and High School. I thought my family was chaotic until I met hers. Her mother was a nervous woman who chain-smoked cigarettes and sold Avon. Always there would be little paper bags with Avon products in them and she'd be looking seriously at her order forms and all business-like when we'd plunk our books down on the table after school. The crazy stuff would happen when she was out giving demonstrations or dropping off orders to the ladies in town. Mostly it was her brother Bobby who did nutso things like one time Arlene and I were working on English homework and there he'd be dragging this carcass of a dead animal into the front room. She had a sister Ruthie and these two kids were always drooling and had dirty faces. Their beds were never made and explosions of garbage, dishes, newspapers and clothes cluttered up the place. To add to all this disorder they bred St. Bernards. Whenever Arlene got into a fight with her dad, which was often, she'd let one of them in her basement bedroom window.

But this story isn't about Arlene, it's about Lyle, a boy a year older than me whom I noticed the first day of High School. Arlene and I were smoking out on the front steps of school, where all of us congregated during breaks and lunch and his hands caught my eye first. They were strong hands with a ring on the third finger. I discovered through Arlene's friend Bob that he lived on a farm a few miles out of town. I found myself circling the hallways at school trying to figure out where his locker was so I could make myself visible to him.

As it turned out Bob became friends with Lyle and through Bob then to Arlene I learned that Lyle wanted to go out with me. We decided to double-date. The night of the big event I went to Arlene's where the boys were going to pick us up. We spent two hours getting ready. Arlene always fretted over whether she had a booger showing. And then constantly checking the mirror complaining she looked fat. Fact was she was beautiful, with her almond shaped brown eyes, elegant nose and rose coloured lips. She had black shiny hair and when she wore makeup she really was stunning and she never ever felt that she was.

That date didn't work out. We waited for hours and I finally went home feeling terribly upset not knowing why they didn't show. The next day at school Bob found us outside smoking and told us the news. Lyle was grounded because he forgot to put the heater in the chicken coop and killed all the chickens. We didn't get a chance to go on a date for two weeks later.

Our dates followed the same pattern for the two months that Lyle and I saw each other. Bob and Arlene would sit in the front seat and Lyle and me in the back. We'd pick up a case of beer and drive out into the country where we'd pull over and drink. Then we'd neck and steam up the windows. For Christmas Lyle gave me a ring and asked to go steady with me. I was thrilled at the sight of that Black Alaskan gold ring. It fit perfectly.

I always thought up until that age that romance and boys and love was something transcending. I figured that everything in life would make sense once I found true love. I longed for that feeling of belonging to someone and feeling loved and accepted. It wasn't long after we started going steady that our passion in the backseat of Bob's car felt so disappointing. Lyle tried second and third base and the night that happened, I remember bursting into tears. He was bewildered by my reaction and the night ended abruptly.

Bob told Arlene and Arlene told me that Lyle thought I was a child crying just cause a guy tried to put his hand down my pants. I gave his ring back. He didn't understand and nor did I at the time, it was just the disappointment of it all.

Love on the Run by Gaboo

Theresa. A doe and a waif. Striking features, beautiful, and probably weighed ninety pounds. I met her when an acquaintance introduced us. But we kids were faking. It was a small town. Theresa and I already had a secret. We had met fatefully the spring before.

Me and and Marshall were touring in a 65′ Simco, ancient, but free. The car was so ugly most other guys opted to walk, but we were not daunted by pride and took a run at the freeway to cruise the roller rink and find some girls who wanted to party at Chucks. We never made it to the roller rink. On the drive up the service road, we chanced upon two girls hoofing it...

"Hey, do you wanna go to a party at Chuck's, you know him?"

"Sure."

Bonus. We pull over, get out, and three point turn the car by hand (there was no reverse), our dates graciously boarded, and off we sped to the mesa where Chuck's would be the rage.

Marshall, in moments of arriving, was pairing with new girl Terri. Very quickly, they barricaded in a downstairs bedroom and began bouncing on something with springs. Even Chuck paused the music so those gathered could listen to the all star wrestling on the other side of the wall. In ten minutes that seemed longer, the love birds emerged, smiles, with weird disconnected looks. I no longer knew my friend.

Theresa was not impressed. She wandered off and I found her pouting under a veranda. I tried talking, but she was not at all interested in being with another human, let alone a guy. I could empathize, her friend did just abandon her for a cirque de la lune performance that now had the party house all chirping. Eventually, I

47

gave up. Polite chatter was bombing. I asked what was wrong. Oops.

The faucet opened and the torrent flowed. She was a run-away, she was broke, she just got thrown out by her boyfriend, who she loved, who beat her, who she loved, and her parents were mad, and her brother was mad, and she loved her boyfriend, and they had plans. Oh jeeesh. Oh yeah, I got played.

Maybe it was a boring portion of my life. When I reflect, I really had no one in my world that was living vitally. Everybody was humdrum. Nobody had plans. But Theresa had something better than plans, she had desperation. That was thrilling.

That night we talked. Talked and talked and talked. She told me all about her life and her struggles, and I drank it up, the nectar of street intoxication. She batted tear soaked big eyes, and I kept the diner coffee flowing. She was fascinating, a wild sprite on the run. I wanted to help her, but I also wanted to impress myself by helping. I wanted to be the knight.

For that forty-eight hours in late May we lived a married life together, me trying to pen her in, and her trying to break free. She curled up on my shoulder a few times, to nod off, or feel secure. She smelled tinkly and perfumey, and frail. She was a kid, sixteen—I was a man of seventeen. In the late afternoon on the Sunday, I convinced her of an option, she would leave her boyfriend, and return to her parents. It was logical, it was resolvable. I was right. And with her safely tucked away at her parents, I could continue to culture my pygmalion filly. That night I arranged the meeting by phone. Her family would be in attendance for an intervention. Theresa agreed to participate willingly. I would mediate.

When we showed up, her parents were genuine and scared. Theresa was adopted, both she and her brother. I was sure I recognized him.

48

He was well mannered, concerned and wanted Theresa to come clean. The parents were of a distinctly different heritage. They were perfunctory and academic. I got the impression that dear brother was their favorite, or at least they used him as a glowing example. Theresa and her brother were fostered away from abusive birth parents by the government. Theresa had been in and out of group homes for lack of control. She skipped school, stayed away for days, and was obsessed with her boyfriend. He treated her like dirt. Her parents couldn't compete. We all talked. Then in turn, each of her parents and her brother professed their undying love for Theresa, no matter her choice. She was forever welcome home, but she had to abide house rules, go to school, don't smoke in the house, be home by ten, no swearing, and take a break from boyfriend. Theresa released in tears, hugging her mom and dad, apologizing and admitting that she did want to try. It seemed to work. I returned to my borrowed car and brought up Theresa's meager luggage. She stayed.

Two days later, I was dumping texts in my locker at school when six of the shaver airheads from the football team circle around me. Great. Now I remember where I knew her brother from. He was a jock. All star, all ego, first string. Doubtful they would hassle me, I was a crazy musician, a party-er, with an ongoing detention record for upholding justice, but having the team neanderthals puffing around all serious in a semi circle was a little intimidating. Then Theresa's brother, supro-jock, asked me aside and shoo'd off the bruisers.

He suddenly pledged his gratitude for my efforts. Apparently, this had been a ray of light. They were going to try. He also swore that if I ever needed anything, some backup, don't hesitate. I accepted his business card to my mental folder. Good to know.

Epilogue: Theresa continued in and out of trouble and on and off with her boyfriend. Like how this story started, when Carol, the alcoholic roommate holed up in the ten by twenty trailer flagged me down because Theresa was getting thrown around by her boyfriend again. What a revolving situation. Theresa seemed to like it on the edge. Now I understand that maybe with her older brother and her family so good, Theresa tried to be just as bad.

Obituary to Love by Adrienne S Moody

I remember his laugh. I remember how easy it was to make him laugh. Whenever he was around me, at lunchtime, breaks, before and after classes in High School, I suddenly turned comedian. I could always count on Mitch for that. Although he was a year older than me, he ended up in the same Creative Writing class as me. He sat in the first row by the door, halfway down. I sat by the window row right across from him. When there were projects to do together, like that newspaper we created, we liked being on the same team.

We eventually had to write short stories and he ran his plot idea by me:

"Hey, Adrienne, what do you think of this idea I had last night? These two brothers are involved in this war and they are on opposing sides and they encounter each other at enemy line and one of them has a gun pointed at the other and he has to decide what to do? Let him go or do his job and capture him, maybe shoot him. Whatdya think?" he asked lighting my cigarette, shielding the flame with his hand.

"Fabulous idea, Mitch. I like it. I like it a lot."

I really liked Mrs. Rinebolt, the teacher and chastised Mitch whenever he called her his pet name for her, "Bird Legs." We never formally went out together, but he'd call me a few times a week after school and we'd have these rambling nonsensical conversations riddled with belly laughs. My mother would poke her head around the kitchen corner and smile, happy to see me happy. I never considered him as a prospective boyfriend. He scared me a bit.

He'd often disappear during lunch and not return till last break and he'd smell of booze. The drinking age had recently been lowered to 18 and many Grade 12 students and younger were sneaking into the Inn by the river. Only Mitch would head back to school as he'd have to catch the bus which took him to his country home. He'd be different during those times. He turned mean and someone I didn't know anymore. He had a weird look to him. One time he picked me up and threatened to drop me to the ground from the top of the school stairs. I never gave it that much thought, and I didn't realize he had a budding drinking problem.

By age 19 I was engaged and was about to move a thousand miles away after my wedding. I was at that same Inn by the river with my fiance and there was Mitch sitting at the table next to us. He leaned over at the end of the evening and said:

"Why are you marrying that jerk?"

But, I did and occasionally wondered about him and how he was doing. My sister told me that she'd heard through a friend of a friend that he said that I was the best woman he ever met. That shocked me. I really had no idea he had that kind of feeling for me. Things didn't turn out so well for my husband and I. We divorced when our only son was four years old. I never returned home, however, even when my parents pressed me to for support and being amongst my childhood friends.

Not that long ago my Dad died. All of us kids returned home for the funeral. Many of our old school chums still lived in our hometown, but I wasn't prepared to find a Sympathy Card from him amongst the stacks of cards left for us at the back of the church after the service.

"This one is for you, Adrienne," my sister passed me a white envelope. "Open it! Who could it be?"

I had no idea.

It was from Mitch. It was a lovely card and the inscription inside was heartfelt and warm. It was:

Take comfort in your family and friends to get you through this difficult time. Your friend, Mitch

I was very touched.

My mother died a few years later and the same scenario. This time the inscription read:

I've always liked your Mom. I am so sorry for your loss. Your friend, Mitch

So we figured Mitch was reading the daily obituaries and sneaking into the back of the church during the service and leaving the cards on the table along with the rest. No one ever saw him and I would've liked to see him after all these years and thank him. I found his number in the book but felt too shy to call.

"Write to him, Adrienne," my brother suggested. "Even if he is married, it is quite appropriate to do so."

I left the following day on my flight home and once I settled into my seat, put my seat belt on and once we were airborne, I pulled my pen and paper out and began this long letter to him. I wrote how much I enjoyed his friendship throughout High School and often thought of him and how his life was turning out. Did he still write?

Was he happy? I ended it by thanking him for his thoughtfulness during my grieving for both my parents and that I would really appreciate his friendship if he felt the same. Maybe we could email, talk on the phone occasionally? I ended it with xoxox, addressed the envelope and licked a stamp and pressed it on the right hand corner. We touched down a couple hours later.

After I retrieved my luggage I headed out the automatic doors, back home, back to my life, feeling somewhat like an orphan. I stopped at a trash bin suddenly feeling very different about my plans to reconnect with Mitch. I pulled the envelope out of my purse, ripped it into pieces and tossed it away.

Lessons from a Mature Woman by Gaboo

Trudy Marshall, a charming neighbor. I hung out with her younger brother, Billy. She was older and gawky, kind of looked like a proud horse, in a Julia Roberts way. She had big eyebrows and a great left hook. Well one day, a hullabaloo broke out in the alley behind our house. Trudy was screaming at her brother, "You felt me up! You felt me up! I'm telling Dad you felt me up!"

Billy was pleading with her. Whatever had happened, it sounded pretty mortal. In the end, Trudy's anger was quelled with the formal grounding of Billy and a lecture from his parents.

This weighed heavily on my mind. Later that murky August summer holiday weekend, I approached Trudy with a soul searching question, "What does it mean if you 'felt someone up'?"

She grabbed my hands and in a flurry, rubbed them over her breasts and made my fingers squeeze.

"That's what it means."

I doubt she remembered that I existed, me being nine and her fourteen. I remained in love with her for the next four years.

Jeff and Me by M Dawn Thacker

He was five days older than me, and my best friend. Two doors separated our apartments and we came and went as we pleased without knocking. Our parents worked and we had keys on strings around our necks that let us in after school. Lemon Cooler cookies and milk didn't taste the same unless Jeff was sharing them with me at the table.

We were ten, and planned our lives in a hideout under the steps in the basement storage room of our building. We stacked milk crates to display our rock collection and kept a paper bag to fill with glass soda bottles. The nickel deposits on each one added up to purchase forbidden bubble gum and chocolate bars. Every day we opened the secret cigar box and selected a treat. Jeff taught me how to blow a bubble. I showed him how to whistle with a blade of grass between his thumbs.

Our mothers were friends. They were both single and went out on Friday nights sometimes. I sat on the corner of my Mama's bed, watching her at the vanity, applying mascara and lipstick, brushing and curling her hair, fussing over which blouse to wear with what skirt and how high her heels should be. She twisted and turned at the mirror trying to see all sides, making sure that everything was tucked in and perfect. It seemed like a lot of work to me. I liked my jeans, t-shirts, sneakers and hair in braids. It was hard to ride a bicycle in a dress, and I knew I'd poke my eye out with the mascara wand.

Jeff and I shared a baby sitter. It was cheaper that way, and fun for us. We got to stay up late, and watch cowboy movies on TV. While Cindy took over Mama's bedroom, locking the door, to talk to her boyfriend "privately" on the phone, Jeff and I pulled sheets out of the linen closet and draped them over the kitchen chairs we dragged in front of the television, making a tent. We pulled pillows and blankets off my bed to create a prairie pallet, camping out in the open range of my living room, and cooked a cowhand's meal of popcorn and chips. We turned off the lights, kept warm by an imaginary fire, star gazed, and listened to the cows in the distance. We planned to drive our cattle over the plains and through the river the next day. We both knew how to swim.

We must have fallen asleep before our mothers got home because when I woke up the next morning, Jeff was still under the tent, curled in blankets beside me. I poked him in the ribs before turning the TV to cartoons. He sat up blinking and rubbing his eyes. His hair stuck up all over his head and I laughed at him. He punched me in the arm. Our range breakfast was two bowls of cereal and orange juice. We sat Indian style and watched the Roadrunner outsmart the Coyote over and over again.

Jeff went home to brush his teeth and change his clothes. We met in the storage room where I scratched around and found a piece of rope. Jeff knotted a loop in its end and we practiced lassoing a broken mule ear chair in the corner.

Outside on our bicycles, we drove cattle all day, down the grasslands of Berkshire Road and through the river of Cedar creek at the foot of the hill. I slipped climbing the creek bank and Jeff caught me by the arm, pulling me up onto the grass. We reached the apartment building patch-of-grass-Ranch by late afternoon. We were tired, having driven five hundred head a hundred miles in one day. Our knees were grass stained and scraped. Our sneakers were muddy. The saddle packed peanut butter and jelly sandwiches from lunch were long gone and our stomachs grumbled.

We flopped down in the grass and stared up at the clouds waiting for our Mamas to call us for supper.

"Look at that one," I said. "It's a turtle. See his shell, and his little tail?"

"Where?" Jeff asked, putting his head closer to mine.

"Right there," I said, pointing. "See?"

"That's not a turtle," he argued. "That's a heart."

"How does that look like a heart?" I asked him, turning my head closer to his angle.

Then he sat up, leaned over and kissed me on the mouth, just like that, right on the mouth. My eyes opened wide and I sat straight up. "What did you do that for?" I asked, pushing his shoulder so hard he fell over. I jumped up, wiped my mouth on my sleeve, and stomped home. Jeff Hentslie sure did know how to ruin a perfectly good day.

Sweet Grass by Gaboo

I can't write about her now, not at this moment. The act would take pages. I need to be somewhere large and open, where grasses meet sky. Then I can find the air and the room to remember. A summer? We were sitting, leaning backs to a fence, plucking stories and grass, hanging on words, ears wide to each other's cue. We were submerged and innocent.

She was talking, or smirking, telling puns and I was so close, casual close and friendship comfortable—when the touch of a finger or a brush against cloth was everything. Her nose was sunburned, like mine, and she had parched lips and a loose gap in her teeth. One lip, the top, was too thin and the bottom one always looked swollen. She had an long face, with heavy eyebrows, and eyes for finding mischief. She was mesmerizing, swift and beautiful.

I keep coming back to that time, out at the fence, where we relaxed one afternoon and chewed grass, talking and kidding. That's when I caught the glint of sweat on her temple. Soaked wisps and strands fell over her ear and trailed back to her cheek. This was profound! She was sweating! Girls don't sweat? I had to know if she had a smell—like shoes, or paint, or butter. I listened to her, giggling and going on and on. And while she talked, I inhaled, gently, so careful not to breathe on her neck. She smelled of mosquito repellent, barn straw, dirt and sweet grass. Freedom and sweet grass.

Read This Please

Volume 2 Edition 8 - Melancholic Habitus

March 15, 2011

Read This Please Online Periodical Edition #8, themed Melancholic Habitus, and all about the turmoil of inspiration. Writers, poets, artists and musicians can relate. We understand the web of angst and rumination coiling in the frontal lobe. We dive in and sort through triggers, flashbacks and mental mazes, organizing fleeting glimpses into verse, or stories, or great solo melodies. For a reader who walks alone in depression or melancholy, we want to share—you have brothers and sisters in the artistic community. Woe is a thought process that we can tap. Those thoughts of sadness and melancholy aren't you—they are tool to creativity. For the Ides of March, Read This Please Edition #8 will offer words of perspective, inspiration, and few ladders up from Melancholic Habitus.

Melancholic Habitus

by Gaboo

I have a chore I keep putting off. Writing shouldn't seem a chore—but I can always come up with the excuse of requiring more experience, "Can't write just now—gotta live something."

The problem: Events and happenstance add up and compound. Experiences are addictive and soon become overwhelming. Then they threaten my creativity, contemplation, and reflection. But experience is so yummy.

So I want to write about depression—what a chore. I've been picking up vibes from my offline friends and the similarities to creative melancholy and literary angst are noteworthy—essay worthy. There's also been some perspectives surfacing, how depression actually advances thought—placing us further up the intelligence tree than many other species. Depression has a purpose. Depression is a biological function. An astounding premise? Not really when you look at how depression works. For the reader, I'll frame it in my own experience.

I get blue, moody, and sad just as other writers, poets, and painters do. Society and the natural world throw a lot of wrenches at an individual and I've learned to duck, but I still get clipped on occasion. I won't get into how far I fell or how isolated I became. Just say, it's part of our experience as a family. I've slid into gray fogs of melancholy and scraped my way out with a strength beyond my own. I'm compelled to share what I've learned—something about the condition that rang true. As I became coherent, stepping tenderly, I began to see depression for what it is, a tool of cognition.

A simple explanation is that depression happens in a region of the brain, and for a purpose—the epiphany, the idea. "The anatomy of focus is inseparable from the anatomy of melancholy," wrote Jonah Lehrer, and I suspect that's why artists are so good at both. Suffering from depression? You're advanced.

What I have learned: Depression takes work. It's managing concentrated impressions and ideas about an inch and a half inside the forehead. For those who succumb to depression, they perceive a never ending spin in painful spaghetti thoughts and tangled memories. What is happening? The mind is sorting out the problems. As I look at what is physically happening, I begin to understand that depression is a focal gift, the tumble dryer whirls in the frontal cortex of focused thinkers and the melancholic. My attitude changes: We focus to sort out the tangles. In the frontal cortex, neurons fire in clusters—this is how we concentrate. One who is depressed is concentrating. Some might concentrate on a musical piece, others on a painting, and another on their past. For the one immersed in depression, they are unraveling issues, examining each knot, and spinning the tumble again and again. They are problem solving.

However, because the issues being examined are personal, painful and internalized, the depression seems never ending. Imagine a groove in a spinning disc, or a song you can't get out of your head. Depressing thoughts wear that same groove. We get stuck in the rut, sink in the hollow. The neurons fire and fire, and this becomes fatiguing, tender. Suddenly, I realize that I must take a break. I've thought too much. We are reluctant to let go of depression in the same way we are reluctant to let go of a puzzle. We are tenacious and want to resolve issues first, in order that we may enjoy the rest of the day. When the depressed or melancholic individual begins to understand that depression can be a helpful tool, a problem solving tactic, then they can schedule breaks—"I'm penciling in some quality depression at nine, to work on an issue and maybe get a poem out of it." The artist realizes that he or she can return to the hard work of rumination and continue where they left off. Just like digging a garden, schedule some breaks. The work will still be there—just rest to gather strength and tackle the issues with renewed energy.

In order not to drive a rented Ferrari into a wall, I learned depression is OK, and just a focal skill I use to analyze issues. Using medication brings relief—it's hard work swirling a tangled ball of dark goo just inside the forehead—but it only buys time to rest. The depression will return because it hasn't been sorted out, filed and categorized. Thinking hard, concentrating, considering the worst scenario—this is all work and drugs and booze are shallow relief—the good work of focusing still calls and needs the deep thinker to be straight.

I learn to use simple, life-based, pleasures to smooth out grooves of depressive thought. Vistas, fond memories, appreciations… I built a toolkit of permanent, simple, positive activities that have become part of my human experience—for me, charms on my bracelet of life. I didn't need to claim 'a melancholy' as my own—depression is not an identity—I only needed melancholy for what it was. Concentrated thought. I began to see depressing ruts as a tool for understanding. Concentrating was a skill: Analyze over and over to find the key and unlock an asset. But I also realized that any tool needs a rest. My mind is a good resource and I depend on it, so I rest it regularly.

My creativity suffers a little when I don't schedule some quality rumination, but I also understand when it's a good time to page through old memories and impressions, and when it's a good time to just go play and rest my little atomic engine. I realize my mind wants to organize and resolve issues whenever it can, but 'Me' likes to have some fun. Now, the depression often waits in line.

Sometimes I don't even get to it. I treat myself when I have achieved some good focusing. And because I've entertained some quality depression over the years getting to this point, I'm due for some special treats.

I am not what I think I am. I am not what anyone else thinks I am. I am just me. I don't have to reach all the answers. Some I let come on their own. I have far more questions now, than I have ever had, yet I am free. All I know, is that I am a little spark in a human shell. And this is the ride.

I'm addicted to living.

The Wounded

by Sarah Scott

I don't remember the ambulance ride, only the frigid metal against my skin. I can't recall the paramedic who attended to me, just the wailing of the siren and the flash of lights reflecting off silver-tinted walls. The truth, I don't remember much at all from that night. Only bits and pieces, eerie and foreboding like a black hole in the mind.

The sterile smell of the paper-towel gown made me nauseous. I clutched the steel pan as round after round of pills and bile exited my over-developed twelve-year-old body. The nurse asked me a dozen questions, none I can recall. The Doctor bombarded me with even more. I don't remember those either. Or maybe, I don't want to remember. Either way, they admitted me, ran some blood work, and sent me off to the seventh floor ward.

Upon entering the double set of heavy metal doors, I was ordered to hand over my artifacts into a plastic container, on which the petite blond slapped a sticker. I was given a set of "clothes" and a bag of "allowed hygiene items" in place of what I had surrendered. Instead of shoes, I was resigned to footy socks, the kind one receives when trying on new shoes. My bag lacked the obvious: razors, shoe strings, shoes, any sort of jewelry; and the not so obvious: shampoo for my hair, toothpaste for my toothbrush, mouthwash, etc. The bag did include a small brush with extra soft bristles and a toothbrush. The shampoo and toothpaste, I later learned, were administered at shower time each day, and my use of such items monitored by female staff, along with daily medication.

The lady, who I later came to know as Pita, had a thick foreign accent, Polish perhaps? Her blond hair was cut in a symmetrical bob that barely brushed the tops of her shoulders; her features were angled and thin, as if someone cutting her out of the magazine accidentally trimmed too far inside the edges. But she was kind, and her green eyes were soft, trustworthy.

The psychiatrist, who I was ordered to see once every day the first few weeks, and once a week the last few weeks, was a burly man with lots of hair protruding from every visible place. He wore thick-rimmed glasses that slid down his nose. He never bothered pushing them up, and so spent the whole of our sessions peering at me over the top of dark black rims. He wore a white lab coat, looked very official, and always spoke with the most condescending air. Plaques celebrating his achievements in education and the psychiatry field lined the wall. Everything about his office made me want to dash from the room.

The residents, of varying ages from 12 to 17, of which I was the youngest, came from all walks of life. Some were more friendly than others. I kept to myself and never said much to anyone, and still somehow became the ugly duckling of two elegant male swans-Eric and Wesley. One afternoon during our free recreation hour, they caught me staring at the ball volleying from one side of the table to the other. They came over, introduced themselves and invited me a bit closer. For the next few days I took up post along the back wall, watching them play, studying their movements, trying to understand the rules. Around day ten, I gathered the courage to accept a game, which they had offered to me each day subsequent the first, a game I wretchedly lost. Playing ping pong helped the days and weeks pass and before long it was time to leave.

I still think of them when I pick up a paddle and ball, and I still lose every game. I still remember the smell of the hospital, the taste of the food, which was always the same no matter what dish I ordered. I still feel like my memory was sucked into a black hole some days, but if it weren't for living, wounded people like Eric and Wesley,

Pita, and Dr. Thick Rims (I cannot remember his given name), it would have been game over- perhaps not at twelve, but maybe thirteen, or sixteen, or eighteen, or twenty-three, or twenty-eight. The faces changed with time, but the lesson remained constant: only the wounded understood the pain of healing. Only the wounded knew the strength it took to look in the mirror and choose life when death would have been so much simpler. The scars remain, but the wounded heal.

Too Late

by M Dawn Thacker

Mama pulled me by the hand, as we ran to the car, "Hurry Baby, come on, we've got to get home. I didn't realize how late it was."

We'd stayed at the park too long. The sun wasn't hot anymore. The slide didn't burn my bare legs when I went down. It was the best time to be at the park, but we couldn't stay. It wasn't a good time to be away from home. I didn't argue. I wanted to get there as fast as she did.

She started the station wagon and we lurched into traffic. Cars kept getting in our way, stopping at lights, or taking a long time to turn. The mailman kept putting mail in people's boxes and Mama banged her hand on the steering wheel.

"Dammit," she said.

My Daddy's truck wasn't home when we got there and Mama let out a long breath. "Let's hurry," she said.

Pork chops sizzled in the skillet and Mama was washing lettuce in the sink when the screen door squeaked. Our heads turned at the slide of the key in the lock. It happened every time the key slid in, even if Mama was humming a song or washing a dish in the sink, she stopped, turned, and watched the doorknob. The key made a scratching sound, then a click, and the knob turned.

When my Daddy came in the house singing or whistling or carrying a grocery bag, everything would be OK. He might pick me up and swing me around, calling me his doll baby, or kiss Mama and dance her around the kitchen. It didn't happen often, but when it did, we had fun. Even Mama looked happy.

When he came in quiet though, I held my breath. Tonight, he was quiet. The door of the trailer opened into the living room. The sofa faced the kitchen and the TV was between the two. I was sitting on the floor watching the Roadrunner outsmart the Coyote.

"Shut that damn racket off," Daddy said.

I turned the knob on the set way down so I couldn't hear the "meep, meep," and backed myself up until I was sitting in the hole between the sofa and the green chair. There was a space just big enough for me to curl into, if I pulled my knees up real tight, and held them with my arms. I squeezed my eyes shut, and waited.

"Where have you been all day?" he asked Mama.

"Here mostly," she said. "It was sunny, so I took Maggie to the park this afternoon, for a little while."

"Uh huh, sure you did," he said.

I heard the refrigerator door open and the beer bottles rattle. He popped the top off of one and the cap rolled around on the kitchen floor. He kicked it, and it hit the wall under the window.

"Must have had fun today," he said, "going to the park and all. That why you're all dressed up? That why you have on lipstick?" He asked Mama.

"I'm not all dressed up," she said in a quiet voice with a shake in it.

She wasn't dressed up. She had on a dress, but it was an old one with a hole at the bottom where she got it caught on a nail outside one day. She always wore lipstick.

"Can't I give my wife a compliment, tell her she looks nice without an argument?" He said, his voice getting louder, as he slammed the bottle down on the kitchen table.

"I'm sorry, Honey," Mama said. She said she was sorry a lot. Most of what she said wasn't right or didn't come out like she meant it to.

"You're sorry alright," he said. "I should have listened to my mother. She said you were no good. She said you'd run around on me and lie. 'Too pretty for her own good,' she said. 'Don't go and marry her, you'll regret it,' she said."

Then their voices stopped. I could smell hot oil in the skillet, hear water splashing in the sink. My heartbeat was in my ears. I opened my eyes.

Mama turned with the lettuce in her hand just in time to catch the back of my Daddy's hand with her cheek. She spun around on the floor, letting go of the lettuce. It smashed into the kitchen window and bounced off the table and ended on the floor. Mama fell in a heap at my Daddy's feet. She was curled up, holding her face, and crying.

"Don't lie to me again," he said, picking up his beer as he slammed out the front door.

I waited a few minutes, until I heard the truck roar, back up, and take off again, scattering rocks against the side of the trailer. I crawled out of my hole and over to my Mama. I sat on the floor rubbing her back.

"I'm sorry I made us late," I said. "I won't do it again."

I looked at the TV. The coyote was pushing an anvil to the edge of the cliff, waiting for the roadrunner to stop underneath.

Life Crashes

by Sarah Scott

Sometimes life crashes in waves of wonder and majesty. Other times it seems catapulted from a meteor shower, blindsiding boulders as big as states on the map. Emotions swing from one end of the pendulum and back in a moment—like the instability of summer winds rushing across open plains, stirring dust balls in their wake. Swing, another shift. Ding, and then it's gone. From moments of joy to the depths of despair so dark I cannot see my own hand in front of my face. Some might suspect it a mental illness, a disorder of the brain chemistry that needs balance through medication and therapy. But for me, it is the bane and treasure of my existence. In the despair I write the ache away. In the ecstasy I bask in beautiful ballads and happy songs of people and places. I've learned to live with my demons and angels, they aren't always in harmony but they're part of what makes me..... me.

Building Blocks

by M Dawn Thacker

It builds, the emotion, like blocks, one after another, balancing, balancing, swaying a little, then shored up with two yellow cylinders, pillars of happy that reinforce an unstable column. Then, the purple square plops hard with force onto the tower and I feel the impact all the way to my foundation. Sometimes I know when it will happen, and sometimes the smallest blue half moon shape gingerly placed on top does it. Then, I'm a mess.

I used to build castles in my grandparent's living room on Saturday nights. Grandpa and I watched David and Chet take turns telling the news. The Vietnam War played out on the small black and white Zenith TV.

While the television screen showed pictures of sweaty men in helmets and dirty undershirts, running, carrying other bloody men out of the jungle on stretchers, I erected dream houses out of colored wooden blocks. I started with a basement, added the living room, and then two smaller bedrooms. I didn't bother with a kitchen or bathroom, but made sure I had a tall tower with turrets and fancy windows, so I could watch for my prince. He would be like my Daddy, wearing a uniform, coming for me soon.

When the gunshots tatt-tatt-tatted one after the other, I knocked down the walls, scattering blocks across the floor.

"Gotta pick those up Tump. Don't wanna trip over 'em in the dark," Grandpa said.

"I know," I said, gathering the pieces one at a time to start all over again.

Listless

by B G Lewis

Listless: silent floating, mists leaving, creeping away from dawn, ambition hung, saturated, unsung and stumbled by the untrod, tangled and never woken by the sun.

Listless I've become: misplaced, the chipped window, a dusted priority misshapen, smeared with avoid, mistaken cares tattered by nonevent, and bent, insignificant.

Listless took me: swept in the down draft of inertia, a crevasse in lurk, tumbling in landslide, a cautious non-participant spied in severed glints from closing doorways.

Listless is hollow: ever waiting, ears pinned to the unanswered wail, never running, in mid-fall, almost love, alive for unwant and a death unfinished, reasoned ineffectual, the faded us.

Listless gazes in might have's, forever pining, enduring blunt points unaimed and maiming, stealing sky blue before the rain, snowfall on lost footprints.

Listless loves me: lulls me from a day no greater than a night, a brush with poisoned lips, woken from sleep in no night greater than another, hate in blur, the embrace of nowhere special.

Listless measures wealth in souls: forgotten epiphanies and half held handshakes, cornered doubts and unspoken non-beliefs, a sink in steady drips of unconcern, never joy and pain, never reaching. Listless.

The Card

by M Dawn Thacker

I wake up and smile. I'm twelve.

Outside my window it's bright and cold. Wind shakes the tree branches. It's Saturday and my party is tonight, a sleepover for me and three of my best friends. I smell cake baking. It's my birthday.

Mama peeks her head around the door frame of my room and sings. She's done this on my birthday every year that I can remember.

"How does it feel to be twelve?" she asks, smiling at me.

"Much older than eleven," I say. "I'm almost thirteen now—almost a teenager."

I sit in bed surrounded by a fluffy pink comforter, under the watchful eyes of dolls on my bookshelf. I'm embarrassed by these things. I asked for a new bed set for my birthday, those bold geometric designs in purple, lime green, and sky blue. I'm too old for dolls now. What I really want? One of those fabric covered journals—with a lock and key—to keep my secrets safe.

I hop out of bed, move in front of the mirror and untame my braids, brushing my long hair into a new wavy style around my shoulders. The phone rings. I wonder if it's my Daddy. He's in the Navy and I haven't seen or heard from him since I was seven.

"It's for you," Mama calls.

"Happy Birthday! How's my girl?"

It's my Grandpa. I'm glad he can't see or hear how my insides feel, all disappointed and flat. I can see his smile over the phone, and I feel ashamed of myself. I talk to him, and then Grandma. A little while later, my aunt calls, then my uncle, and then two of my cousins. Each ring of the phone makes my heart beat fast. I try to stay near the phone all day, waiting for the next call.

My cake is done, three yellow layers with chocolate icing, and 'Happy Birthday' written in green script. Twelve yellow candles are waiting for a wish. Two presents sit on the table wrapped in shiny paper with curly ribbons. One is big, my bed set, and another is the size of a notebook, my journal. I can open them at the party after my friends get here.

I hear the crunch of gravel as the mail truck pulls up to the apartment building. I slam the front door and run up two flights of steps to the landing where the mailboxes wait in a neat row. I shift my weight from foot to foot as the mailman opens each box and sets letters inside. Ours is next to last. I see birthday envelopes in his hand, pink, yellow, and blue. I know they're for me.

"Looking for something special today?" the mailman asks, smiling at me.

"It's my birthday," I say.

"It is?" He looks in disbelief. "How old?"

"I pull my shoulders back and stand a little taller. "Twelve," I say.

"You're growing up. Hope you have a very happy day," he says and hands me our mail. He walks out the door to his truck.

"I am growing up," I say to myself, sitting down on the steps and focus my attention on the cards. I go through the envelopes—I know his handwriting—it's bold print in black ink with strong, straight marks. He underlines the important parts. I have the postcard he sent me from Cuba five years ago. It's stuck between the mirror and frame of my dresser. Every morning, when I get ready for school, I look at the photograph of a sunrise over the ocean, and then again every night before I go to bed. I take it down at least once a week and read the note. I don't see his handwriting now.

There's a card from my Grandma, Grandpa, my friend Jeff, and my aunt Margaret in Mississippi. I search through the envelopes again and again. I hold the catalog from LL Bean by the binding and shake it, just in case the mailman stuck the card inside by accident. I take apart the sales flier page by page and look on the floor under the mailboxes. It may have fallen out of the mailman's hand. Nothing. Maybe my Daddy put the card in the mail too late for it to arrive today? We live a long way from Cuba. Maybe the post office lost my card? Maybe he will show up in person—with a present?

I stand, head down, shoulders slumped, dragging my feet back to our front door. I feel the tears start deep in my stomach and then travel into my chest. The tears hang in my throat, choking me, and press upward. My eyes burn and then flood. I stand with my hand on the door knob, squeezing my eyes shut. I take a deep breath. I will not cry. It's my birthday.

I square my shoulders, try to smile, and go inside.

"Did you get any mail?" Mama asks.

I show her the cards. She opens each one, frowns for just a second after the last, then smiles at me.

"You are one lucky little girl," she says and then hugs me. I have never received this many birthday cards before.

I walk into my room and tug out the postcard. Turning it over, I read the words again:

Sweetheart, I miss you. The ocean here is the same color as your blue eyes. See you soon. Lots of Love, Daddy

The words 'miss', 'soon' and 'lots' are underlined. I press the card to my chest with both hands, and close my eyes. I imagine my Daddy walking on the beach, looking out at that blue, blue ocean, thinking about me. Missing me. Then I slip the card back into its home on the mirror, leave my room, and close the door.

It's my birthday. My friends are probably waiting for me. Two are already thirteen, and one is twelve and a half.

Mrs. Tilly Ambert

by M Dawn Thacker

Mrs. Tilly Ambert lives in a vacant lot that used to be the foundation of her home. She owned her house and lot outright until her neighbor's dog, Sweetie-Pie, made her mad.

"Tilly has always been a strange one," her next door neighbor states. "She has never been a friendly sort. She scowled at me when we met at the curb with our trash cans on Monday mornings, years ago. I tried to make pleasantries, but she had none of it."

Mrs. Ambert never liked the little dog that lived across the street, either. Sweetie-Pie barked at her, ran to the fence, stood on his hind legs and screamed at her in K-9 obscenities. She actually hated Sweetie-Pie.

One morning, the dog's owner, 'Mrs. Sweetie-Pie', had the dog on a leash, walking him on the street in front of Mrs. Ambert's house. Tilly was rearranging the rocks in her yard, moving them from the north side of the driveway to the south side of the oak tree. Sweetie-Pie made a dash toward her and snapped at her ankles. Mrs. Ambert snapped back. She kicked out and caught the little dog right in his side, sending him hurtling into the street. The slack in his leash tensed and Sweetie-pie recoiled, landing in a small, whimpering heap at his owner's feet. She picked him up, ran home, and called the police.

The deputy arrived an hour later and rang Mrs. Ambert's doorbell. She came to the door and when the officer asked to talk with her, she assaulted him.

"He was trespassing," she told the judge in court.

The deputy, in his official uniform, testified against Mrs. Ambert when he sued her. He won a $30,000 settlement. Mrs. Ambert refused to pay; and the deputy put a lien on her property. Her house was scheduled for auction to pay the settlement. The deputy was smart. He took out an insurance policy on Mrs. Ambert's house the week before the auction. Word got to him that she threatened to "burn it down, before I give it up to the likes of him or anyone else."

The night before the auction, Mrs. Ambert set fire to her house and burned it to the ground.

She's lived in the vacant lot, where her house once stood for thirty years. The deputy received his settlement money and the city dropped the arson charges against Mrs. Ambert when they couldn't definitively determine that she had set the fire. She had no insurance.

Mrs. Ambert is now in her eighties. She uses a wheelchair. She lives in two tents, surrounded by five extra wheelchairs, 12 large garbage bags contain her belongings, piled up around the outside of the tents. She also owns four ladders and two wheelbarrows. The trees, shrubs, weeds and brambles make Mrs. Ambert's lot look like an suburban jungle. The neighbors on either side constructed privacy fences bordering her property and try to ignore her.

The church in the neighborhood buys her a new tent every two years and has Meals-On-Wheels deliver directly to her tent. Sometimes she accepts the aluminum covered and sectioned food, sometimes she throws it at the volunteer.

The city has debated buying Mrs. Ambert a 'yurt'. A yurt is a round igloo-styled abode that is more substantial than a tent. A yurt is also insulated. Habitat For Humanity, and the local church, are willing to offer some of the funding for the yurt, but the city was not willing to foot the rest of the bill. The City Council felt that Tilly had already used enough of their good will over the years.

"There are several matters regarding the history of this person and the use of city support," said Jack Miller, the city's head planner. "It's dead as far as I'm concerned."

Mrs. Ambert's neighbors dislike her enough that they didn't care to offer support at the public hearing.

Mrs. Ambert said she didn't care one way or another. "If people would just mind their own business, stay out of mine, and stay off of my property, there wouldn't be any trouble," she said.

Cello Notes

by Adrienne S Moody

If I were a cello—

I'd play a melancholy piece at the first sign of snow pinging on your window pane and make you stop what you are doing, look outside and remember—remember yourself as a child and remember the smell of pine needles...

Before November snow—

I'd follow you through your day and you'd hear my aching melody and remember...

The full moon above the prairie grasses illuminating that desolate night on a train— late and moving ever closer to her. Remember the quiet before the November snow, just hours before she died— remember your sister's face at the station, fatigue and fear lined deeply—so young for such sorrow, and you could see her like yesterday from the family kitchen window, as you wash dishes and watch how sweet she is, standing on the porch, shaking crumbs from the checked tablecloth in the summer breeze, and she turns into a princess, she wraps the cloth around herself and ties the corners under her chin...

I would play for you at the railroad crossing and the bells would fade, the wooden arms would raise, and I would let you go.

If I were a cello—

It's That Time Again

by Jac

7:00am, Thursday, July 14th, 2005…

Some day's are just going through the motions; today I wake up filled with the promise of the day.

Only working a half day.

Dogs have an appointment with the groomer this morning; all three of us always feel a bit cheeky after.

Best friend Michelle is meeting me and the pups for lunch in the park.

Dad and I are getting together this afternoon; he has news about a surprise we're working on for Mom.

Brother Tom has been working on a new CD and is recording a couple live songs tonight at a very cool blues club. I'm part of the live part. The whole family will be there.

Just danced out of the bathroom singing along with Kelly Clarkson's, "Breakaway".

Phone rings. Caller ID displays, Mom and Dad…

"Hello", I say with a smile.

"Good morning, Honey", I hear my Mother's voice.

"Hi Mom, what's up? Kinda early for ya, isn't it?" I say with grin. Mom is a night owl.

Feigning indignation she replies, "I've been up at this hour before!"

Her reproach doesn't slow me down. "Wasn't me, it was always your sons."

But, I can hardly keep from laughing. "So, why ARE you up so early?" I ask.

"Your Father is taking me to breakfast." I can feel the happiness in her voice.

"What's the occasion?" I ask, knowing she would prefer a lunch date.

"We're going to Albany this morning, I'm meeting with Leslie, we're working on donations for the buses, and who knows what your Father is up to? He suggested we ride together and stop for breakfast first." She explains.

"Probably wants to show you off" I say.

"Yeah, right!" she retorts.

"He just wants diner food," she sighs.

"Mom, you have to go to the "76" then, the blueberry muffins are incredible. Michelle and I both had one, then split a third Monday night." I tell her.

I can hear her eyes rolling. "Jennifer, I'm trying to get him to lose a few pounds you know", she says.

She continues, "I called to remind you about tonight. Oh… and hang on a second; your Father wants to talk to you, something about a project you two are working on…. I won't ask" she quips.

"Mom, I can't. I'm late. Tell him I'll call him later" I begged. "I'll be there, I talked to Tom last night, and he's excited."

"Okay, you know he's going to ask, 'Who's more important, me or work?' and, 'Don't be late tonight!'" She replies with in jest. Tom is the one who's always late.

Laughing at her late comment, I just say, "Tell Dad, he is and I'll call him or stop by later, love you, bye Mom."

"Love you, have a good day, Dear," I hear her say as I hang up the phone.

…

Getting to work on time was just too damn important, for the really important thing. "Have a good day," still rings in my head with the clicking sound of the phone.

My brother Tim took me aside just before the wake and begged me to stop asking my Mother if she had told him. I didn't realize I was.

Dear Traveling Companion

by B G Lewis

I gave the steering wheel to another. I am a humble dog, led where I can be of best employ. A long time ago, I relinquished my fears, willing to accept whatever comes my way, only asking that I may recognize the deeds that I must do, and a little joy.

To clarify, I should be dead. There is no reasonable explanation why I am alive other than to teach or learn.

There is no great answer. Joy is elusive, as it is precious. But the more I am willing to reach out and share joy with someone, any person, animal or living creature, the closer I come to my home. You are a sister, or a brother. Float the river with us, be amazed together.

It's taken a long time to quiet my mind. Alcohol worked effectively in masking the problem for twenty years, all the while I knew I was too scared to face anything without it. If I quit, then would come the great alone. I would be left to my own thoughts, without the soothing forgetfulness of booze.

But something happened, when I gave up, when I admitted I couldn't do it alone—I gave up responsibility, even for my heart beating. I crashed. My brain blew itself out. I was a living shell. Like a babe, I would only have what came to me. No more seeking, no more questions, no more wanting, or fear, or guilt, or vengeance. I was done and a seed in the wind. This day was the beginning, my beginning. The chain was broken. For six months I gingerly twitched, letting new experiences feather in, recoiling like a timid mouse at even a sour look. I wanted nothing of the world, only what life deemed necessary to make my heart beat and my lungs fill. I eat the food I am led to. Each day, and even today, has been one of awakening. The person who was trapped in fear and anger, resentment, was only reacting. Today, I am the person I was when I was two years old, three, and four... If you want to know what I was like as a child, look in my eyes. I am me again. And with that, I accept my faults. I dwell on things, I am quick to flash, I can be sarcastic and morose—I can sink easy. Knowing these self truths, means I don't have to pretend, I am what I am. And even if I am shot up or crushed, I know that my job is to spread joy. That's how I am heading home.

Individual moments can take hours, and I love it. Making rice for example. I have a connection with every single grain that goes in the pot. Outside, every blade of grass who bends that I may walk—I consider. Every shovelful of dirt I lift, I genuinely ask whose home it is, and what their world is like, and if we would be friends. Every relationship, handshake, glance, word or nudge is a precious consideration. How do I not go nuts? Because in the embrace of every life form, honoring every footprint, I can immerse in life, and feel its percolation around me like a spring shower. The bog cleanses my thoughts as much as a good friend. When I fall in despair, a bird will sing and gently guide me back to my feet. And on I go, in full appreciation of millions of little heart beats around me, laughing with them, crying with them.

I walk in conversation, not burying my thoughts, but expressing them. And life understands, it lets me drop my burdens. That's why I come and go on here like a butterfly, I am easily led. What adventure will my children teach me? How can I let my love know that I have been in love with her for 10,000 years? How can I give more? And grow stronger? The doors open, a bird sings and I listen. I have no answers, only one path to peace of mind. Take from it what you need. I love a traveling companion.

Window Thoughts

by Sarah Scott

The rain falls in sheets, heavy droplets plop on the pine needle blanket beneath my open window, singing me a lullaby. Hush child, the rain whispers to me. Rest sweet, the wind speaks through tree branches hanging low with evening tears. Ebony sky sheds tears for me, for I have none left to cry, exhausted of precious buckets of water long ago fallen from my eyes, evaporated into dismal night. I listen, steal a glimpse out my window, the cool breeze on my face, dew drops refresh my scalding skin, satiate my thirst for a few moments. Tender hands reach to trace the falling rain, tangled fingers in a spiders web on the window sill. A smile for a living thing taking solace in an undisturbed corner of my world. Hanging by a thread, the world spun in his web, of such a small entity, I am in awe, mesmerized.

Digital Mind

by Trularin

I have a digital mind with scattered bits of scattered data that transcends the boundaries of space and time. Should the fragments collect, a thought splatters itself into my consciousness and I know… something.

Losing my mind is always an adventure in trying to find it. One never knows where the blasted thing will run off to. In the case of any word, it jumps between the letters with no particular pattern of progression yet arrives at the station in time for the next space ship.

But the thing that really gets me is when we land, I never know what planet we are on… even if my mind knows and is just playing with me.

Resting My Mind

by Adrienne S Moody

Climbing rock in the heat of summer

Channel surfing

Silly talk with childhood friend

Rifling through a box of old photos

Watching silly commercials on Youtube

Driving and parking at the dike and watching birds land on the mud flats

Sneaking into a matinee with popcorn and indulging in a film only I would enjoy

Biking along Mud Bay

Sitting in the corner table at the new cafe with laptop and people watching

Powering down the mind by extreme exercise

...

Click.

Sarah is my son's new girlfriend. She's 19 years old and pretty like Snow White. She has this soft voice; it reminds me of the breezes through poplar trees back home. The poplars have soft white flowers that fill the air in the late spring and may fool you into thinking the trees are frail but they have to be hardy to survive the Alberta winters. And so like Sarah. The voice and manner, gentle, and lowered eyes when attention is on her, lie about her strength.

She studied my dream book while my son and I talked after dinner.

"What dream are you looking up, Sarah?" I asked, curiously. She closed the book and put those hazel eyes onto mine. "I have this dream often—more often when I was little—but I still dream it. I dream of crows pecking at this… carcass."

"Crows?"

"Yes. Lots of them. And then there is a slide that I know I have to climb to get away, and there is water on the other side. I want to get there—badly. So I climb up, but I keep sliding down to the crows."

"Did you dream this while you were having a difficult time during your childhood?"

"Yes, I did. I still dream it now."

Jeff had his eyes lowered.

Sarah's mom has mental health issues and Sarah rarely sees her. All I know, and it's not much, is that the girl lived mostly with her father. Child support money sent to her mother went to a drug addiction.

Sarah now works at a gas station saving money for her education. She's taking early childhood development. A few months back, while at work, she was held up at gunpoint. I asked her if she was scared.

"I was after they left."

Sarah has a library at home that holds over 250 books. She was given a notebook that can download books. It came with 50 classic novels. She took ballet, hip-hop and jazz dancing when she was younger, just like I did. As we talked and bonded, I felt we were leaving out my son, So I told her when he was in grade eight, he was frustrated about his perceived failure in school. Everything he wrote came back with red marks circling spelling and grammar errors. I knew he had wisdom that he displayed often to me.

"'If you can think it, you can say it. And if you can say it, you can write it,' is what I encouraged. I told him to go into his room with a pad of paper and write me one little paragraph, forgetting about spelling. I didn't care about that. I wanted him to write down what he feared the most in life. He returned an hour later and what he wrote was poetry—and I told him so. I showed him how to lay it out like a poem and told him the next time the teacher asked for poetry to hand this in. So a month or so later she did and Jeff handed this piece of work in. Well, it was displayed in the staff room for the teachers to read. He was invited to take a special creative writing class as he obviously had talent."

"Did he go?" Sarah asked.

I laughed.

"No. Jeff had trouble sitting still in the classroom. Just like I did."

She laughed with me.

There are moments in life, if we are aware, that we realize life is perfect right there, right in that instant. And it doesn't get better than that. There aren't thoughts on what will happen, or an hour later, or the next year when the car is paid off, or on our vacation. It's usually a simple time, like with us that evening, after our meal, sitting together, Sarah with her dream book and me touching Jeff's arm.

Click.

Gloomster

by Bruce Reisner

Guilty of not being cheerful. And for spreading the sad condition like noxious berry jam. I've been accused of wearing my heart on my sleeve, to the detriment of people who didn't want to hear it. I've tried to defend myself by explaining how stupidly patient I had been when they were last depressed. But it doesn't help my argument, because they were having a great time on the occasion I told them I could no longer afford to maintain my car.

I've been told, "Buddy, I was better off not hearing that."

It's habitual, though, and there are always sadness-invoking troubles, of which some jerks have to go squawking. There are worse gloomsters than me, else I wouldn't just heave my own dry chicken bones in the juice can and throw them down on the spotty bedspread. There are those people who don't merely describe to others, but draw others into their germy imbroglio.

A frenemy from my distant personal past left a message on my answering machine last week. It's as good as knowing that he is in some form of need, and said need results from the squalor of his ways. Before you slam me for being a materialistic bigot, this is a gent who evaded material support for about five kids, and is retiring on largess begged from the same abandoned kids, now of working age, and grudgingly obliged to help their dirt bag father. This is a fast biography of someone I used to drink with in some days of my melancholy past. There is alcoholism involved, so the melancholy is clinical, like the sheep skin on the wall, but the voice on my answering machine was one of "mendacity central," the guy who was always telling his troubles, so convincingly the victim of other people's wrongfulness, a word that by itself begs assistance.

See, the gloom I got on the slate is the entangled form, squalid tales and a person, decades hence in consistent dipsomania, dancing a sailor jig in front of saddened lives he is organically one half of. I wouldn't be in a position to tell of my sad evenings out skirt-chasing, when we were two young bucks, with the aging gloomster, whose voice on on my machine made me go fessing the blues, to you, feeling melancholy. I'm not ready to talk about the women I met, when the Gloom Dealer and I were still drinking buddies, but the sadness chronically dependent people traffic in, stays with people. So I lament. I'm not sad to have met so many saddened people, just sad to think it wouldn't have been so grim, if not for at least one gloomster who made webs out of his vices. Beamed his viscous threads of 'usery' like a spider. People got caught up in them and spent months in a state of melancholia. You get awful depressed from drinking with people like the one who left me a message last week. For now, it's enough to write memories of melancholia. Don't care to open up a fresh one.

Class Question

by Sarah Scott

Slumping into another chair and looking around the room of angled faces with creative bents, all eagerly anticipating the arrival of another professor. Filled with nervous energy and momentary brain spasms, we introduce ourselves and share a story. Truth or fiction, the fare for today. Only we alone truly know, but everyone enjoys guessing anyway. Crumpled balls of paper fly, filling the tin can with broken sentences. Perhaps where the mind fails, the creative eye will see. My turn came. I loathe storytelling. Writing a story is another matter, uses another part of the brain. I stumble through and the baton passes to another unfortunate soul in the sea of faces. We all applaud politely, even if halfheartedly, as our ears are filled with memories, tales, and wonder. Tonight I must dig through the yellow pages and deliver a name and address for the next in-class torture session. Someone remind me why I thought this class was a good idea?

Why do we write? I ask myself time and time again. The question tumbles around inside my head, like some old record that doesn't play well anymore. And if we don't know, if we have no purpose in writing or our words, are they just as valid and valuable as the words of those who understand their purpose in writing? How do we know that our writing is good, or even wants to be read? I've come to no conclusion, except that through asking these questions, we prod ourselves on to greater ability. Through the creation and analysis of poetry and fiction we exercise our muscles and grow stronger. But still I sit and wonder, why do we write?

I suppose it's an easy enough question, which we all have to answer. Some write for expression, others for healing, but is there more than self-gratification? Do we write to share a perspective that the world might need to hear? To challenge modern day thinkers and policies? What do we have worth saying to the opiate masses that are comfortably droning in the same old fashion, following the machine?

It perplexes me without end, this question spinning round my head. It's constantly evolving, morphing into something new. Perhaps for today I'll just write for me, and tomorrow I'll write for you. I used to write for self expression, to give voice to my pain, but even that grows dull as the years change. Now I'm not so sure why this pen keeps dribbling ink, why my mind keeps filling with words that I can't seem to speak. I write them down; I pour them out; I drip ink from my veins. And still I do not understand, why the writing stains my mind, and reality, as if it were my friend. I do not understand what is my purpose here if all the words I muddle over fall upon deaf ears. And still I write, and still I muddle, and still I make this mess. So I can only assume that in this grueling process, I must find some piece of value, or pride, to keep me slaving so. And so for now, back to the papyrus I go.

Trade Places

by B G Lewis

It's been quite a ride and along the way, I've learned to see the universe in a rain drop. There's a whole journey inside one.

And every creature gets a chance, chuckling. We're not really creatures, we just happened to this place. Quite a ride.

There's a lot of time spent looking at the envelope, the cusp, the meniscus—the edge where we blend into mineral and magnetic. From shoe polish to bush paint, from reflection to mirror, we are enthralled with this place.

A gray and black chickadee darts and squawks, bombarding my attention. I'll give him a peanut if he's willing to trade places.

Strange Country

by Steven Bird

Awakened to rare country,
strange, lost, we see:
Odd this flat gray plain,
this low place
Valley of shadows
Walk here, observe
the mournful visages
Wan ghosts rattle and
dance in a formidable line
Do not linger there long, wander
Journey
Seek the rim of the low country
Find where land begins
to rise
It will be there no map
but open eyes to sight
down the parallax
of passing suns

Climb

Climb to the line of trees
A row of cedars
supports a temple
A row of cedars
supports a temple,
the long sky
Part the rustling boughs
The arc of heaven abides

dawning beyond leaf fronds, near
A finger's length
Rest there, await, the eternal
wind free speaking secrets
Await waking

In Good Company

by B G Lewis

Angst? You're in good company.

Morrison, Joplin, Moon, Keats, Nowell, Cobain, Hendrix, Shelley, Lymon, Kossoff, Honeyman-Scott, Bolin, Ace, Drake, Wilson, Lawrence, Jones, Johnson, Byron, Mondragon, Ham, McIntosh, Curtis, Beiderbecke, Williams, Lang, Richardson, Sappho, Fjume, Murcia, Neimand, Feliciano, Vicious

… and Coleridge and Wordsworth because they deserved the honor of a young death. Poets, musicians, artists all.

Demises: OD, suicide, crash, gunshot, wither, broken hearts. All tormented, gifted to see great beauty, and condemned to recognize great pain. But for the stilted walk of the artist, all would be warehouse shades of gray. I note this trivia because I read their lyrics and poems to gain perspective. Not all were wise, but each had a wonderfully unique way of expressing the inexpressible. You, like many, may hear those passionate thoughts, and better, you hear them with pen in hand, fingers on keys. Write for the reader who is in torment, alone.

Muse

by B G Lewis

Win didn't consider the elevators anymore. Double bays swing open. People enter. They close.

Third floor—take a breath. Peri-Operative is always busy. It's bright, aesthetic and acrylic ocean swirls guide visitors to Palliative and beyond. Plants set in ceramic pots provide a pleasant distraction, but for Win, there was no appeal. All faded into the mission of coming and going.

At the floor station, Win looked for a familiar face.

That nurse? Where was she? She was efficient. No, no, she's not here. Just two different ones. Breathe.

"I'm here to see Nance—I mean, I'm here to see Nancy Dwyer."

"Sure, one second please. You are—?"

The nurse turned to a docket, glanced, and was in mid conversation with a passing tech when Win began to respond.

"Ah, I'm Nancy's husband, Winston Dwyer. She's been here before. They called me at home. She was in geriatrics at St. Augustine's. They said it was the same surgery as before. They had to—do it again?"

"That's right. Nancy Dwyer. Bay 7. Please come through the door."

Volume 2, Editions 7 - 12

To Winston's left, an access lock released. One shoulder to the door and it swung open. Then the sign, 'Always wash your hands entering or leaving.' The door closed. Click. Then the people.

"Winston?"

That was familiar.

"Denise? Oh you're here! Thank you."

Winston let out a breath and then searched the corridors with his eyes, "Someone phoned. She's had another operation. They said she's here again. Where's bay seven?"

"This way. She's asleep. The operation went fine. But we have to see if there's a change. She woke up on her own when we brought her down. That was at two. We're letting her rest."

Bay 7 is draped in uniform green and set against a wall of post op monitors and panels. Nancy was on her back and propped slightly. Her hair was lop-sided and shadows traced under her eyes. A thin tube trailed from her nostril while one lurked over her shoulder and into her arm. She was in a pink gown and covered by a blanket to her shoulders. Her arms were left out at her sides. Two ID bands looped around her wrist. She looked a mess.

"Denise, I'm just going to sit here for a bit. I won't wake her. I'm just going—-going to sit."

"That's fine, Winston. Stay as long as you like. If you need anything, let me know." Denise left through a fold in the curtain.

Winston sat. The space was small and the lighting subdued. Voices from other post-operative bays drifted over the curtain. A hidden speaker carried announcements in muffled tones. He wanted to hold her hand, but waited. This seemed too technical a room for Nancy, she wouldn't like this place. Nothing seemed natural. He could hold her hand, that was real, but Win waited. He didn't want to reach out and find hers was different, or unresponsive, or not there.

He knew her hand, every nail on every finger. He knew her knuckles, the creases, the folds, the very bend of her thumb. He knew her hands as well as his own.

His own. Winston looked. He barely recognized his bones. They were foreign and old. His hands were spotted, and withered, and sore. When did he become frail? When did he lose his strength to protect her? Winston strayed into memories filled with younger hands and younger faces. Those times had seemed spry and magical. When all was soft, and supple, and life lay before them.

"Nance? It's our anniversary on Monday. What do you say we go for a night on the town? Just us—no kids."

Their children had grown and moved on. It was Win's little joke. And it was Nancy's habit to giggle. They were teenagers again. Both retired, work had since faded as an obligation. Their sons were independent and educated with families and friendships and love. Win and Nancy had flicked a switch and were suddenly seventeen again, flirting and teasing—and living. Then her stroke.

Nancy's breathing was steady and relaxed. A panel array blinked in unison.

"You know," Win proposed, "there's a nice drive that opened up past the housing development. Thought we could do some cruisin'. Maybe this year we don't buy any gifts for each other. Let's just get some take-out and drive up to the view. We can listen to some music. I'll write you a love poem—"

Win knew his moment. He touched her finger and snuck his hand around hers. They were joined again, if just to wander back along the path one more time. They fit so well despite the years. They could still let their fingers entwine. They could still be each others. Win thought of flooding his own energy into her. Could he just cure her with love and want? Could she just wake up and feel him?

Win sat waiting and the moments clicked onward. His thoughts settled and he wondered why he felt peaceful. He realized he wasn't paying enough attention to Nancy.

The panel blinked and then changed. Green became yellow. A tone started. This wasn't good. Win reached for the page button, but Denise appeared at Nancy's side. She pressed the panel and set a stethoscope below Nancy's clavicle.

"What's going on? She was sleeping. She didn't move."

"Don't worry Winston. We suspected this might happen. One blood vessel is having a hard time sealing. The surgeon will want to reset a patch. I'm afraid we have to do it now."

The rear curtain slid aside and a gurney was ushered in. Denise moved along side an orderly and they lifted Nancy up and over. Winston barely recognized Nancy's frame. She looked so small and insignificant. She was a stranger hoisted by strangers. She was a lone shape.

"Winston, follow us to the door. We're going straight into surgery next level. Can you wait in the lounge? I'll be down as soon as we have her prepped. I'll let you know what her specialist says—okay? Will you be alright for a little bit? Winston?"

"Sure, I'll be okay. I'll wait. Just hold on to her for me."

Win couldn't stay in the lounge. It was busy, noisy, and smelled of trauma and recovery. Win couldn't think. He had to leave. He had to walk.

Two blocks up Regens Street, the thoroughfare turned a corner and passed a high school. Just beyond was a small cafe painted in bright colors with a window papered in concert notices and photocopied art. It was a hangout, but school was in session and only a few teenagers sat inside and sipped coffee. Win pushed open the door and a bell chimed. He slumped in a booth by the window.

"Coffee?"

"Sure."

"Cream and sugar?"

"Just coffee."

The cafe was ratty and eclectic. Dim light revealed trinkets of all shapes hanging on the walls. A low counter was covered in cups and muffin trays. Someone's knapsack was left on a chair. Books and cds were loosely piled in front of a stereo unit while a strange music floated in the rafters. The shop was different and vibrant; not a place Win had ever found himself in before. It was comfortable and it was young.

Win held his coffee and didn't think. He just stared between posters that obscured the glass. Win wasn't even looking. For that moment, he just was.

When a man thinks of his love lying, broken and in distress, he reaches for anything he can control. A man looks to what he can do and Win was no different.

"Would you like a refill?"

"No thanks. I'm fine, but—could I borrow a pen?"

"Sure, here ya go."

Win pulled a serviette from the dispenser and squared it on the table. How small it all was—a page, a life, a marriage. Win picked up the pen, but no words came. It seemed trivial, writing what he felt. How does one sum up a lifetime of love and compassion? Win drifted back into memory. This was all happening too strangely. He wanted Nancy beside him. Nothing was right anymore.

A bell rang somewhere. He looked to the school and a flurry of young adults trampled down the steps and spilled onto the courtyard. Noon. In seconds the door of the cafe chimed and a bustle of voices filled the space. Jackets and books flooded onto tables. In minutes the shop was full.

Win watched the commotion, pen still in hand. These young spirits were mesmerizing. Full of vigor, alive, and unstoppable. They reminded him of a another world—when he was a part of it. They seemed so distant.

"Whaccha writing?"

A teenage girl slid into the seat opposite Win.

"Sorry? Oh, nothing—" Win paused, startled.

The sprite began unloading binders and texts, "You looked pretty deep in thought. Mind if I—?"

"Go ahead. I'm just waiting for someone."

"Thanks. So, whaccha writing? I'm in Lit this afternoon, two essays and a short story due. I'm dead. Oh well, we had a party last night. Priorities, heh? I'm Holly P—that's for Parmoni."

The young girl smiled. She was buoyant and cheerful. Her hair was in three shades of disarray. Piercings jangled on her nose and lip and her eyes were thick with liner. The girl's slight frame was plunked into an over sized winter jacket. She was oddly infectious.

"I'm Winston. Just waiting for a bit. My wife—she's at the hospital. She's in surgery."

"Oh," Holly slowed, "that's too bad. She's gonna be okay—right?"

"I don't know. It's our anniversary on Monday. Fifty-four years," Win looked out the window to the school, "I should be buying her something. I promised her a love poem, but it's not a good time to write. I don't know what to say. I guess I don't know anything right now."

"Wow, fifty-four years. I can't imagine that. You two must really love each other."

"We do. At least, I think she does," Win managed a chuckle, "she hasn't complained much lately."

"So you're going to write her an anniversary poem—how sweet!"

"I wish I could. I'm not much of a word person. Maybe I should just get her a gift."

"Sometimes," Holly brushed blond and black strands from her eyes, "when I'm stuck on a big project, I just take one bit of it and write something. You know, like the heart of the message. Then I don't have to worry about the rest. What's her name?"

"Nancy."

"So—what does Nancy like to do? What do you like to do together?"

"We like taking drives, talking, holding hands, going for walks."

"Okay, what's something that Nancy does that makes her special?"

Win considered this young girl. So fresh, almost naïve, but she was deeper than he first regarded her. She had a wisdom.

"You know," Win smiled, "whenever I felt down or angry, Nancy would take my hands and start to dance. I would be all grumpy and she would laugh and start to whirl around. In no time I'm laughing. She dances my blues away."

"There you go. Write about that. She'll love it."

"Yeah, you've probably got something there. Maybe I'll try it." Win was wondering if he just learned something. "I should get back to the hospital—you know."

Win extended his hand as he rose to button his coat. Holly hesitated, then took it. To Win, her skin was warm and electric. Her thin fingers squeezed once. He felt her energy and drifted to another place, with another girl. It was all similar, but in a different time.

"Thank you, Holly. For your kind words. I'll work on it—the poem."

"See you, Winston. I hope Nancy's doing okay. You two have a great anniversary!"

The bell chimed and Win left the cafe behind him. He walked slowly, returning to the hospital, and the tubes and blinking panels.

What drew Win back to the small cafe? He did not know. He had been wandering for days. He would sleep, then rise and walk. He didn't consider the passerby or the city. He simply wandered, looking, searching, and for nothing in particular. Walking was easy. It took little effort.

The place hadn't changed. Posters still littered the windows. The door chimed on entry. A stray student crammed over notes in a corner and strange music still filtered from the dark ceilings above.

"Coffee?"

"Sure. Just plain."

Could he jump to this world? Could he return to this future and start again, full of hope and promise? Here was a bliss without time or tomorrow. It was a pleasant thought and his gaze wandered back through the glass, between the posters and on to the school. No, this is their world now. It's their chance. Win could watch and sip coffee—and remember.

A long bell sounded. Young adults emerged from the school and bounded down steps in arms and legs and knapsacks into the sunshine. Within moments the cafe was full again. Their voices laughed and cajoled, cups clinked, and the music grew louder.

"Hey! Whaccha thinkin'?"

It was Holly. And this time with different hair color, different jewelry, but her eyes were the same. She slid, jostling with books and papers, into the booth.

"Winston? Right?"

"That's right. How are you?"

"Always running late," she laughed. Holly was still carefree, living a moment, and she had a sharp memory. "So—did you write that poem? For your wife?"

"Yes, I did. Thanks for your help."

"And—what did she think? I bet she loved it."

"I don't know. She never regained consciousness, Holly. She's gone."

The girl paused to let Win continue, but each sat without speaking.

Holly broke the silence, "I'm so sorry, Winston. This is just so sad."

"Yeah. It's been hard. Harder than I thought it would be. I don't know where I'm going most days—" Win stopped himself. He had slipped, burdening this innocent, young individual.

Holly could see he was trembling. Win set down his cup and tried to focus attention on his words, looking to the window. He took a breath and then returned focus to Holly. There was an expression that carried through her eyes. The future, the past, the now: He had seen those eyes before, when he had been smiling, looking into promise—young, beautiful eyes from long ago.

Win longed for Nancy's gaze again. The last time was the afternoon he visited at long term care, just before her final stroke. Her eyes were tired, but aware and still lovely. Was it fair not to have one more glance? Just to hold—just to remember?

"You might as well take this," Win reached for a small card in his coat pocket, "I never got to give it to her, but you inspired it. I kind of new I was coming here today—you can have it."

Holly opened the card. A single watercolor rose was printed inside. Opposite was a hand written verse. She read it and closed the card.

"That is so beautiful, Winston." Tears ran on her cheeks and she reached her hands forward, a simple gesture, to hold his from shaking. "I wish I could say something, Winston. I can't."

"No, it's okay. You take the card. Keep it for Nancy. She would want to know it was read—for me."

"If that's what you really want, I will. I'll keep it for her. If you're sure."

Winston nodded. They sat a few moments longer, then he stood up from the booth and turned to leave.

Holly still fingered the card and she looked upward at him, her support and remorse unspoken, compassion without experience. He felt her virtue, her plea for his serenity. Win paused and smiled. There was a bridge to this world; there always would be. It spanned from Holly's eyes to where his wife had gone. He gathered up the music, the chatter, and the exuberance. "Here is a memory."

He looked once again to the girl, "You know, Holly, you should be a teacher."

"Why's that?" her lip trembled.

"Because I think I'm going to write some more poems. I think that's what I'll do. For now, anyway. I thank you."

Holly's expression widened into a smile.

"Goodbye Winston."

"Goodbye."

For Nancy

We are the dance

We are the wind and the grass

We are the long drive and the distance

We are the laughter for the blues

We are the hands and the embrace

We are the seeds and the trees

We are

We will be

Forever

Love

Winston

Expectations

by Gaboo

The human animal strives to find the best, to excel and exceed. If some of us live the flash and bash Coliseum lifestyle, it's because we painted that picture for ourselves.

We're a tribe of legends. And legends are expectations. We expect of ourselves–to exceed and excel. Someone came before you and painted this picture. Even these words I type, all invented by another.

But we humans, always questing for unbroken snow. Such a shame it's all been done before. All been done before? Such a shame. There will always be new deeds, but the exhilaration of discovery is the same for Alexander the Great or a child in play—don't you think?

So, how do we come by these expectations? Early on, we watch others, interact, and see how attention is ladled out. Desiring group, wanting family, it's a survival technique. Otherwise, we'd go wandering off without any sense of loss. And to make the life of the organized tribe easier, certain expectations are prescribed. There's an expectation of how we should grow—what we should accomplish—in order to achieve standards set by our sibs and parents. A set of expectations has been placed upon you by your family, peers, friends, bureaucrats, mentors, and when an individual is full up on the rules and mores for group behavior, maturation takes place. Splash—get a haircut and get a job. You are initiated to the realm of adulthood. Now go do something nice that lives up to all our expectations.

Just jokin'. I'd rather receive your cooperation voluntarily. Do something fun and be proud of yourself.

Read This Please

Volume 2 Edition 9 – Everyday Magic

April 24, 2011

Read This Please Edition 9 is all about the little clock stopping moments that happen to each of us daily. There is a swirling essence that seems to have fun with our sense of reality, despite our plans. Many know when the phone will ring, or when events stack up that are a little too coincidental. Often these pauses are brushed aside, but if a bird lands on your head and tells you a message, heed that bird—because birds don't do that very often. Let us know about some of your 'magical' experiences. Serendipity, phenomena, wonder, and awe, this is your life and you have many dimensions to explore. We invite you to read some quality short stories by the creative scribes at ReadThisPlease and journey into Everyday Magic.

Flash Magic

by Adrienne S Moody

White Lace

A late model white Cadillac screeches to a stop in front of the brick steps of the Catholic Church. One white high heeled sling back shoe followed by billows of white eyelet lace emerges into the June sunshine. Late for the ceremony, the bride and her heavily perspiring tuxedo-clad Father lift handfuls of antique-lace train and race up the stairs. The ancient wooden door slams shut on her veil.

Northern Lights

Don't Walk. The pedestrians stop and traffic moves slowly forward. The smoky white exhaust lingers. Minus 35. Wind chill factor: minus 45. Ice fog. Frosted eyelashes. Look up to see the sun is wearing a halo. Walk.

Polar Bear Swims

I wait at the shoreline dressed in ski jacket, mitts and double-layered track pants. On cue, four hundred and thirty-two men, women and children, most of whom are wearing bikinis or shorts, stampede into the frigid ocean. Splashing, screaming, laughing, and my camera captures one crying. Seagulls circle high above screeching their disapproval.

Leo

His majesty lay sleeping soundly in the tall sun burnt grass. Black flies circle his mouth looking for a meal. Suddenly he rises to attention, bits of grass tangled in his dusty mane. With little effort he opens his mouth and vocalizes his displeasure at being disturbed. A blond toddler in her stroller claps her hands and squeals with delight.

I See You

His strong bare shoulders catch my attention. I can clearly see his hands from the passenger seat of the vehicle I am in. They push the wheels of his wheelchair with ease. I guess him to be around 35 years old. I sense a recent injury—a motorcycle accident? That's my guess.

Amongst a group of pedestrians, he appears frustrated as he maneuvers around them. No one looks at him. He looks at me and for a moment we share a flash in time. His hands freeze on the wheels of his chair and I smile.

"I see you,"' I try to tell him with my eyes and we pass on by.

The Invisible Unicycle

by Gaboo

So much I could lecture on the workings I've gleaned, but the very act of forward behavior nullifies the effect. Love was always the seeker. The one with horizons to seek, sought.

Control, control, control, control. We all want control. From the raindrops pinging above to the toleration level of humming, what came before and what will be—all in our control. Never was, why start now?

It's fun to watch people run and splat into the wall, until they hurt themselves. Then it's kind of disenfranchising. I wince and turn away at horrid things, thankful I came with the gauge of time that runs rewind around bends, a chance to head check and measure options and depends. Ha.

We control our rising, on who we associate, and our opinion of things outside the head box. So much we control: to where we travel and to where we can escape; how comfortable the backrest and how long the bondage. We seek to control everything. Unless we offer control to others. C'mon, cordon off some of that defiance and acquiesce. Personally, I want responsibility for running into the wall as an individual. Some tyrants cut the tongue to prevent suicide, they want to control so, thus I avoid discussion. Seekers will seek.

Relaxing control to something you cannot see or logic—that is a feat, an individual accomplishment, because there's no reference. It's a path and a balance as specific as your own DNA. Gulp. Plunge in submission to the alpha wave, the big dog of happenstance, and a will that, oddly, perceives and retrieves circumstances, presenting them in front of the observer within a frame that sometimes only one can see. Yikes. Have ye the gumption to confront an intuitive sense that rallies with nature to bring about the best in an individual and in the instance of occasion? Now there's top-level, wee and wondrous, all inside and out, catch a sideways glimpse of infinite control. Behold, a ladder and a doorway. We are tugged to the inevitable.

Big towers and monoliths are sunk into permanence. Such control. The great fear of the past and the anxious future, surveyed and hacked, dredged, plowed and whacked, all in the grand attempt at control, and all for little ol' us, with fingerprints for picking berries and teeth for grinding nuts, and knees to scramble, and ears for headphones.

I gave up the cell phone a long time ago, because I knew it was going to ring anyway, because when I started talking about someone, they phoned. I don't remember who hinted that they would phone, but you know it, the whisper. I got into riding the invisible unicycle when I moved to a meadow with room for spills. It was always available anyway, the chance to ride. Comes with a bell.

"All things return to the ground, even the crows." I took that whisper to mean something galactic when I first heard it, but now I consider the phrase a tenet on humility. Crows just have to eat. If I get too busy, with too many plans and obligations, I become a high flier, zooming in multiple directions, placing emphasis on my own priorities. A humbling bout or an unplanned interruption soon demonstrates that while my head was airborne, my feet are entirely land-based. The more I want for control, and control of others, the harder the smack into simple humility. I could build walls and layers of scaffolding to prop up my plans, however, the result is isolation. Then I'd have to pay or control people to be around me— a life of regal comfort.

You have to want to ride. I mean you have to want to ride bad enough to convince yourself to accept what was already there, despite the screams and taunts of ego. Oh, my misery, oh my pains. Mostly from scraped knees. I look for help outside for something I claim within.

Oops. Reverse that. Oh, that misery. Oh, those pains. Within is the help I seek.

At my core is my bridge, my doorway. I can step with the freedom of being guided or I can go it alone—my choice is an affect that I have. And I choose based on my whim and my desire. Each person is different. Each person is unique.

For the choices I make within, I seek validation from outside. I seek the praise, appreciation, acknowledgment, understanding, and agreement of others. But that is unnecessary, because the path was within all the time.

On the outside, I experience the external interaction with material objects and living beings. I can see their defined roles, character foibles, their choices expressed. Each individual is already attempting a balance: convention, conformity, security, whim and desire, fears. What is the well-balanced participant supposed to find? Peace of mind.

As I spread joy, more and more, I notice spirit manipulates the material world and the affect of other choices to coincide with a path toward joy. There is no singular route to meet and greet spirit, only a doorway of connection to spirit. Each life teeter totters between choice and recognizing the will of spirit. All human pursuits are merely games of experience toward all knowing understanding and control of living. Enter control: Successful birth to clean death, with food and amusement along the way. If someone can control an outcome to put some happy in your joy cup, they can make a buck. I know this because I got all jiggly saving a hundred bucks on a cool mountain bike that symbolizes a dream to be free and ergonomic. But chance is that the stuff we buy will always leave us feeling empty, or wanting more. Material joy, and prideful joy, biochemical joy, those are material solutions to a spiritual loneliness.

Hopefully, the bicycle I bought will help me pedal in the direction of some good stuff. I hope the guy who built it was joyful? And the guy who plowed the mountain side for aluminum? What tangled webs. The human attempt at control and manipulation, to fashion and create, to organize life and defy death, all are deeds to achieve a material replacement for joy. And yet, a babe might perish, never to leave the nursery and still achieve a fulfillment of a life. So tragic, yet this was the experience of one individual in participation with the living. This was the ride, and there is no rip off, or exchanges. This is a tangle of wills and lives in the gift of experience for each participant, brief or long.

Joy is not necessarily happy. Joy is the fulfillment of divine will. What should be… is. Will is done. And our acceptance of spirit's intent brings us joy. Spirit leads us to deeds of life and creation, and spirit leads to the acceptance of passing and transition. The shivery, shimmery sensation of fulfillment is the fulfillment of will. We sense joy when we are led to like, and in opportunity, and in wonder. We experience the sensation of joy in balance.

You may have heard the old song, *Amazing Grace—blind, but now I see.* Pretty much true, or an expression of one person's testimony. It was here all the time, almost with a sense of humor, sending a little bird shit on your lapel when you were trying to look pompous. Or letting you appear encouraging and confident to a child in a memory that will last a lifetime. Spirit was ever upping the ante toward joy, will be done.

This path to grow joy like limbs of a tree seems ever opportune'd by spirit. Feel the percolation. Our energy enters the shell of material, and then exits when we pass. There's a constant interchange occurring in a meadow—birth and death, striving and wilting. This is a purr of life that abounds. Within the foam of life humming and percolating, we sense the will of spirit bearing fruit in all things. And interaction with spirit is an individual perception, for the ant and the oarsman. The will of spirit is intricate and surrounding like a river. We flop and dog paddle our choices, but spirit flows and swirls, full of current and happening. Stand against spirit like a rock in a river, or let spirit swim you upstream, like a fish to the lake.

Funny how we make our own paths to joy. Drugs, new furniture, esteem, celebrity, adrenaline, inhibition, satiation—so many routes. Drive a strip mall in a '59 Cadillac. I have. See all the signs? New, better, best, fine, faster, value, insure, protect, more, grand, big… These are messages designed to fill your joy hole with a service or a gimmick, or a need, or a dream, or a want. Or a hope. Everyone's got an angle on joy. Do this. Do that. Release this. Control that. Just follow my plan—because if you're willing to follow, then I must be right.

Anytime a human starts spouting rules of order, my eyes glaze over. Where we sit in this meeting was once an inland sea, and before that a primeval glade. (Funny, they put those vistas and scenes on dog and cat food packaging, so you can think you're spreading joy to your pet. The animal likes living in a pack. They'd be happy to pick through dead road kill with you.) Everyone has an angle on joy— usually their own methodology to succeed at convention, to follow prescribed plans and then leap for the gravy. Splat. Or chill out--- that was in a message from this king of yore named Solomon.

So, I did it all too, spun the wheel, lived the dares and the chances, hunger and broken bones, busted hearts and living alone, but in the end, just like the old sages said, I found freedom through humility, giving up control and following spirit to a veranda with my family playful, and a few friends, a relative hanging out and sharing some music, watching the animals roam and the flowers loam... now that was living. Forget all the power and the conquering, that's just another drug for a sorrowful joy hole. Job was similar, but from the flip side.

The fulfillment of spirit's will and sensing the rush of participation, that's a ride I get into. And it's not for everybody, or at every time. We have a certain amount of navel gazing to do. We have to skin our knees and get punched back. This is our individual ride. When we were swirls you said "Pick me!" The gong sounded and you plooped. There's an element of bumper cars involved in living physically. Spirit has us participating in a changing and shaping planet with an over-sized brain in our noggins and lot's of individual choices. Imagine a bunch of sophisticated four-year-olds running amok and wreaking havoc... welcome to Earth.

Sure there's taboos, religions, politics, head games, pursuit and property, blood and sweat, hither and thither. It's a tough job trying to live in a world that some dead people control from the grave. Oh well, they must have had a powerful influence on their children. I didn't buy into the traditional scheme. Instead, I witness choice and an ancient plan. I witness a planet that undulates and reshapes itself to the will of spirit sharing the experience of aging, and time, and dimension.

Most people, if endowed, can manage to look within, rap on the window, and say, "Hey, help me do thine will." Are you sure? Are you positive you don't wanna be king of the castle, or queen of the castle, or big cheese in charge? Because the karmic flow of what will be done is sometimes not what I've expected.

Generally, serendipitous events and paths have coordinated with my present state of affairs, but some of the more in-depth experiences could be categorized in the leap of faith folder. Yet, I was never led to cultivate pain, only healing. And never led to chastise or judge another. I was never led to shun, or corrupt, or influence another. It has only been with my sense of freedom within, projected outside, that I can participate. I am not to influence, but only charged to experience, and mindful of the will and purpose of spirit. None living speak for spirit, but spirit might speak through you. Many times I wasn't aware until afterward. Gee whiz, no glory. Oh, well.

We all experience this. Atheists, fanatics, kings, queens, paupers, slaves, spectators, skeptics, victims, perpetrators: Each is given a window, a doorway to recognizing the 'ever there' of spirit. You already knew the phone was going to ring.

It's OK if you are blissful and scientific, fact-based and three dimensional. We all are to some extent. Doubt and skepticism are valuable learning tools, just like questioning the limitations of our dimension. To each, their own experience and their own participation in the percolation of the meadow. You are your own bubble, and you have your own private link with spirit.

I cannot tell you your purpose or if you have one, for to understand karma of spirit's will is like trying to plot the path of a raindrop back to the sky. But joy, now that is a something I asked on. You can imagine a person would have to be pretty low to only beg a wee bit of joy before they die. I finally had my priorities figured out. Up til then, I'd presented my own will like a child laying out some wrinkly laundry. Cute attempt, but useless.

It's amazing how much of the world I want to control. Something scares me, threatens me, is objectionable to me, and immediately I jump to control it. I'm learning to pause, and ask first, "OK, where are we going now?" Bring good shoes. If things start lining up for you, and the path is to the core, a doorway, or a chance where life and joy branches can sprout—and if you start thinking you're a little bit oddball for tuning in while everyone else is obsessed with material, corporeal self, then step back...

Go to the meadow or the window, and listen outside and within. Watch. A gentle comfort will guide you to ride the invisible unicycle, and you might sense the joy of participation, the fulfillment. It's not 'on' or 'off'—more of an ebb and flow, like we are playing in the ripples of life. You see, the thing about the invisible unicycle is that you can't expect to control the journey, but some lives are having fun riding it, and some are freaked out. Sometimes things seem ominous and in other situations it's just like gliding. Be kind, spread joy, and happy trails.

Despite The Odds

by Sarah Scott

A week passed and Hanna was out of immediate danger, still Melody found she had little hope of her daughter ever being normal. Hanna still didn't look at her when Melody spoke to her through the incubator, but Melody took comfort in her daughters strengthening grip. Twice in the past week the infant's fingers had found Melody's and held on for brief moments.

Melody stared at the list of phone numbers and picked up the hospital phone. She needed to find a family member or friend to stay with while Hanna grew strong under the watchful eye of Dr. Charles and the hospital staff. She dialed the first seven digits and waited, wondering why none of her family or friends had come to visit in the hospital.

"Hi Grandma. I need a place to stay in town. Hanna may not be discharged for several months and I can't afford the gas back and forth from Milo."

Melody slammed the receiver into the cradle. Grandma Miller was a long shot anyway, she consoled. Maybe I'll have better luck with Aunt Ruby. When she had gone through all of the phone numbers on her list, Melody stretched and left the hospital room, headed for the NICU and the little comfort she found in being near her daughter; the only family she seemed to have left.

Melody felt lost in thought, watching the rise and fall of Hanna's chest and recalling her earlier conversations with family and friends. They'd disowned her, all of them. Even Aunt Ruby said she couldn't help. Melody didn't understand. What about all that stuff they believe about God's unconditional love? Heat seeped through her bones. What about helping the orphaned, widowed and destitute? It's not like she was asking them for permanent shelter or money. She just needed a place to stay for a few months while Hanna was still in the hospital. How could they disown her? And since they disowned her, did that mean they disowned Hanna too? Melody pounded clenched fists into her thighs and winced with the pain that shot through her.

Turning her mind back to her little girl, she stroked a few wisps of hair on Hanna's head. Melody's eyes studied her daughter. She had beautiful round cheeks with the smallest dimple on her chin. The gauze removed, the scar grimaced at Melody reminding her of Hanna's rough road ahead. She whispered Hanna's name and a smile curled around Melody's thin lips. The color in Hanna's body was slowly becoming ruddy. Doctor Charles assured her this was a good sign, and that soon the ruddy color would become rosy. Melody longed for the day when she could cradle the little girl against her chest and feel her heart beating. She imagined Hanna's wispy hair growing in thick and blond just like Melody's had been as a child.

"Hello Miss Atkins," Doctor Charles' presence in the room had gone unnoticed, but she couldn't mistake the creamy baritone voice or the rich cologne permeating the air. "I would like to discuss what we will do next in regards to Hanna." He motioned for her to take a seat in one of the teal hospital chairs nearby.

"Okay." Melody situated herself, her long legs stretching well beyond the edge of the seat. "How is she doing today?" She tried to read Doctor Charles' eyes, but he kept his thoughts well disguised. The mark of a professional.

"Well, she's doing much better than she was this time last week. She appears to be trying to breathe on her own, but it will at least a few more weeks before we can safely take her off the machines. Her scar is healing well."

"So if she won't come off the machines for a few more weeks, what's there to talk about?" Melody struggled to keep the frustration out of her voice.

"Between now and then, we want to run some tests. As you have probably noticed, she doesn't appear to be able to locate voices or noises in the room, turning her head side to side as if she can't find the source."

Melody gulped. She had noticed, but dared to hope it was just side effects of the drugs. But she couldn't deny that Hanna's ability to find her hadn't improved when they began weaning her off the medicine. "I understand."

"So you will allow the tests then? It won't be anything invasive. An ophthalmologist will come and look at her eyes. Nothing more than that. It may be something that we can catch early and correct. We won't know until Doctor Peterson comes. He'll be here next Tuesday."

"Yes, I agree." Melody stood and strolled back to Hanna's incubator. "How long before I can hold her?"

"That depends on her continued progress. It may be possible to hold her a minute or two next week if she is stable, but we don't want to risk more and compromise her immune system."

"I can wait another week I suppose." Melody sighed and slid her hands back into the gloves.

"I've waited this long." Her eyes glistened, but her heart filled with hope. They were talking about next week and beyond next week. Melody took it as a good sign. She smiled and reached for Hanna's hand. The child turned her head towards Melody and held her gaze for a few seconds. Melody's heart slammed against her chest. "Did you see that? Did you see it?"

"Well, I'll be." Doctor Charles smiled and patted Melody on the shoulder. "I'll go confirm with Doctor Peterson. Check in with you later. Hang in there."

Led To Overcome

by B G Lewis

A little every day magic? Me, wife, and both kids (then aged five and one) headed downtown for an outing. Our intent was to reach the park and pick up some vibe the wife was on about. (She would get those often and away we went to palaces and back alleys alike.)

As we approached the park, much construction was going on. An older gent who was trying to be helpful, told us not to go 'that way' because the road was a mess. We thanked him and went anyway. He was adamant and insisted, even arguing. The interaction was spooky, like we were being forewarned. We went anyway, as the wife's GPS was cosmic.

Industrial fences were blocking the route, and another man approached, complaining. He said there was no way that a baby carriage and a tot on a training bicycle would get through, even with adults—a tall, chained gate permitted no access into the park. This soothsayer was equally forward and insistent. We smiled and continued, to shouts of "You will never get through!"

Eventually, we reached the infamous barricade. Seven feet tall, locked, chain link. Almost on cue, an elderly gent with his grandson showed up on the other side. We all looked through the impasse and laughed. Then, without plan or barter, we began an exchange. He picked up his grandson's bike and hoisted it up. I grabbed it over the top and brought it to the our side. In turn, the baby carriage went over, then grandpa's bike, then my eldest son's, the kids, grandson, the wife, grandpa, and me. All over the top. Now we each stood on opposite sides of the barrier, intact. We all laughed and went our own directions.

Remember That Night

by M Dawn Thacker

Do you remember that night in 1996? I think it was November, because it was cold outside. The weatherman on TV... what was his name? Norm, I think. Yes, it was Norm. He greeted us every morning that week, encouraging us to take advantage of the Leonid Meteor Shower. Do you remember that? We always laughed at his serious tone, the way he took the weather on his own shoulders like he had some control. And those smiley sunshines he drew on the seven day forecast, remember them?

I was more excited than you, about the shooting stars. I wished on them when I was a little girl and felt myself lucky if I saw even one or two in a summer. The thought of seeing as many as a hundred in a night gave me such hope. I didn't want to miss even one. Do you remember rolling your eyes and sighing? You did, but you went and got the ladder anyway, and leaned it up against the roof over the back porch.

"It's the flattest part of the roof, the safest," you said.

We didn't go out much anymore, not like we did before the kids were born. We had a hard time staying up past nine o'clock at night. Remember? We laughed and called each other "old fogies." Meteor showers shouldn't begin until after midnight. I was so excited that I didn't feel sleepy after the boys were tucked in. I gathered blankets and pillows for an adventure.

"I think it's too cloudy," you said, peering up at the sky from the back door that night. "Are you sure you want to go out there in the cold?"

I came up behind and pushed you out the door, remember? You pushed back, making it hard work for me all the way to the ladder. I called you 'chicken' and made a 'bock, bock, bock' noise, remember? You grabbed the blankets and huffed up the ladder like you were mad. You made me laugh and I followed.

We made a cozy nest up there on the roof. The shingles were a little hard and you said the bed downstairs was much more comfortable. Remember? It really wasn't so bad, the feather comforter and our warmth as we waited. I loved snuggling under your left arm with my head on your chest.

I pouted as we watched the clouds drift over the sliver of moon in the sky, remember?

I said, "Norm promised us clear skies."

You mumbled something about Norm's track record.

More clouds gathered and we lost interest in the sky, all snuggled up together, under that huge expanse of night.

Look at you, still blushing after all these years. Isn't it funny how I'm the girl and you're the one who blushes? Oh now don't get mad, it's endearing. It's one of the things I love about you. Your Mama taught you modesty. Mine taught me exhibitionism.

Alright, alright, enough about that. It's just that when I pulled into the driveway tonight and got out of the car, I saw the stars and remembered that night like it was yesterday.

Now look at you, blushing again.

Wake To Walk At Daylight

by M Dawn Thacker

Sometimes late at night , when the wind blows, the sound whistles through me like I'm not solid. I shiver wide awake, and think of glaciers and polar bears, snow and ice, walking on powdery flakes in big wide snowshoes with knotted rope soles. I lean into the wind, taking one small, slow step at a time, into the darkness with my parka pulled tight around me, the hood, cinched so that only my nose peeks through. I want to breathe.

I walk into those northern lights we talked about, they are green and wispy in the sky. Their iridescent arms and fingers reach to touch the ground and wrap around me, lifting me up so that I can embrace the color, bask in the light, feel their heat. They hold me, cradling my form and pillowing my head. I am cozy. I close my eyes and sleep, dreaming of a cold April night under down blankets.

I wake to walk at daylight, watching the sun rise from the earth, all orange-yellow in a ball of hope over the flat, open, expanse of prairie. It spans ahead of me on and on and on to where the grasses are scorched by the rays. The wind picks up and even though it's cold, and I shiver, I stand there, alone in all my solitude, feeling freer and happier than I ever have. Loneliness feels good. The sun and I are friends. Even though the grass separates us, we embrace each other right there on the prairie in North Dakota, a few miles out of Fargo.

Old Slippers

by Adrienne S Moody

Jessie would tell you that she decided to marry Tony on the day they sat at the end of the pier with their feet dangling in the tepid water. They met while she was on holidays, the first year after her Grade 12 graduation. It wasn't that she felt this blood pulsing lustful attraction, nor was it that deep soulful connection. No, it was what he told her as the sun went down and the mosquitoes began to bite.

"My brother shot himself when I was twelve years old," he spoke softly. "He wanted me to play a game of chess with him, but I was reading a comic on the lower part of our bunk beds and I just didn't feel like it. Just one of those things, you know?" Jessie nodded in response and squeezed his hand. "So when I heard the gun go off in the carport, I knew. I just knew. He tried before and failed. This time he succeeded. I was the first one to see… what he'd done. I won't ever forget what I saw."

They sat side-by-side and watched the sun drop low in the summer sky. He told her that his mother left the home and ran screaming down the street. She didn't return until much later in the evening after the body had been removed. Jessie could imagine Tony alone, abandoned, and feeling responsible.

His parents went for counseling, but the three remaining children did not. They were left to their own devastation. It would be years later when they would discover what each other was doing on that day. Everyone had secrets deeply buried. Jessie surmised that people back then didn't think children needed psychiatric help, but children were probably the ones who needed it most.

She felt this connection with Tony upon hearing his tragic story. She had her own, but didn't tell Tony until years later. When she was a child, she was assaulted and told no one until she was twelve years old. When she told her mother, she did not get comfort and understanding like she expected. Much like Tony's mother, Jessie's parent turned her back and walked away. Jessie and Tony were damaged people and somehow they found each other, and within only a few meetings, they felt that they belonged together.

Eventually, they married and their relationship was, at best, tumultuous. But neither one of them could imagine being without the other.

"We're like your old pair of slippers that no one wants, Jessie," Tony whispered to her in the middle of the night after one of their near break-ups. "We belong together. What good would one tattered beat-up slipper be to anyone? Don't ever think I'll leave you. I've got nowhere else to go."

Whenever their fights turned especially nasty and the silence in the house became unbearable, Tony would place a twig or a stone into one of Jessie's old pink slippers. The first time he did this, Jessie laughed at his attempt to reconcile.

"I love how you made the effort to do this, Tony. Such a little thing, but it made me laugh. How silly to think I would ever want to leave you."

"Don't forget, Jessie. I'll always be there for you," he'd whisper in her ear when she embraced him.

They didn't go to counseling during the two and a half decades they were together, although if they had they may have lived their lives with less discourse. Their childhood injuries were always resurfacing with the most unexpected triggers. Their fights would take a turn and suddenly one of them would accuse the other of something they never did.

"How could you leave me!" Tony raised his voice to Jessie one Christmas Eve, after she arrived home an hour late from Midnight Mass.

Eva was a close friend, and together they attended the service, then went for tea afterward. Jessie was an hour late arriving home, but that wasn't anything alarming in a marriage, so she was very surprised at his outburst.

"I didn't leave you, Tony. What are you getting so upset about?" Jessie spoke in a calming voice as she pulled off her winter coat.

He just stood in front of her with a strange look in his eyes. At times, he was seeing something she couldn't see. He left the room and she knew to leave him be. He would always come back to her as the Tony she knew and loved. They never had to explain behavior such as this. Being damaged people, they understood what no one else ever could.

They didn't have any children, so most of their time was spent together. Even if Jessie was shopping, Tony would sit in the car doing crossword puzzles. Jessie took her time browsing the stores. They rarely went alone anywhere. They would visit friends and play bridge, where their strong connection was especially evident.

"I think you two cheat somehow. You seem to know what each other has," said Eva's husband, Ned, as he stared over his glasses at Tony, "and more suspicious, is that you know just what the other is going to play."

It was an especially cold winter day, when Tony went to the store for Jessie. She was ill and they were out of any medication to take down her fever. It wasn't unusual for Jessie's fevers to reach alarming temperatures. Often she would become delirious and hear voices, or see visions. He cursed when he saw an empty bottle of aspirin placed back in the cupboard with the lid on. They had run short.

"It's too cold out, Tony. The roads will be icy. Don't go. Just put cool cloths on my head and the fever will go down," Jessie pleaded with him.

She was shivering from her rising temperature and he knew that he had to leave. He tucked her covers tightly around her and promised he'd only be half an hour. The fever was causing her to become irrational and he kissed her hot forehead.

Jessie fell into a fitful sleep. She woke with a start, thinking she'd heard her name.

"Tony?" she called out into the dark.

The windows were shaking from the blizzard wind. The pinging of snow told her it was still snowing outside. The clock read almost midnight. He'd been gone for hours. She knew before the phone rang, that he was gone.

…

Jessie went to his grave site every Sunday and talked to Tony like he was still alive. She scolded him for leaving her alone to fend for herself.

"How could you, Tony? You promised me and I believed you. I begged you not to go out into the storm that night, but no, you had to go and get yourself in an accident and leave me here by myself. And you are right, no one is going to want someone like me. No one will ever understand me like you do," and on and on went her rambling, every Sunday.

On the first Christmas after his passing, Jessie decided she'd put up a tree and try to make her home festive. She loved the lights and the smell of pine. After all the tinsel had been strategically placed over the branches, and the lights set just so, she poured a bath and submerged herself, relaxing in the hot, fragrant water. Afterward, she wrapped up in a bath towel, stepped out, and slipped her feet into those same tattered slippers. She drew her foot back sharply.

"What on earth?" she muttered and sat down on the ledge, reaching into the slipper, and there it was—a small twig from a tree.

She smiled.

Bench Warrant

by Sheila Cano

After my mother moved to Bellingham from California, I used to take the bus down to visit her on weekends. At the U.S. border, we all got off for questioning while a Customs inspector checked the interior of the coach. Not everyone was interrogated, but I always was. When they punched my driver's license number into the computer, a lot of information came up. They couldn't refuse to let me in, as I was a U.S. citizen, but apparently my life was of some interest to them and I usually had to wait several minutes while it was scanned. At first the process made me nervous, but I got used to it after awhile.

One time, I got on the bus in Vancouver and sat down beside an aboriginal guy. There were lots of empty spots, but all the window seats were taken. We were silent most of the way. However, as we approached the border crossing, the man clapped his hands to his head and mumbled to himself.

"Something the matter?" I asked.

"Aw, I just remembered. There's a bench warrant out for me in Whatcom County, for breaking and entering," he groaned. "I'd forgotten all about it. That was two years ago."

"Never mind," I said. "Just stand behind me when we get in line and they won't pay any attention to you. They'll be too busy with me."

"Really? What did you do?"

"I was married to a draft resister once," I replied. "But I've never done anything they could arrest me for."

As usual, we filed off the bus into the building. I was about tenth in line, and when it was my turn, the officer typed in my driver's license number. We stood there for five minutes while paper spewed forth from the printer, piling up on the floor. He began waving people around me without questioning them, and the native guy went over to sit on the bench with the others. Finally the officer said I could go, and we all got back on the bus.

"Gee, thanks a lot," the man said, as we sat down again.

"No problem," I responded. "It happens every time."

Moon And Venus

by Jac

I'm sitting on the back porch of our new home, I should say, soon to be new home. Over the weekend I signed a lease for the next years plus two weeks, a bonus of two weeks because the last tenant left a month early.

It's Monday morning, February 28. When I stepped into the yard with the dogs (my girls) the clock read 4:28am. I'm not exactly sure of the time now.

Eight inches of new snow fell Friday night, my two girls and I have spent the weekend trying to get our fill of this winter wonderland. This morning is our last chance to play in it for a couple of weeks, or possibly until next winter.

We've enjoyed the snow from Saratoga to Albany, in Upstate New York. We haven't seen much snow this year and miss it. The girls were born for snow and spent their first few years in this part of New York. I uprooted them and they've been sad that Northern Virginia has missed almost every storm this season.

The car is packed and we have to start back to our adopted home within the hour. Sixty months of accumulated stuff needs to be packed, loose ends tied, and many goodbyes' said. Who knows if the snow will be here when we return?

For everyone else in the neighborhood it's the middle of the night. For us, it's our normal playtime. In the last hour we've run around under the lights of our new backyard, trying to find the bright orange ball I've thrown. The ball disappears as soon as it touches the surface of the snow.

The two girls run and pounce on the spot they believe it landed. First, it's whose eyes are the quickest. Then it's whose legs are the fastest. Finally, it's whose nose can detect a ball submerged in snow, each trying to be the first to find and return it to me.

They're evenly matched in size and stamina; Silver has the advantage of athleticism, while Nova's asset is sheer determination.

When either of them finds the ball, the object is to return it to me. The others objective is to force the finder through a gauntlet of sorts, designed to shake the ball loose.

When Silver finds the ball, Nova grabs at her tail, collar, fur, or skin around her neck, anything she can grip with her mouth and teeth, and then she puts on the brakes, often managing to pull Silver to a complete stop. When Nova finds the ball, Silver runs ahead trying to cut her off, using her body like a football player and ramming into Nova.

Both tactics are sound and the unlucky can become the lucky. I have treats for the lucky.

Those infrequent times that they can't find the ball, it's my turn to run and pounce. I end up buried to my knees in snow with the two of them trying their hardest to find my boots, which have also magically disappeared. Or they try to find the pocket that holds the treats, and that combined pouncing and grabbing always finds me covered in dogs and snow.

We have exhausted ourselves and are now enjoying the rest of our time here, relaxing on the porch. I, with a steaming cup of coffee, sitting in a soft chair wrapped in a comforter. The girls each have a chunk of rawhide to chew, lying on their favorite, thick, warm blanket we've brought along from Virginia.

The view from the porch is east, southeast, and the dark, early morning sky is incredible. I see the shimmering silver sliver of a crescent moon, its razor-thin iridescent hands reach out for an equally brilliant and dazzling Venus.

I can't take my eyes off them. I don't ever remember seeing the two together like this. As I watch their slow journey, my thoughts drift to the last five years. The accomplishments, lessons, places, people, friendships, and love I found in Virginia can never be replaced and will never be forgotten.

Now in New York, as we prepare to leave our new home for a couple of weeks, I can't help but imagine the three of us as Venus— with the Moon beckoning to us, "Hurry back home soon."

Mothers' Bench

by B G Lewis

I write this as testament to the simple path of an ant.

I wanted something to do, a job, being so remarkably adept and skillful with my new opportunity, I reasoned, though oblivious to my own certainties. Exuberant with the gift of chance and perception, I often found quiet contemplation to wish upon a task, to be a good doggy. All roads were leading to thrills full of learning, and understanding. The tuition was paid for, and I a willing student. So it happened that I awoke one morn with an impending task to do.

"I get this thing about 'mothers'," was my announcement to the wife at our next opportunity.

If her eyebrow raised, then I was too naive and questing to notice, and continued, "All day long I've been getting 'mothers', or 'mother'. I don't know. It seemed important. I even got the vibe, and I saw an ad, Mothers' Music, some store downtown. Musical stuff."

"Do you think you should go?"

"Where?"

"To the store downtown."

"I don't know."

"You have to ask."

So I took my guitar. Mothers' Music? Packed it in the case and walked up to the train station, pondering what the heck 'mothers' meant. The sky's a little overcast.

On the train, nothing forward or noticeable. I get off downtown and wander the thoroughfare looking for signs, symbols or symphony to join. I met up with old Bob, a moderate term panhandler that runs his gig where the high-rises turn into low-rises and three story, cheap hotels. Lots of adult shops and bars. Good stake for spare change, but busy—you have to fend off intruders for real estate. Bob's doing a talking bit, winning over gripers in his stained plaid meeting suit and a two week old beard.

"Buddy, buddy, c'mon, give a guy a break, man. C'mon, spare change… Hey, Ma'am, Ma'am, hey, I'm just dirty, not scary. Need some food, c'mon lady… Hey buddy, slide some change c'mon buddy…"

Bob's hit-to-walkby ratio was terrible. I was getting the sense Bob was far too serious, too intent on getting the cash and getting out. He needed something to lull the crowd. This could be an opening.

"Hey, I'm gonna play some guitar."

"Whatever, man."

"I don't know, maybe get a bit of coin. Sing something."

"Nah."

I start in with some meandering blues chops, but I'm not really getting the vibe from old Bob. He's growing antsy, more abrupt with the clientele. He's looking like I've crashed his gig. Then the break up.

"Hey, dude…" Bob interrupts my twiddling solo bend. I've been oblivious to the passing annoyed.

"Yeah?

"I kinda work better alone."

"Oh, OK."

Not much more from Bob. He seemed to have things handled, and not really the 'mother' type. The topic didn't come up.

Onto the music shop. Lessons learned: Zilch. Feeling of idiocy: High. Still listening.

…

Four more blocks and the destination, Mother's Music. The outside is security glass with display windows and papered in posters and notices. An artiste's supply nook. I'm through the belled door and turnstile, then into the emporium.

I can no longer remember what I specifically looked for, but nothing struck. No signs, nothing cosmic. A busy store, but my thoughts were preoccupied with a need for some event or instruction. I was looking for evidence of a mission clue. I was without a signal.

I left the music store dejected and foolish with myself for indulging this trip of faith, spurred by a surreal tingly feeling and an overwhelming moral compulsion to comply. I was nuts.

I wandered in an aimless fashion south and west, walking with advantage of a sloping grade towards the water. The guitar and its case were becoming a burden and I switched hands often. I was wondering if it wise to bring the crate. The commercial zone, and my transportation, was now many blocks behind me, and I caught glimpses of a brightening sky over the harbor. I was walking through apartment blocks and en route to the shoreline.

I had a decision, stay on level ground and head west, perhaps running into a downtown bus route saving me effort, or turn and descend towards a park and open green space. Drawn to the open expanse and the possibility that my quest could indeed exist toward that which I was naturally compelled, I marched to the sea and the sunshine.

I turned and took twenty steps. On the sidewalk was a lopsided square of purple construction paper. It caught my attention because it was a glimmer of color and creativity on a stark, concrete slab. I picked it up and examined the handiwork: A serious crafter, heavy into crayon pen and glue. Bright, and good use of perspective and media. Probably grade two, or three. Alas, all that work. I couldn't leave it there, in the event rain started. The idea of some kid's art going to mush without appreciation seemed a little harsh. It belonged on a fridge door, getting good praise and warranting much gloating. I surveyed the art, a night theme with a sky full of stars, all twinkly and evenly spaced. They seemed to flutter. My interpretation—given my ethereal, wannabe disposition—angelic.

I picked it up and placed it flat in the guitar case, then continued walking.

I should take pause and express the dilemma that was going through my thoughts. The concept of leaping downtown with no more than an intuitive sense that I was to perform some todo list item about 'mothers' was affecting my self confidence. What was I doing?

Why was I doing this? I felt I was playing some obsessive game, seeing it through to the end and the scenario was planned in my unconscious. Was this an elaborate ritual or proving ground for my own lapse in reality? With each step I was daunted, then compelled. The whole process was exhausting. A witness might have thought me out on a day pass.

Finding the little picture, the kid's art, gave my gnarled disposition a glimmer. The harbor shared the outlook. As I approached, the sun broke and flooded a patch of open water. The brilliance brought me comfort. Nature again.

I walked confidently toward the sand and the lapping waves. The wind picked up and few beach goers were present. Some huddled behind logs to escape the wind and wait out the overcast sky. I continued southwesterly in the warm beams that confidently shone out over the sand. The day seemed to be turning fair, and I loosened off my jacket, trudging, and toting the cement guitar.

In another hundred paces, I began to realize a little phenomenon. The sunlight was encircling me, in a rough outline fifty feet across. Everyone else on the beach was in a cloudy day. As I walked, the sunlight traveled with me and I became self conscious. The brightness splintered through the clouds and the entire harbor was darkened, but I had a carpet of sun glow that was moving with my pace along the beach, over the grass, past the picnic area, and onto a slope leading up a hill to the park gates. It felt a little Hollywood.

Looking at the knoll and the park entrance, I watched the accompanying sunlight suddenly speed forward, dash up the slope, and rest on the forested hilltop. And then, big vibe. I knew that was it. Whatever I was searching for could be found somewhere on that view site, among those trees. I asked within, and got back a wordless affirmation that wiped doubt from my mind. My direction seemed as obvious as a runway beacon. Mothers, hey?

When I reached the top of the rise, I saw a bench. The sunlight pointed at it like a giant, blazing finger. All very dramatic. When I approached and set the guitar case down, the patch of light moved off and fled out to the water and hovered over the bay. This was the place.

The bench was a memorial, as well as a rest stop for the weary wanderer. There was a brass plaque and an inscription:

To My Cherished Angels,

Know That My Spirit Is With You Always

Love Mom

Somebody lost their kids. Maybe they still returned to contemplate their loss? Maybe a mother? I unlatched the case and pulled out the little kid's picture, then set it on the bench with a small stone on top—so it wouldn't blow away. Suddenly, there was a great sense of ease, like "mission accomplished" or "you did well." I felt thankful for the little journey, a bit puzzled, but I sensed participation in a larger significance. Maybe someone forlorn would walk to that bench and find that picture and hang it on their fridge. I didn't know, but it didn't seem to matter. I felt I had done a minuscule part. I plucked a tune, packed up, and left. I know it seems like nothing, but I had to see if it was real.

The Girl I Left Behind
by Adrienne S Moody

Kenny was very sick when Vanessa was hired to care for him. He was diagnosed with bone cancer and his wish was to remain at home as long as that was possible. Sixty-five years old and with his jet black hair, crystal blue eyes and a wicked grin fronting a sly sense of humour, he seemed much younger.

They laughed easily together. He called her his angel. Together they organized his medication and she soon detected he needed her to listen, just be there beside him.

Vanessa made mistakes during that short time she knew him. It was her first experience with morphine patches and didn't realize they contained varying percentages of the lethal drug. She left him one day with only half the amount he needed to manage his pain. When she arrived home later in the evening there was a message on her machine. In his raspy Scottish accent voice, he told Vanessa that an ambulance was called and he was admitted into hospital—would she come and see him as soon as possible? She left immediately.

She wasn't surprised to see they placed him on the seventh floor. Patients there would not leave the hospital and their stay would be short. She sat beside his bed in his private room. Moments passed before he opened his eyes.

"Hey, Kenny," she smiled at him.

"There's my angel," he put his hand on her cheek. "I guess I'm here sooner than I thought."

"I'm so sorry, Kenny."

"Don't apologize. I've done that myself…they need to mark the patches better. They gave me a heavy dose…put me right out…dreaming," his eyes glazed, rolled upwards and his mouth moved wordlessly.

She sat for a few moments and then left. The sound of her heels echoed as she walked down the sterilized and polished hallway. It was late and there were a few visitors. The patients were generally heavily medicated or in drug-induced sleep. Vanessa glanced into a few of the darkened rooms and could see the lifeless forms on beds. She nodded her head to the two nurses at the desk before taking the elevator down.

The cool night air welcomed her; she breathed deeply and could detect a hint of spring—the smell of the earth warming and promising growth. She thought of Kenny and his love of poetry. Rudyard Kipling was one of Kenny's favorites and years earlier he had given a copy of the poem If to to his son, Micheal.

"My Father didn't give way to lectures on what it was to be a man," Michael told Vanessa one evening, after Kenny had gone to bed. She sat with Michael while he drank whiskey and reminisced. "He just demonstrated by the way he lived his life. The only time he came close to lecturing me was giving me a copy of Kipling's poem, If. I can recite it for you…" Michael stood and raised his glass and spoke:

'If you can keep your head when all about you

Are losing theirs and blaming it on you,

If you can trust yourself when all men doubt you

But make allowance for their doubting too,

150

If you can wait and not be tired by waiting,

Or being lied about, don't deal in lies,

Or being hated, don't give way to hating,

And yet don't look too good, nor talk too wise:'

Michael's voice broke with emotion at the end of his recital and his eyes filled with tears.

"I'm going to miss him. Goodnight Vanessa." He turned abruptly and left the room.

Kenny was a fighter. The nurses were getting impatient with him.

"He won't sleep. He's fighting this every step of the way. His pain is excruciating and he's refusing medication because he says he's afraid he won't wake up," Morgan, the day nurse, complained to Vanessa.

They walked together from the desk to his room. Kenny was sitting in a wheelchair staring out the window; a lock of black hair hung close to his eyes. He looked up and beamed a smile when he saw Vanessa at the doorway.

"Angel," was all he said.

"Yes, here she is… here to hold your hand," Morgan's voice was sharp and she abruptly left, responding to a patient alarm.

"Kenny, how goes it today?" Vanessa walked closer and put her arms around him. He held on weakly.

"I want you to bring me a bottle of whiskey tonight, darlin'. It's under the sink—a bottle of Black Velvet I'm saving. You'll join me and Michael for a drink tonight? Don't worry about them," he waved his hand towards the door. "Hide it when you come–they will never be the wiser." Kenny instructed.

Vanessa nodded her head. Whatever he wanted she was determined to do. "Take me outside, dear. I want to smell the air. This hospital air is enough to kill a healthy man, let alone a sick one."

Vanessa pushed his wheelchair down the hallway and they took the elevator to the main floor.

"Will you ever marry again?" he asked her on the short ride down. She was surprised at the question.

"Yes, I think I would. If I ever found the right man, Kenny," she smiled at him and her fingers brushed his hair from his eyes.

"What would be the right man, Angel?" he asked and she detected a mischievous look in his eyes.

"Let me think. He would definitely have to be Scottish and love poets like Kipling and Burns... I have a weakness for that kind of man... and that burning intensity in his eyes... and, of course, he would drink Black Velvet Whiskey and break all the rules to do so." They grinned at each other and the elevator doors opened.

A young man pushing a very pregnant woman in a wheelchair, waited for them to exit and Kenny placed his hand on the expectant mother and said, "You'll be fine, dear, just don't eat the food," and winked at her.

It was 9 pm when Vanessa arrived back at the hospital, the bottle of whiskey hidden under her jacket. A nurse whom Vanessa had never seen before stopped her before she could enter the room.

"Are you a relative of Mr. McGregor's?" the petite nurse asked.

"Yes, I am his niece," Vanessa lied, knowing the hospital protocol about only family visitors near the end of a patient's life.

"Okay, go on then. His condition is very grave, I must warn you. I gave him a very heavy dose of morphine a couple of hours ago and he's not stirred since."

The nurse waited while Vanessa stood at Kenny's bedside. She felt his spirit had left and all that remained was his shell. His breathing was labored and Vanessa did not want to stay. A paperback book on his meal tray caught her eye. She picked it up and read the cover, 'The Girl I Left Behind.' "

"What's this? Where did this come from?" she asked the nurse.

"He got it from the patient lounge down the hall. He asked me to wheel him there and he went through the bookshelf and picked it up. Strange fellow, this one. I'm trying to get hold of his son. Do you know where he might be? He needs to be contacted."

Vanessa shook her head and the nurse left the room. She opened the cupboard door above the sink and picked a plastic cup from the shelf. Vanessa pulled the curtain surrounding Kenny's bed for privacy, then opened the bottle of whiskey and poured a shot into the glass.

"To you, Kenny," she toasted him and drank the burning liquid. She sat close, touching his arm and listening to the hospital noise around them. Urgent voices, clicking of heels, murmuring, doors shutting and Kenny—his breath turned to a rattle and she waited anxiously for each one. And then all was quiet. She kissed his forehead and picked up the book. She knew Kenny had left it for her. After slipping it into her purse, Vanessa left.

Blind Date

by Adrienne S Moody

His internet picture revealed a man with broad shoulders and an intensity in his eyes, and reminded her of a man she was obsessed with years ago. Although he was twelve years younger, she felt compelled to meet him and so they met. He shed his broad shoulders by peeling off two jackets and a vest. Her profile stated she was a non-smoker, but she pulled a package out of her purse and asked him for a light. Just when she was about to rate this date as dismal and deceptive, he told her he recently hit a blind woman crossing the street and killed her. They sat huddled together like conspirators at the North Shore Quay and she listened to his story as the gulls hovered and tug boats chugged across the bay.

The sun was setting low in the late summer sky, painting the cotton ball clouds pastel shades of pink and purple. Her date was of Hungarian descent with golden, wolf eyes, a ski jump nose, and nervous hands. Touching his arm gently, she urged him to tell her what happened. He lit another cigarette and ran his slender fingers through his thick black hair.

"I wasn't speeding... it was just another day at work. She came out of nowhere and it almost seemed like she jumped in front of my truck. It doesn't make any sense. I remember the sound of hitting her body, but the strangest thing was, I heard a voice whisper in my right ear just before I turned the corner."

"What did the voice say?" she coaxed him on.

Seagulls suddenly swooped down and converged on a box of french fries two teenagers had left on a table. The couple waited for the screeching to subside. The Seabus hooted its horn and pulled away from the dock. The smell of deep fried fish filled the air.

He took a deep drag of his cigarette and blew rings that floated up into the air, perfect little o's.

"It was like my guardian angel. The voice said, 'Prepare yourself. Something is coming to you.' And I did prepare myself, like this force field that suddenly covered my body… and when I hit her, it just wasn't real to me. It was like I left my body and I was watching from above. Weird, I know," he acknowledged the puzzled look on her face.

"So you did hit her?"

"Yes, I did. And then, it was just, crazy. She was down and I kept saying, 'It was just a bump, just a nudge, why isn't she getting up?' I remember saying that. It didn't make any sense. One minute I'm driving back to the station and it's Friday… and I'm happy it's the weekend. I've got four more blocks to go and I'm done for the week. And then this? This woman, carrying one of those white canes, is down on the street and she's not getting up!"

The sky held onto one red streak. Crimson red. He was breathing heavily. His face was shiny and deep furrows made him look much older than his 32 years. Three Asian girls wearing matching school uniforms burst through the doors behind them and with their arms linked, passed, their voices like instruments playing the same tune, lovely and light.

"After all the legal stuff I had to go through—I was found innocent, by the way—it was just a freaking accident, I parked my truck at the station and I tried it. I tried falling into the front fender the way she did, still trying to figure how such a little tap could kill someone. But it did. It did."

"That's such a sad story. What do you think that voice was, anyway? You think it was a guardian angel?"

"Yeah, that's all I can figure. Prepare yourself. Something is coming to you. Man, they weren't kidding. I hope I never hear that voice again."

A Puzzle In The Night

by M Dawn Thacker

Grandpa talked in riddles, rarely giving the answers straight up. I always had to work his puzzles. Sometimes I had to fit the frame together, or gather all the blue for the sky. Other times, I built mountains from the valley floor and climbed them so I could appreciate the view. When I finally had the picture together though, I never forgot the lesson of the piecing.

He was eighty-nine years old, bent, but strong. Near the end, he shuffled from his favorite spot at the kitchen table to his red leather chair in the living room where he rocked his memories to a slow, gentle rhythm.

I went to visit him in late August. He was reflective and quiet, holding my hand with the same firm grip, removing his cap, so I could kiss his bald head. He didn't have much to say. We sat in comfortable silence for a long time, he with his eyes closed, me watching him. When I had to leave, I leaned in close and said, "You have a birthday coming up."

"Nope," he said.

"Of course you do," I insisted. "You'll be ninety. We'll have a big party, with caramel cake and vanilla ice cream, your favorite. The whole family will be there and you and I can dance."

He looked up at me with watery blue eyes and smiled, but re-stated his earlier, "Nope."

I squeezed his hand, smiled back, and chalked his statement up to lack of oxygen, or confusion from the stroke. If I had known he only had eight more days to live, I would have stayed and held his hand a little while longer.

He was the nearest man to a father I had. My mother and I moved from apartment to apartment when I was little. His house was 'home.' He built my swing in the maple tree, and taught me how to reel in a fish at Abel's Pond. He gave me a quarter for raking leaves even after I jumped into the pile and scattered them all over the yard again. The two of us watched David and Chet tell each other goodnight. He called me "Tump" in a baritone voice that I can still hear when I close my eyes late at night.

Garth Payne would have been excited to learn he was going to be a great-grandfather. The doctor broke the news to me about the baby several years after Grandpa died. I was a little excited, and a lot scared. I sat on the examining table feeling lost. I was an only child, and the youngest of Grandpa Payne's nine grandchildren. I had no experience with babies and didn't know what to do with one. The responsibility terrified me. Suppose I broke the baby?

Grandpa was wise. I could talk to him about anything. He would sit and listen, chin resting on his walking stick, watching me.

"What should I do?" I'd ask.

Then he would tell me a story, one of his riddle lessons. He never handed me the answer, but by the end of his tale, I was pointed in the right direction. Now he was gone.

I knew his footsteps and the squeak of the floorboards. I'd grown up in his house and now it was mine. This was not a dream. I fought to wake up, to open my eyes and see him again. It was the middle of the night, dark in the room, but he was there.

"Wake up," my mind told me. "This is important," but my body wouldn't listen.

I felt the mattress give as he sat down on the bed next to me. I knew my Grandpa, his touch on my face, his warmth.

He leaned down close to my ear, and whispered in his distinct baritone, "All the worry in the world ain't gonna help, Tump. Just love him."

I turned, and headed in the right direction. On March 13th the following year, Benjamin Garth was born. He was named for the man who taught me the most about love.

Everyday Magic

by Steven Bird

A strong chubasco moved up from Baja and blew over the desert basins spread north to the San Joaquin. Heat poured over the coast range, drawn by convection to the cool Pacific. The furnace wind hit at sunrise and blew open the back door.

I woke to find my bed exposed to the world. I threw the covers back and stretched, gazing out into the yard where the wind shuttled stray leaves from under the plastic chairs while the hot breeze wafted into the room. It smelled like magnolias and orange blossoms. Then something flew by the window, and reappeared in the doorway.

It was a bright, foil balloon. A child's balloon. It hovered at the open door quivering on the breeze, long enough for me to read the message.

Happy Birthday!

And then it was gone on the wind, a long red ribbon trailing. I rolled out of bed and ran outside to follow, watched the balloon meander above the street until a strong gust blew it into the grid of power lines. The ribbon tangled in the wires. The balloon remained stuck for awhile, the heart shaped head furious against the wind. And then it pulled loose and flew up, up and out over the highway, then across the beach, and kept going far out over the clear expanse of ocean. I watched until it was a tiny exclamation point above the horizon line, and then the sky absorbed its form and it was gone.

Magic, I thought. Nobody will ever believe it.

The Magic Hour
by Adrienne S Moody

Photographers often refer to this time of day as the Magic Hour and it is during the last hour of sunlight, or the first of the day. I've walked the beach during this time and pebbles that look nondescript will suddenly take on a hue that causes me to bend down and examine more closely. The next day I will wonder what inspired me to carry it home. In normal light, it is, indeed, just another stone.

I will always remember the first hour of daylight. That was when my newborn woke and demanded attention. I would rock him on the glider, bought especially for the occasion, and together we would greet the day. The first crack of light, through the large picture window in the home we lived, would light on my baby's face and nothing compared to that sight—for me, a new mother. There was nowhere I'd rather be. We lived in this cocoon, he and I, and the world moved all around us. We'd watch, he in my arms, or perched over my shoulder, wide-eyed at everything he saw. Nothing touched us.

It was a time of holding, rocking, changing, bathing, and feeding. And at around 4:00 am every morning, he'd stir and not even cry to wake me or summon me. I began to enjoy this time, a time for he and I to greet the light, in our magic hour.

Night Along The River

By B G Lewis

Morning, beautiful and horrid. Unknown seeps and ebbs from appreciation. Arising to hope and promise misplaced, a fear lost in sleep, until shock with reality. I miss the night when day arrives and I miss the sunshine when night sweeps in, never long enough, but I understand the visit. If all was night, I wouldn't appreciate the intricacy of solitude.

There's a valley with an emery sheen that dances on a river. The scene unfolds, breathtaking and forlorn. Rocks and boulders sit scattered, draped in tangled pines like broken bystanders, wild and changing. The banks are shaped by cascading torrents and in the motion, I become mesmerized. The water's relentless turmoil calls me at night, so I walk down the path to water's edge and feel the rocks speak. They rumble low, and I listen, a guest. Then another is revealed, in prints that cross the sand. A large one makes the night home. The rocks bid me "go no further" and again, I listen, setting a stick to mark my furthest intrusion. The journey along a river ends, the night in living combination was brief, my prints pacing alongside the beast's. I ran back in the morning, but the river has worked the prints into sand, washed a night into sand.

Morning dream, beautiful and horrid. Fears ebb and unknown seeps, raising hopes briefly with the dawn. Conscious comes and lulls the hidden again to sleep. I miss the night when day arrives and I miss the sunshine when night claims all. Still, the night's never longer. And in ever stillness, I would kick and scratch until the daylight bled again.

There's a a crystal sheen who dances with a river, breathing in the gills of earth, tumbled wild and ever. Changing, shaping torrents in cascade, a swirling fray, reduced and sized as me, mesmerized to see the night spectacle, padding in a path held by all to water, and a greeting to flowing spirit, a speaker in currents and eddies calling, frothing. Still, I come as a guest, not at home, and still the icy chill forbids me, singing, that I go no further. I listen into the journey alone, a shadow turns me, and leaves memory in return, the night ours and briefly, my presence entwined with the river beast. Until I arise, running into morning, a strewn connection with sunlight, the water sifting memory within dream shimmer, escaping, beautiful and horrid.

A river finds me lurking for a seat where the world can pass, and I never have to gaze, or lift a stone. So effortlessly the world changes in the rush of moving water. A blanket embraces the river valley at night, dulled in fog and busy to the edges of earth tugging, sipping on frozen rain who will wake on high plateaus to tumble and cajole on mission to the sea. A river is a promise of always getting somewhere and torrent can slip log and limb to another realm beyond the corner or the bend. To sit in the river blanket at night, is to paddle a raft of thoughts and stories and ever changing what if's. Those paddling, they look fondly on the earth bound manor or the shack and see a chance to root and sink into a day of stationary thought. While the shorebirds watch the river parade in passing, free of foundation and commitment. The landed are left to daydream on the river traveler. She pauses, the witness hanging laundry, and wonders, what if?

Pink Snow Day

by Sheila Cano

Cherry trees are giving up their blossoms today. Petals fluttering like snowflakes on the breeze resemble the flight of moths, up, down, and sideways until they settle in drifts on the ground. The gutters are lined with pink snow. It is time to have the snow tires on my car exchanged for the all-season tires. I call the tire shop to book a time, and plan to go out for breakfast while the job is being done. There is a cafe a few blocks from the row of auto repair shops down near the harbor.

The day begins with a deep conversation with an acquaintance about karma. We each have friends who are Buddhists, and we struggle with the concept of karma. Buddhists believe that every action you make has a cause-and-effect relation to your circumstances in life, and that you are reincarnated in successive lifetimes with the opportunity to improve your chances of attaining enlightenment through practicing good intentions. While both of us adhere to the golden rule of 'do unto others as you would have them do unto you,' we find it hard to accept the notion that our current status in life has been determined by our actions in a past life. By this notion, someone who is born into poverty, or with disabilities, is marked because they have done something bad in their past life. Those who are born into wealth and good health are deemed to have deserved this status due to their virtue in a previous incarnation. The relationship between the oppressed, and the oppressors, is seen as a dynamic of cause-and-effect: the one seen as a victim must have done something to deserve that from their past life actions. The two of us find this to be a challenging concept.

I used to go to a small, two-person tire shop. The last set of snow tires I bought there were a cheaper brand, and I wasn't happy with them. The next time I wanted to order a better brand, and they were unable to do it, so I went to a bigger tire shop a few doors down. On this tire changing day, I head to the shop, and find myself pulling up in front of the small outfit instead. I am surprised that my car has guided me here, like a horse that knows its way home without the rider using reins. For a moment I waver, then decide that it must be 'car-ma', and besides, it will be about $20 cheaper for the job than at the larger place. I leave the car and walk to the restaurant. On the way, I pass by the shop I called in the morning.

"Hi, I called earlier today to book time to have my snow tires taken off."

"Oh, you're the Toyota Echo?"

"Right. Something's come up and I don't have time to do it today."

"Well, just give us a call anytime. Plan an hour to an hour and a half for the job."

The restaurant breakfast is an indulgence. Maybe a couple of times a year – when I get tires changed, I order a two-egg platter and pay for it before taking a seat: sausages and scrambled eggs, brown toast and fried potatoes, black coffee. I sit near the window, but out of the sun, and read the morning paper. There is an article about an artist who travels to the Arctic and Antarctic, and his exhibit includes photos of cows in Tierra del Fuego, animals who travel on icebergs to get to new pastures. The image is startling. However did the cattle decide to do this? Did their herd-mates mutter, "Teach them this unfathomable procedure, urge them to have faith that they will survive the trip without drowning…"? The server brings breakfast and I munch, visualizing a cow leaving the security of the land for unknown fields in their imagination. Homeless, in a sense, for the duration of the iceberg ride.

I leave half of the fried potatoes and a slice of toast, too stuffed to eat any more, and mindful that my body doesn't need any more carbs. As I step outside the cafe, a tall, thin man with long stringy, matted hair approaches.

"Good morning, Ma'am," he says.

"Good morning," I reply.

His clothes are ragged and soiled, and his face is lined and dirty. I think he is probably younger than he looks, living on the street or in the bush. His voice is calm and polite.

"Do you think you could buy me a coffee, or something to eat, Ma'am?"

"A coffee? Sure, I can."

"And something to eat? I'm really hungry and I haven't eaten in a while."

"OK, I'll buy breakfast for you. Come on inside and tell them what you want."

"Thank you. I really appreciate this, Ma'am." We go in, and I approach the counter.

"I'd like to buy breakfast for this gentleman," I say to the cashier.

"What would you like?" she says to him.

"I'd like bacon and eggs, sunny-side up, and white toast," he replies. "And coffee."

"For here, or to go?"

He deliberates. I suggest to him that he could sit inside if he wants to.

"I don't know about being in a restaurant. I haven't had a shower lately," he says quietly.

"Well, it's up to you," I say. I pull out my bank card and pay for his meal.

"To go," he says. The cashier hands him a take-out cup and he helps himself from the coffee urn.

"Thank you," he says to me. "Thanks very much, Ma'am. I hope you have a good day."

"You too," I reply. "Take care."

I walk back to get my car. The bill is, as I figured, about $20 cheaper than the other tire shop. That more than covers the cost of my meal, and the one I bought for the man at the restaurant. I drive home, pausing before the garage entrance to let a grandmother and a little toddler walk by. The tiny girl chortles as a big swirl of petals blow off the cherry tree, enveloping us in a pink blizzard. I'm still thinking about karma.

Last Wedding Gift

by Adrienne S Moody

I was surprised that he let us go. It couldn't have been easy to see his wife and son pack up and leave like we did. What motivated me most was scraping ice off my windshield in the month of June. A freak snowstorm, yes, but far too common, having lived in the Prairies all of my life. The ocean beckoned me.

I had sat in a doctor's office flipping through magazines and there it was—an article about the ten best places in North America to live. One was a tourist town close to the US border. "Had it all," the article claimed. The scenic town boasted the most hours of sunshine compared to the rest of the region—and then that picture of a couple hiking in the mountains. That was for me—year round, outdoor recreation. The Prairies are beautiful, that big sky is like no other, but the bitter cold and lengthy winter season was killing my artistic spirit. I will never forget the change in the air at the end of August; the winter wind makes its presence known, as only it can do.

I burst into tears upon telling my ex that I could no longer remain. If I didn't move where there were four seasons and warmer weather, I would surely perish. Dramatic? Yes, but my spirit suffered and would take no more.

It was still so difficult to leave. And he let me. He helped me pack. We moved around my apartment in silence as I wrapped dishes in newspaper and piled them carefully in boxes. Linens were rolled together and placed in large plastic bags. I threw out so much, because I was traveling by car and had to conserve space. I discovered minimalism during that time of my life. There was freedom taking only the essentials.

We stood in the middle of the barren kitchen after we finished the bittersweet chore. Sadness. Fear. Then something else ended. A ticking stopped suddenly. We both looked up on the wall where the last of our wedding gifts hung. We'd forgotten the forest green wall clock that had lasted right up until that day.

My ex reached up for it, brought it down, and held it out to me.

We didn't speak.

I took it from him and packed it along with the rest of our belongings.

The Little Death

by Gaboo

Is it our human nature to protect ourselves from eminent darkness, or death, to feel that our time here is limitless among the cosmos? Why do we look to the sky, endless with no gravity or fear, just stars and comfort?

There's an old saying, la petite mort, the little death. The French coined it and I can see how they would. There's a beautiful, romantic tragedy in its offing. They meant at orgasm, or the height of bliss. A sneeze. The shiver urinating. The gasp losing balance. Sometimes the heart slows a beat, pauses, and we let go of the reins. There's a pinnacle of being alive suddenly juxtaposed with leaving the body—the freeze frame when all is happening and all stops—the verge of death.

I get the same sensation from heights. I envy you mountain climber types, but I'm afraid to look down. I don't trust myself and fear I would go into lala land or pirouette off the edge. But the crazy thing is, I wouldn't care at the time. The vertigo would have already put me between dream and waking, swirling. In that moment of the little death, I am not afraid.

Sense Of Wonder

by Adrienne S Moody

I remember the feel of my bare legs holding tight on the horse's back.

"Nah, you guys don't need a saddle. Ride 'em bareback!" my cousin, Ralph determined.

Ralph loved to see city kids scream and to show them how little they knew about 'real' life. Farm life was, in my mind, far more exciting and interesting than any city could be. I was hoisted up on this old mare's back and clung to Patsy, who was five years older than me. She couldn't have known, that her brother was going to swat the horse and yelp, startle the animal and make him bolt, but that's what happened. I learned from that experience; anything could happen at my Uncle's farm. As I clung desperately to Patsy, I rallied off a few Hail Marys, begging her to make the horse stop before I toppled off to my death below. Part of me thrilled at the sheer excitement of it all.

I was never bored.

The cycle of life played out in the glare of sunlight and at times witnessed by me, a mere city girl, there for a summer vacation.

"Come here, Adrienne. Follow me," my Uncle gestured, while I gathered eggs.

I followed, knowing I would see something worth writing in my journal later that day. He took me to the back of the barn and suddenly put his hand up, signaling to stop. I did. There ahead of us was a cow giving birth. The calf dropped to the ground all shiny and gooey, and as its mother licked him, he slowly emerged into this world, wide-eyed and unsteady. He stood on shaky stick legs, found his mother's food source, and drank greedily.

"A calf is the only animal I know that in five minutes after being born, it learns everything it needs to survive," my Uncle smiled at me.

I loved to gather the eggs and it was one job my Aunt and Uncle trusted me with. It was like hunting for treasure. I pestered those poor hens every twenty minutes. The coop stunk and feathers floated in the air, but I relentlessly checked for those warm splotched eggs. Sometimes there would be specks of blood, but I didn't care. One fussy hen pecked at me when I got too close, so I called the same cousin who talked me into riding bareback, Ralph.

"She won't budge, Ralph. She pecked me too—look," I showed him the little mark on my hand.

"I'll look after this, Adrienne," and to my absolute horror, he took a whip that he kept clipped to his belt buckle and slashed her one. Squawking and feathers flying, that poor creature fled the coop. There were two perfect eggs left in the straw.

"There ya go, Adrienne," he smirked and left me feeling distressed and ashamed that I caused such harm. I learned to never ask him for anything, ever.

My Uncle, on the other hand, could see that the farm was a magical place for me, with all kinds of hiding spots that only he knew. And even then, he couldn't know them all. Upon hearing of my chicken coop fiasco, he called me again. I followed him, always ten or so paces back, tentative I was. There were bales of hay stacked by the pig pen and he reached down, pulled a loose bale and there were three perfect, little white eggs. I gasped. He smiled.

Every afternoon it was Patsy's job to go get the cows from the pasture and bring them back to the barn for feeding. I walked with her trying to avoid cow pies hardening in the sun. The flies were like busy clouds hovering and by my third day there, I ignored them, just like I ignored the overwhelming smell of manure and spoiled milk.

"CO BOSS! CO BOSS!" Patsy yelled out and miraculously the cattle lifted their heads. One-by-one they obeyed her command and started filing in. Once back to the farmyard, they'd crowd around the troughs for feed that my Uncle shoveled from bins. They scared me a bit, those animals, so big and stupid looking. They were not my favorite creatures, but I could see how valuable they were for their milk and for the beef.

There were always a couple of bulls around that would stare at me with their beady, little black eyes—scared me to death! Especially when I was shown by Ralph (always up to something) the little holes in the barn door when the bull allegedly charged my Uncle, and how he moved just at the last minute. The bull gored the wood.

"Really?" I questioned him with my heart pounding at the thought.

"No kidding, Adrienne. Keep clear of them. They'll charge ya for no reason at all. They love city gals."

In the early morning, I'd hear my Uncle bellow to the boys to get their "lazy asses" out of bed and start their chores. I'd blink in the dark and cuddle under the blankets, grateful that I wasn't a boy and would not have to do the milking in that cold, dank barn. But, that was farm life, chores morning until nightfall.

Mealtime was a feast. My Aunt would often send the boys out to go kill a chicken and that was something I watched only once. Seeing that poor bird madly circling the yard without a head was an experience that gave me nightmares. The boys seemed to relish the sight.

The table was an extravaganza with clouds of mashed potatoes stacked high in two bowls, roast chicken, three kinds of steaming vegetables from my Aunt's row-upon-row garden, stacks of homemade buns, farm-churned butter, and fresh milk straight from the source. The cream for tea and coffee was skimmed off the milk cans that very morning. I swear I could taste the sunshine in all that we ate there.

After meals my Uncle would always sit stirring his coffee looking out the window scouring the sky for the upcoming weather. His crops were dependent on Mother Nature providing an equal balance of rain and sunshine. His toothpick sat in the corner of his mouth and I examined the crinkles around his sky blue eyes. His face and hands were like worn leather. He didn't speak much, but I loved being around him. I'd just sit near him and watch.

At night Patsy and I would read or play board games and the house would settle in for sleep. The floors stopped creaking and quiet permeated the old farmhouse.

"Let's sneak out!" I'd always ask and she'd comply.

We'd open her bedroom window wider, so we could slip through, and we'd sit out on the roof with a flashlight. We could hear the sounds of the animals, braying of the horses and mooing of the cattle, but it was the stars in that black prairie sky that captured me. A million lights up there, so bright, and they made us feel very small sitting on that roof. The warm prairie breeze picked up my hair and cooled the back of my neck. I don't think I ever felt the sense of wonder that I did during those brief weeks every summer of my childhood.

Gifted To Notice

by B G Lewis

Hearing a whisper chanced
in a feather's frantic tapping
above the din, tender rapping
gasping 'neath a window's ledge

And peering through garden's thickest
where nettle and thistle bury quickest
forgotten trinkets of occasion
ceremony, and might have's

Kneeling, considering, I cupped it
clearly fallen from commonplace
from song flown into reality
slipping dire into disregard

And in a wounded one's stillness
came tears, long lost to fulfillment
not of fear, but loosened in purity
on a stumble in death's humble garb

In regret came the muse wondering
delightfully draped in obscurity
charming a seeker to sorrowing
and teasing the silk through the shards

To glimpse and behold, unfaltering
as worlds fade below golden
in seasons forever flown splendidly
on the pillow of the one soul.

Read This Please

Volume 2 Edition 10 - Ticket To Ride

July 03, 2011

Let's go! ReadThisPlease.com Edition 10 is all about travel and motion, getting somewhere, and what we do when we arrive. Traveling takes many forms, so buckle up—we invite you to read some road-ready short stories by the wandering scribes at ReadThisPlease. Journey with us on a Ticket To Ride.

Need For Speed

by Gaboo

The city decided to open up the highlands to development and paved a new road called Pine Bluff. It was a winding coaster road with curbs that achieved a trucker-terrifying eight percent grade before grinding to a four-way stop then crossing busy South Main. Hehe

We started with bicycles and tore a dozen set of brake pads and tennis shoes practicing the downhill mile run—me and the other neighborhood dare devils. Then we switched to skateboards.

There was time when I could slalom asphalt on a clunky board like a dolphin surfing waves. No fear and quick enough legs to run out a tumble. We lived for the wind, reaching terminal, and growing testicles to one day shoot across South Main in full blur.

Some kids from the bottom of the hill built a go-kart. They were a little younger and didn't have the daring to start from the top, and instead hauled their wobble-wheeled, plank-steering calliope to the final chute and clamor on. Us bucks, watched with amusement as the newbies lost control in the final stretch and careened into a hillside full of poison ivy and cactus. Hehe. There was a girl on board who had guts even when she took a hard tumble and a face plant into the spike shrubbery. Amazingly, I would marry this individual years later.

But the buddies and I were the masters of Pine Bluff and eventually the ride became commonplace—we moved onto motorcycles and cars, fast women—and the hike up to the top of the road, in desert heat, became a drag. I do remember the last run.

On ten-speeds, crouching, with no need to pedal, gravity pulling like an invisible anchor falling full tilt with three tucking monkeys riding an inch of rubber on the road. Faster, faster, the chains and cheap Shimano gears whining in distress, bearings hot and losing tolerance, every ripple and bend in the rims magnified into frame-fracturing vibration. Three of us, buddies, screaming down Pine Bluff wearing hell's bells and no regard. We hit the bottom doing no less that sixty miles an hour and there was no stopping, no second chance, no alternatives. You make yourself real small, like a bullet on wheels, close your eyes, and sail straight through the busiest intersection on South Side and into the future.

On Driving

by Sheila Cano

To grow up in California is to live a life ruled by the road. Public transportation, other than city buses, was almost non-existent in the 1950s. You had to have a car. And the car made living in the suburbs possible. Vacations were always taken by car; and visiting friends on weekends often meant 50-100 mile round trips. Children brought their pajamas and slept on the way home.

Getting a driver's license at age sixteen was a rite of passage. You were nobody in high school if you couldn't drive, or borrow your parents' car for dates. Many of us even had our own cars. Mine was a slightly compromised eight-year-old Renault Dauphin. My next-door neighbour was given a brand-new red Mustang when he graduated, as a reward for not getting into trouble for drinking. He was an expert drunk driver.

I didn't give Mom a hard time when I was an adolescent. She had enough to handle, working full-time, raising me, and always at odds with the stuffy rednecks in the school district who thought of her as the "headshrinker" or "mindreader." I kept a lid on teen-age rebellion. My outlet for all that energy was driving.

I used to go up the winding mountain roads nearby, setting time trials for myself: I'd pick a spot about 40-50 miles away, then see if I could get there and back in an hour. I learned how to handle curves at speed, how to deal with a skid, honing my reflexes like an athlete. Basically, I drove like hell. Always with a desire to preserve life and limb, not go too far overboard, and above all, be home on time.

I could beat out any car at a stoplight; used to embarrass other teens in their Pontiac GTOs by popping the clutch of Mom's Fiat roadster when the light turned green. There was nobody who could keep up with me, ever. I had one cardinal rule: never take anyone with me. I didn't want to be responsible for someone's life. Once, I broke that rule. I took my boyfriend with me on a jaunt to the airport one rainy day. When I slammed on the brakes at 100 mph to see what a 360-degree spin was like on a wet surface (it produced three of them), his eyes bugged out and he turned even whiter. I took him home. We broke up a few months later.

Years later, after finishing a media project with a friend, he said, "Why don't we go up to Whistler for a drive?" It was the only time I've taken someone for a ride to let off steam. He didn't know that I was familiar with each and every curve, having driven the route many times just for fun, and to clean out the carburetor. By the time we got to Squamish, he had slumped down in his seat and gone to sleep. When we got back, he asked, "Do you always drive like that?" "Only on curving mountain roads," I replied. He was 39 years old and had never held a driver's license.

I didn't burden Mom with the knowledge of my road-warrior driving. Only twice did the car register evidence of my flat-out illegal driving. The first time, I broke the tachometer while speed-shifting. The second time, I broke the speedometer, which only went up to 125 mph. To spare her any grief, I fibbed and told her, "It just broke and flopped over to the right." She never hassled me about either incident.

The notion of becoming a race-car driver occurred to me. But I was on track to go to university, and I knew it would be foolish to throw away that opportunity. Besides, I didn't think I had the stamina—or the guts—to hold my own among other drivers. It's one thing to race by yourself, quite another to do it day after day in grueling competition. Nor did I have any experience in the man's world: the real world, of auto mechanics, of black fingernails and gritty toughness. So I kept my fantasies to myself and went to college.

A favourite activity for Mom and me on Sundays was to take a drive in the country. Later, when she moved up here, got old and couldn't drive anymore, I often took her on Sunday outings. We'd go to Bellingham, go shopping at Fred Meyer's where we could get Tillamook cheddar for $2 a pound, and eat in a Mexican restaurant. Or we'd to Sumas, or Glacier, Washington, around American Thanksgiving and have a turkey dinner at a diner. Once I took her up the Fraser Canyon, where we had great hamburgers at the Spuzzum Cafe. There were seven different kinds of wallpaper in the place, everything from red-and-black flocked velvet pizza-parlour stuff, to a dreamy, almost abstract, photographic image of river rocks underwater. At the end of the day, when we got home from these excursions, she would always say, "Thanks for the buggy ride."

Now, I no longer drive like a racer. My favourite type of driving is on gravel Forest Service roads, dodging logging trucks and potholes. Bombing along sometimes at highway speeds if the surface is good; or poking along to avoid damaging the undercarriage of the four-door sedan. I admit to enjoying the incredulous stares of other campers at seeing a mud-covered Mercedes with a canoe on the roof racks. One moonless night, hauling down the canyon on the way home, a locomotive flashed its high beam and blasted a greeting. The engineer no doubt was intrigued at the sight of a white canoe flying over the highway upside down. We blinked and honked in return, a human bond in the starry darkness.

Living at Mach

by Gaboo

Middle of the bald prairies on a Saturday, day off, with thirty straight miles from junction to junction. Nobody on the road. I get on motorbike. It's a rice rocket with six gears. Top gear has little torque (force) but by then you're moving and the big gear just keeps the chain at a reasonable speed.

So, I'm wound out in sixth gear, tach reads 9500 rpm and I've got one grand left in the red. Doing about 150 miles an hour. If I reach back and tuck in my t-shirt, the rpms go up to 9700 and I hit 155. Now the bike sounds like a sprung bat on a mosquito hunt. I realize if I can lower my line of vision, below the instrument cluster, just playing peekaboo with the yellow line, the rpms shoot up to a blistering 10300 and I'm doing 162 miles an hour. Terminal velocity for me, on that day. Don't sit upright! At 163 miles an hour the front bearings lose balance and the handle bars begin to shudder violently. Creepy, and needs modification on the model. But sliding along the ground, eyeballs to the wind, clinging to a screaming block of pistons was a rush at the time.

Ah, memories. The kid called at 4 pm, "get me to the airport". Dang, sky was too beautiful. Off we went. He got in a plane, went to 12000 feet, and jumped out. That was a long 30-40 seconds waiting for that chute to open. He had a great experience—a little ear pressure trouble. I'm glad he did it. I will have the parental shakes for days. Mom nearly dropped when we told her. She knew it was going to happen soon, just not when. She didn't want to know.

But we're all living mach now. Whirl of do's. Anxiety on the state-of-order popping everywhere. Here, and in seconds to be there, double booked, obligated, lurching forward, and pushed back, jostled by the absolutes of people desperate by extremes, choices and libations, in need, or breaking. Overflow, in a tempest of birthdays, and mothers, and kids, and Labradors, racoons, bears, coyotes, cats, chickens, neighbors, crashing in a commotion cauldron. Someone's yapping on about self and see the joy sink and wither, fade to orbiting dead rock, and the demeanor sinks, a sucking noise creeps in the nearby. Smudge, smear, paddle and grip, or let go a take the solemn chat, the affirmation of acknowledgement. Humbled by opportunity to take less for myself and extend more of I am. Full throttle busy is vibrant. Hit the pillow running.

But first, twenty comings and goings. Faces smirk through jiggling pretend plastic. Wordy notion pulls like cartridges to a frantica. Hmmm... living fast, living meddlesome. I don't ever want to be slow.Pudgy crease stretch skinny bags of bones and water little sparks connive yip yak conspire attack in biddy bags of bones and water scrub waxy show posey flippity flap tonguing goes plot planning pluck dumb lucky and confounded by bags of bones and water giddy poly rolls cling oink bouncy bray nasal rickety splinter within proud flashing mean scolding chiding lip lashing wet leaky stink hides robed on bags of bones and water clotted pudding puss freck moled in hairless iddy squish crunch dipped warm wiggly spark squealing bags of bones and water. oi.

48 hours. It all started when the wife showed up sicker than a three-legged hound dog with kennel cough. Twas her intent to enjoy a couple days off, puttering. Instead, she spent the weekend holed up in the fetal position. I suspected meningitis, then pleurisy, or the deadly brain sucking ear worm. Thus the doting began. Meanwhile, I'm actually doing a little venture capital fun and starting a furniture

business. No kidding, left field, but something I've been putting off for years. I've got a order for four units and need to prototype two units for jigs. My own design—it's all about the height of the seat and the slope of the back. Meanwhile, Saturday, I actually find out I have a hernia. I've never had a hernia before, but it ceremoniously signals the last time I WILL EVER HELP MOVE SOMEBODY. I feel good about the new resolution. Oh, yeah, and the twenty year old loon crazy tabby cat that is the darling of my eldest son decides with the nice weather, she'll take to exploring the deep backyard in coyote country. Wanders off if we leave the back door open, then it's a frantic search to find her usually sipping brackish water near the back creek. Anyway, had to run around and price lumber, bolts, hardware, resins, get the equipment. But I was already halfway through tiling the kitchen floor on whim from Friday night because the kid's doing his thesis on my computer because the cat fell asleep on his and gave it a fatal error. I finally got it back but he's lurking around looking for a proof reader. Late last night I flew to the hardware dealer for more stuff and ran smack into the latest 12 inch sliding compound miter saw on sale with an extendable utility cart. This prompted flash rejigging of equipment needs, and went in this morning and bought the thing and set it up in the driveway. But not before the entourage of Sunday sunny day friends and associates began piling in for there on personal Sunday sunny getaway to the farm vacation business. We're on the jogging route. L at 8 am. W at ten. C at 12. L again at 3. Intermitant pop-ins by others. Occasional hobbling to backyard for senile cat. Neighbor's hounds got out and terrorized the place at 3:20. Now keep in mind, the reason these people show up they have deep, ingrain needs for one on one discussion, to vent. The dogs as well.

Wife emerges, eating soup and comments, "Hey, you re-tiled the floor."

Gotta go… bear got into the garbage… Back again. That was a big one, the bear, 400 lbs, young, fast, moves like a cat, timid. He spread garbage all over the yard. That will draw in everyone with a snout. So, I head out with shovel and, ten minutes later, the wife comes out with paint ball gun, a long barrel, nitrogen, and I'm like—whoa, point that downward! I explain it's a tool, not a weapon. Fire one in the air, if you have to, not at an animal, and NOT at me. Point the damn thing upward! Or down. She's paranoid of anything that looks like a gun, but within sixty seconds, she's standing like a prison guard, chewing grass with a high beam on me. She wants to rap one off. I admire that she overcame great fear to step out and protect me, but I say no, the neighbors are having a sit together will think we're firing at them. Bag more garbage. Bungee cord cans, stick tire irons in the ground around the chicken coop. Wife's still escorting me and toting her piece like paid staff, complaining she wants to go to sleep. Go, go. Look out back, more garbage. Gack. Pick it up. Tag corner posts with carburetor cleaner, a deterrent. Come in. Heat a burrito. Sit down and type this.

Hold on, my producer just emailed an audio re-mix. I might just have a musical career! 1, 2, 3, 4…

My Favorite Family Vacation

by Jac

It's early Saturday morning.

Last night, we all helped to pack the station wagon. We're about to leave for a week long family vacation. It's the last vacation that the seven of us will have together—and the first I remember at all. My memory isn't filled with the details. Chevy Chase and his movies fill in the blanks, because I imagine our family vacations had a little National Lampoon in them. What I remember most about this journey are the different emotional pictures.

I'm excited. How could I not be? I'm six and about to drive off with my parents and brothers on an adventure. I have no idea what the St. Lawrence River is, or what the Thousand Islands are, but the thought of a place named after a saint—with one thousand islands— has excitement oozing out of me. There are other reasons, too.

A couple days earlier, Mom and Dad sat down with me and explained the route we would take on a map, naming the cities we would pass: Amsterdam, Utica, Rome, Syracuse, Alexandria. They explained we would stop for lunch, how long it would take, and all the things I'd see along the way. It's hard for me to understand that the Mohawk River will be the same river one hundred miles away.

I'm positive they have a different opinion, but I'm excited about having all four brothers with me. I know they'll tease me in the car, but I love when all of us are together.

Tom, the oldest, will call me Little One, like my Father calls me, but without the affection I hear in my Father's voice. Tom will replace it with the arrogance of an extra fourteen years on his younger sister.

Terry will tickle me until I nearly pee.

Ted will ignore me. Tom? Terry? Tim? Did you guys just hear something?

Tim, nearest to me in age and still receiving his share of teasing, will touch me when I'm not looking. Ceaselessly!

I endure all of that and am rewarded with a special treat. I love to watch Tom's fingers dance on his guitar, but this time it's special. He's playing and singing my favorite song to me, The Baby Tree by Rosalie Sorrells. When he's finished he starts over and all seven of us sing it together.

There's an island way out in the sea

Where the babies they all grow on trees...

After that I only remember a few things... seeing such a huge body of moving water (I'm told that I wanted to do nothing the first day except stare at the Saint Lawrence) and my fear that first night. A large ship passed on the river, directly in view of the darkened hotel room. I screamed, because all I could see were the ship's lights and a faint outline. The vessel looked like it was coming directly into the room. It took my Dad a long time to help me understand what was happening.

The last is another happy memory... Twirl-a-Paint. It cost my parents a small fortune after I encountered that delight.

I remember that this was my favorite vacation, though I can't remember much of it—just the important parts.

Gasquet

by Sheila Cano

Eighteen twisting miles through the redwoods, up the Smith River canyon, brought us to Gasquet: a tiny community among evergreen trees beside jade-green water. Mom and I moved there in November, hoping to spend a snowy Christmas in the forest, with tall pines and deep moss our world for a time.

Mrs. Plaisted was in her sixties, or perhaps early seventies, a strong woman with thick white hair that must have once been blonde. She wore plaid shirts, jeans, boots, and tied her hair up in a bun or French twist. She was tough and resourceful, a person of few words, and not nosy like landladies sometimes can be. Her house, a barn-like wooden structure, was about fifty yards from ours: a grand two-room log cabin with a stone foundation and a huge river-rock fireplace.

Each night when we came home around five-thirty, we first built a fire. The oil heater in the bedroom did little to heat the rest of the space. Unfortunately, every time we started the fire, it smoked up the room, and we had to air it out, losing any warmth we had gained. Usually we got it under control and had the big room cozy before we froze. I sprinkled crystals from a can onto the blaze, and vivid spectral colours of turquoise, pink and red flared up. I could gaze at the hearth for hours, looking at the flickering flame-shapes as you would clouds changing form in the sky.

That Christmas we decided to have a 'natural' tree, with decorations we had made, and real candles. We strung popcorn and cranberries, fashioned ornaments from paper and nutshells, and gloated at the result. We clipped Mexican tin candle holders on the branches, and watched the tree like a pair of hawks when the candles were lit. There was an out-of-tune upright piano in one corner of the room, where I pounded out halting versions of Christmas melodies, and old labour songs from a book with a green cover and red lettering: "Fifty Famous Favorites". We found some aging rolls of wallpaper with a sparkly frost design on a pale ground, and from these I made greeting cards, drawing tree branches and little birds in pastel chalk. Pa sent me a beautiful wooden Swedish maze game, played with a steel ball bearing, the board tilting according to the operation of two knobs. After Christmas we took the decorations off the tree and put it outside so the birds and animals could have the popcorn and cranberries. The only thing missing from our log cabin Christmas was… snow.

Mrs. Plaisted had some loggers take out a big pine tree. It had forked into two trunks very high up. Perhaps it was dying, or just in the way—whatever the reason, it was to be cut down. We were fascinated by the process, and took photographs: a silhouette of the faller up in the sky, the tree like an immense tuning fork or slingshot framework.

When we had some trouble with a young man hired by my mother to do our woodchopping, Mrs. Plaisted showed her fiber. The kid, who was staying with some friends of ours nearby, had taken a shine to me. But he was jealous because I spent time talking to their little boy. I was fifteen, Armand was twenty, and Angel – Robert McCollum – was nine years old. Angel and I used to sit in the old apple tree, studying the scabby bark and talking about life and art. Armand began to go about glowering, and accused me of not liking him because he was part native Indian. I looked at him with his light brown hair and his green eyes, and said: I'm probably more Indian than you are. And jumped down off the barbed-wire fence and walked away. The next thing we knew, Armand was prowling the outskirts of the property carrying a rifle. Mom told Mrs. Plaisted about this, and she said, never mind, I've got a shotgun, and if there's any nonsense he'll find out what's what. We were impressed. Nevertheless, we began to think about moving.

In the new year, we had a rainy spell. Across the road from us, the Smith River began to rise. At about twelve feet above flood stage it spilled over its banks into our front yard. The water crept halfway up the wheels before Mom figured she'd better move the car to higher ground, behind the house on a slight rise that crested at an abandoned airstrip. The building itself was several feet higher than the driveway, and in no danger of being flooded at the moment. However, the slope uphill to the back was muddy, and the wheels were spinning uselessly. I was too young to drive, but in some intuitive or logical way, I knew that if the wheels turned slower, they might grip. We put burlap sacks under the tires, and I said to Mom, try second gear. It worked, the wheels caught, and the Fiat Spider was soon high and dry. The chilly jade-green waters receded and the river went back to roiling and boiling within its banks.

The eighteen-mile commute, though exhilarating, was also dangerous. Always watchful for the huge trucks with sometimes only one giant log, coming around the bend over the line, you'd better be quick getting onto the shoulder if there was one; or squeezing your car into the smallest space it could occupy on the road for that instant that the dragon barreled on by. One stormy night as we headed towards Crescent City to attend an historical society meeting, we encountered a boulder just after rounding a sharp curve. Rather than drive over the cliff, Mom drove over the rock, which tipped us up on the two left wheels and made an horrendous scraping noise underneath the car. We were rendered mute until we got to town. We skipped the meeting in favour of an emergency contact with our mechanic, Smokey, who loved working on our car, one of the few sports cars around. He met us at his garage and confirmed that the only damage was a long scratch on the sealed undercarriage of the doughty little Spider.

Eventually, our unease about Armand wore us down; and it didn't look like it was ever going to snow that winter, so at the end of February we moved back to Crescent City. Sure enough, shortly thereafter, it did snow up there. Though somewhat disappointed, we still treasured our time at the log cabin in the woods. We were sorry that we felt compelled to return to the relative safety of town. Those four months were packed full of experiences and explorations which we could never have imagined. We left the jade-green river and the sweet smells of the forest, and went back to the pavement, the street lights, and the briny air beside the blue-green ocean.

Scooter Tale

by Bruce Reisner

It's a cruel economy, and this pedestrian is in a pecuniary nose dive. My last car got hauled to recycling glory a couple years ago, and ever since, each day has been visited with dreams of transportation less depressing than a city bus. So I've been exploring some options of the two wheeled kind.

Sure it all looks easy, breezy and cute. A nice looking guy or gal zipping down Penn Avenue on a mod looking Vespa or Honda motor scooter. Looks like a charming little way to get around. Well, there's a grim subset of factors that may determine just how easy, just how breezy one of those motor vehicles truly is. I'm working on the problem, right now, having bought one of the very dirt cheapest imported bikes available by mail order.

"Why doesn't he join a support group and leave hard, greasy, hairy chested work to people who are playing with a full deck?" a burly biker might interject. That is how an experienced motorcycle personage may well respond. "Why should I care what a misguided novice learns from his own poor judgment?" some heartless, illiterate gear-head might add. But for people who value the process more so than the outcome, my experience buying a motorscooter off the Internet has been a newsworthy farrago of steel parts and poor communications.

I know you will like hearing that it took over two months to assemble the 50cc scooter, and I could have done it in eight hours if the instructions had been written by someone both familiar with the bike and fluent in English. To further the insult, a sane engine mechanic can put the things together in one hour. If you're planning on doing something therapeutic, don't get a cheap-o ride mail order.

Like finding your buns in the dark. Unless the project is a total failure, there is a moment of clarity when, like in Come Back Little Sheba, a big gluteus comes bounding over the horizon. I got the scooter to work, but arrived at it worse for wear. It was mostly the abysmal instructions. Here are some of the things that went terribly wrong. I hadn't planned on breaking some dainty cuticles removing it from the package it came in. The thing weighs more than I do. It's jangling, greasy parts were bolted to a steel frame inside a cardboard box as thick, tough and cheerful as a brig in the Somalian Navy. While the thing was delivered nice enough by truck to my dystopian hovel, there was no way possible to get it up the two flights of concrete steps between it and the front door. Don't mind that it had been raining all day, so there was no good option of putting it together road side. The best kind of muscular pain was in the works, but first I had to chew through the box and unbolt a metal fixture. Once that ordeal, pain of a thousand stubby bolts, was complete, I had to drag the heavy parts up the steps, to the kitchen, which is the only room in the house that's suitable. Note that no one comes here for dinner. The heavy lifting act was well in the hernia/heart attack zone. Soon false hope arrived when I managed to get the front wheel on.

What happened next caused me to think that its clutch lever was some sort of Flying Dutchman, or else someone in the Smiling Happy Communist Motorcycle Factory #6 forgot to put one in the package. It said in the instructions that it had one. It doesn't. The wispy motorcycle was manufactured in China, and has no brand name. It's a generic imported bike. The political prisoner who wrote the instructions seemed to wish the thing had a clutch lever, or he hates Americans, and is laughing at the thought of guys like me taking it the hard way. It took over a week to ascertain that it has some sort of hybrid clutch, not quite an automatic, but made for people with minimal riding skill. This was worse than The Manchurian Candidate for the way it dissolved ordinary cognition.

The battery was scary because you have to pour a sinister plastic package, like a cross between a bladder implant and a part of the space shuttle, into six or eight matching holes, all eager as puppies for a nice drink of sulfuric acid. There was no way of knowing exactly how to do it without getting third degree burns, suffice I got through that part, but then came the next thing someone in the imported bike biz should have known. It said in the instructions that the battery had an overflow tube. It didn't, so the time spent looking for it was both frustrating and pretty as meat packing. Motorcycles are called, on the street, a 'crotch rocket,' which caused worry about an explosion.

I won't continue to cry over everything that destroyed my nerves, but by the time I got the engine running and adjusted, it was nearer to the Second Coming than hoped. I haven't learned, yet, how to ride it, that will start in a week or so, when I fully recover from stress injuries and a nervous breakdown. Shouldn't be a problem. I'm a quick study.

Rocket Pool

by Gaboo

Me and Skinny Carlson, 12-years-olds, middle of summer and bored silly. We were hiking up a dusty hillside to the windswept flats 400 feet above town level. It was a good vantage. Worn pine roots were exposed and easy to climb, twisting over the rocks and propelling branches into the sky. Below, my father leased a industrial yard, a depot for propane tanks and cylinders and sprawling an acre beyond the debris slides and rock falls. Older kids visited the cliff edge to party, and occasionally lazy residents threw garbage over the side. The view of the vista below included auto wreckers, lumber yards, a dog kennel, and a small assortment of cottage industries. A veritable cornucopia for two bored preteen prowlers. We could also look down to see if my father was on a gas delivery. If he was gone, the shop yard was ours. Good mindless fun full of poking and prodding the old vehicles and industrial gizmos. All we had to do was pick our way down the embankment and onward through the rocks and cactus.

And then we saw it, the kid's pool carelessly tossed next to the slope like beautiful, circular, flying saucer. It was an obvious castaway, but still seaworthy. Why walk? We would ride in style the full 400 feet downhill in our man sleigh.

We flipped the pool over and examined the bottom. The craft was worthy. The terrain: cactus, sagebrush, tumbleweed, and slick off-ramp of broken rock shards and boulders. Would there be adventure ahead? Check.

Once on board with pre-flight plans reviewed, we performed a quick shuffle off the gully rim. Acceleration was immediate. There was no control, no steering, no handling—we bombarded forward in a slow, teacup spiral of oblivious stupidity. A wrenching plastic scream erupted beneath us. Skinny Carlson's eyes went wide enough to know we were approaching a rate at which doom occurs. I was equally alarmed. Below, and thusly approaching, trees magically appeared on our flight line. This is where time slows to black and white, tick tock, stop action, full of life affirmation. The rocks sped toward us and there was no way our recycled K-Mart flotsam would have the structural integrity to absorb impact. We were en route to disaster.

In those instances, life changing decisions are fashioned with clarity: you predict, you react. So I reacted, in that shear moment of self-sacrifice; I pushed Skinny Carlson out of the pool—to save him. "Bon voyage." I turned to face death alone, but Skinny went cartoon on me. He bounced back into the pool. I pushed him out again. Once again he tumbled down the slope as fast as the pool, caught air, and ended up beside me. "Fool! Get out!" I heaved him again and this time he fell behind in dust and cactus. I turned and faced death alone, hands clenched to the sides of the careening plastic and jaw set in determination.

When I hit the rocks, the pool bucked and romped navigating between chicanes of Volkswagon-sized basalt boulders before ditching into a friendlier gravel bank. It was as if by a greater hand, and I was alive and unscathed. Miraculous. Skinny trekked down the fall line and stumbled forward to where I parked the pool. He looked like a confused pup left at a kennel. "Why did you push me out?"

"I saved your life! You're welcome!"

"But you made it…"

"That was luck."

I don't think he ever forgave me for that, I don't recall. We ended the outing by trudging in dust and burrs into my father's shop, with a full gaze of the treacherous slope leering at our bruised backsides. Unfortunately, we didn't anticipate the welcome. My father was, in fact, laughing with a group of business acquaintances in the parking lot. They were all having a good heehaw, pointing at the hill, and discussing idiots around town. That's when we walked up. My father looked at us incredulously and then blurted out, "It was you!" He stomped into his office. The other men laughed royally, though, some of the jokes we didn't understand at the time.

For The Love Of A Trailer

by M Dawn Thacker

We're sitting at the kitchen table. My eyes are closed as I savor the smell and taste of my first cup of morning coffee. I have a whole day ahead of me with no plans. Bruce has his nose up close to the screen of his computer. He's reading out loud, reciting the specs on some heavy equipment. I'm not paying too much attention. He does this a lot.

"Look, I found one in Alleghany County," he announces, turning the laptop so I can see. "It's what we've been looking for."

I focus my attention to the rusted hulk on the screen. "I haven't been looking for a trailer. You have."

"OK, I found the one I've been looking for. Its tongue is longer... it's more heavy duty... it'll carry the backhoe..."

"We already have two trailers," I say. "They look big and heavy enough to me."

He looks at me and sighs. This is where he can start talking like he's explaining something to our youngest son, in simple words, bullet-point specifics. I'm not interested in the explanations. I give up listening and start packing for the trip.

We head out a half hour later, toward Clifton Forge, that's the location listed in the online Government auction. We've been there before. We honeymooned at Douthat State Park, just outside of Clifton Forge thirty years ago. Our cabin was rustic, built with logs and a huge fireplace. I remember spreading a blanket there and eating our first meal picnic style. The food was left over from our wedding reception. The bubbles in the champagne tickled my nose. At nineteen, I wasn't old enough to drink legally, but my new husband was. We planned our honeymoon week—and our entire life together—that night.

I'm more excited about the drive than I am the trailer. I'm a traveler. The road is straight, the mountains are beautiful and the leaves are turning. It misted rain all night, but the clouds are lifting and the weatherman forecasts sun by afternoon to our west. I pack the camera and two books. I never know exactly how long a three hour trip will take. Journeys in the past have sometimes carried over into the next day.

When we leave home, the trailer lists for $365. We climb up into Bruce's new dump truck, my first time in it, two steps up, grab bar, hoist self, sitting on top of the world. This dump truck dares smaller vehicles to pull out in front of it. It's a diesel road tractor with air horns. When Bruce makes a decision, he goes all-the-way-big. We can barely hear each other over the roar of the engine. I wonder why the International even has a radio.

We bump along the interstate and the further west we drive, the lighter the sky becomes, but clouds still drift along the tops of the mountains.

"Help me watch for the exit," Bruce says.

I've been taking pictures from the passenger window, but the side mirror is hindering my artistic abilities. I'm glad for the diversion. The Dabney S. Lancaster Community College is at Exit 150-B in Clifton Forge. I'm amazed that Clifton Forge warrants two exits.

"There it is," I say. "At the end of the ramp, take a right."

As we pull off the interstate, the entrance to the school is right there. The road dead ends at the school.

Clifton Forge is a small railroad town set in the midst of the Alleghany Mountains. Houses and businesses line the sides of Main Street. At one end is the train depot—I remember that. At the other end is a community college—that's new. I can't imagine what they teach there, Coal Mine Management, Train Engineering, Principles of Logging? I'm surprised that there are enough young people living in the tiny town to attend a college.

Bruce follows the parking lot around to the rear of the college until he finds what looks like a buildings and grounds garage. It turns out to be the welding shop. Students are busy at work, helmets donned, sparking metals together. A man hurries out to Bruce and points him in the direction of the saw mill. That's where the trailer waits.

We backtrack to a small gravel path, just wide enough for the dump truck. It's guarded by a *Keep Out* sign. Bruce drops into a lower gear and we descend a steep hill. A saw mill appears on the left, students at work there, too. A bulldozer and log truck with knuckle boom seem to watch us from the parking lot. A tree planter squats in the bushes. Bruce pulls up to the trailer, where it lies dying in the weeds, tires flat, metal rusted, floor rotting. It's worse than the two we already have. Even I can see that. We couldn't even drag it home if we bought it. We'd need another trailer to haul it.

Bruce drops from the cab to the ground, and I struggle, trying to find my footing on the steps and grab for the handle to ease my landing. We walk over to the trailer.

"It's ugly and broken," I observe.

"Let me measure it," Bruce says.

How he finds promise in these wrecks, I can't imagine. I get back in the dump truck and open my book. My decision is already made. Leave the monstrosity here.

It takes Bruce an hour to inspect the behemoth. He puts on his coveralls, takes out his tape measure and begins calculating. He's busy with numbers and schematics. He lifts parts, slides under on his back, shines a flashlight, measures some more and decides it could work.

"Needs fixing, but it'll work. We can't haul it away like it is," he says. "We'll have to pull it out into the parking lot, repack the bearings…." I've stopped listening. I shake my head and wonder again just why I married this man.

He pulls himself up into the truck and starts the engine. "I'm taking you to lunch," he says. "Where do you want to go?"

On our honeymoon, we had stopped at the Outdoor People Store in Clifton Forge for fishing supplies. It was right across Main Street from the C&O Railroad Depot Restaurant. I remembered it as a small, square building, next to the railroad tracks. The interior was bright and clean with a lunch counter and several small wooden tables. I also remembered that we had opened the door to the tinkle of a bell and the aroma of fresh baked biscuits. The food was almost as good as what came out of my Mama's kitchen.

"I wonder if the old C&O Restaurant is still there?" I muse.

Bruce starts in that direction . The small building remains, feeding railroad workers and townsfolk. The door bell tinkles and suddenly I'm nineteen again, just married and hungry. A sign boasts Today's Special: Chicken and dumplings, mashed potatoes, green beans, biscuit. All comfort food. A glass case displays home-baked apple, cherry, and peach pies. We decide on two specials with sweet tea.

Bruce orders cherry pie. I choose apple. We sit at the counter and watch trains filled with coal roll slowly by the window.

As we eat our meal, we reminisce about our time spent here years ago. Bruce taught me how to bait a fishing hook—and fry the catch over an open fire. I taught him how to make a bed, only to have it in complete disarray a few minutes later. We laughed, talked, and made plans for a house, and babies. He lifted me up under my arms and sat me on the hood of his truck. He laid his head in my lap and told me he didn't know he could be so happy. I was a tiny thing back then. Thirty years later, we've spread about the middle, and we're contemplating practical repair of broken down trailers.

Bruce takes out his wallet, pays the tab, leaving a few bills for a tip. We head to the truck and turn toward home. The auction ends at seven p.m. and the drive is several hours long. At exit A, Bruce unexpectedly veers right, and turns in the direction of Douthat State Park. At the entrance, he pays the fee and we rattle over the speed bumps toward the dam and cabins. It hasn't changed in thirty years. We park in the lot overlooking the lake. The sun is out and the wind has picked up. The ripples on the lake sparkle and a few boats bob on the surface.

"Want to get out and walk around some?" Bruce asks.

"Sure, that would be nice."

He opens the door to the truck and hops down. I reach over, lock his door, slide my purse under the seat, and turn to open my door. Bruce is standing there waiting. He reaches up, puts his hands under my arms and lowers me to the ground. He kisses me and we walk hand in hand toward the path to the lake.

"Wonder if they have a cabin open tonight?" he asks.

"What about your trailer? The auction ends at 7:00."

"We've already got two trailers," he says. "I can do without another one for awhile longer."

Now I remember why I married this man.

Turn Left at T's Corner

by M Dawn Thacker

It's the first time I've been excited about the government auction website. Bruce trolls it like an online dater of heavy equipment.

1999 Ford F350/Powerstroke/Dual Wheel."No Title" Morganton, NC; BUCKET Gallatin, TN; John Deere Bush Hog 1508 Nashville, TN; Greenhouse Frame Beaufort, SC...

You get the idea—junk. I have dragged myself into the dump truck on many occasions to ride along for the inspection of some rusted hulk, dying in the weeds, at the back of some city yard, in a distant town. I've rolled my eyes at Bruce's taste in scrap.

I'll be honest, though. He's never bought a piece of equipment that didn't return an investment, or that he couldn't fix and resell for a profit. He finds what he's looking for, researches the make and model, or he looks for a better deal somewhere else. He calls for information and more pictures, then he sets his limit and bids only to that amount. I really can't complain, except that online government auctions seem to be his entertainment of choice lately.

After our last trip to Chincoteague, we decided we want a boat. When I think about a boat, and the coast, I think of a sixty-five foot sailboat with crisp white triangles of canvas snapping in the wind, or a fishing trawler with big nets hoisted on booms, or even a speed boat with swivel captain's chairs and a sporty little windshield. I don't think of a little flat-bottomed Jon boat. That's what we're looking for.

I'm not much of a sailor. I get motion sickness, but I can handle being on the bay or an inlet when the water and weather are calm. Besides, I've been informed by my husband that vomit makes good chum for fish.

What we're looking for is a Carolina Skiff. It's a fifteen foot, flat bottom tri-hull with bench seats and a stow-away compartment for fishing equipment. The Evinrude motor on the back is a hundred-fifty horsepower. My Honda CRV is big enough to pull the trailer. It's the perfect size boat for Big Glade Creek.

Bruce found it on the government website. It belongs to the fire department in Seaside Heights, New Jersey. The boat is even a pretty color green. Puke green. There's no title, but that doesn't seem to raise any red flags for Bruce, so I'm OK with it too. The price is right at three-hundred-fifty-one dollars with a little over a day to go.

I've made up my mind. I can ride along to New Jersey to pick up the boat if we win it without complaining. New Jersey is six hours north of us. I've mapped the route back. After we pay for the skiff, and hook the trailer to my car, we head due west from Seaside Heights to a place called Manchester Township. I-295 South will take us into Dover, Delaware. There, we pick up Rt. 13 South. That highway takes us right to T's Corner and a choice—to drive home, or turn left and head ten miles due east to one of my favorite places to visit. I know exactly how to get to Chincoteague from T's Corner.

Stone To Fire
by Steven Bird

When the full moon of July spins the wind up from the south

and clouds advance down the sky to converge

over the river, bringing thunder

She walks the shore when rain wets the stones,

anticipates the crack and flash of heated sky

Gathering lightning in a jar

When the sky turns injured red, she

gathers lightning in a jar

She rows a boat over conflicted currents; her sweeps cleave

dark water where she points out shapes in the depths

She laughs then sighs and sees no desolation in the flow

and all seems perfectly well

She makes the sound of water rushing by tilted fingers

of savage rock, and when the moon and sky go mad

she bends her back to pull the oars,

when the river writhes insane, she bends

her back to stroke the heavy oars

Turning from the shore beneath the ranks of cottonwood,

her eyes, two silver trout alert and ready to flee

She holds out to me a small brown feather

in the cup of her palm like a child's found treasure

And the feather turns to fire

Her fingers close around the flames and she dances,

laughs, gathering lightning in a jar

When the world turns from stone to fire,

she puts lightning in a jar

Eun Hye

by Casimirr

"My Korean name is Eun Hye...un-hay." She stood in a better posture of Michelangelo's David, with correct weight distribution, and with the same confidence from that Angel who stood behind David when he sank a stone into Goliath's forehead. She spoke in a comforting tone to thirty-four worn down tour members at five o'clock in the morning and carried on from a pause, "in case some of you didn't get my name right during briefing."

Not a sound came from the passengers.

"If this is your first trip..." Eun Hye adjusted her svelte physique, ran her gaze up and down the aisle to avoid eye contact the way most Japanese prefer, and spoke in a tone with pride indicative of a South Korean, "I see, maybe one or two have been to this country before, and know how strange this country is."

Everyone remained in silence.

"To me, things were not really that strange from the first day I was here," she said, "not until I understood every word they said."

"..."

"Whenever there was time, I traveled, but never far enough to any other western city besides Boston, where I had my first and only Boston lobster, thanks to my uncle over there," Eun Hye sighed,

"Korea is the only place I prefer so far. What I have from here, I cannot have elsewhere, but no matter how many years I stay, devotedly, and become one of her countrymen, this country still says I am alien. That is exactly what I have on my Korean ID card, but I happily live to see this country, to better her future, and be in her future… starting from now. You have a lot to hear from me, we have hours and hours of journey on this coach. I am your tour leader. I take charge from here."

Still no sound from the travelers.

"Dong-Sun is from Korea University, the same university I earned my language degree—I am his CEO on this tour."

Eun Hye called this shy, good-looking, young Korean man to the front and said, "Give him your warm welcome, he cannot understand a word you say."

Rounds of clapping stirred up a commotion, with chit-chat buzzing.

"Yes, he is another handsome man from Seoul. South Korea gives birth to good looking men," Eun Hye carried on and said, "Hey, I don't know if he is married, and I'm not going to ask."

Lady giggles fluttered lightly down the aisle.

"As I thought…" She said with a twitch on one corner of her beautiful, thin lips, though marked faintly with a cleft lip scar, "…not from men."

"Ha ha…" Horselaughs burst from her audience.

"Dong-Sun looks like a gorgeous, easy-to-get-along, Thai man and acts like one, darker skin and all that, but he is one hundred percent local, and very proud of that," Eun Hye smiled and carried on. "Our driver – Kand-Dae is roughly what is meant by native Korean, and would do perfectly if he has no need to drive you around on these slippery highways. No worry, I'll bring him a bottle when he's done for the night. He will drink to that."

"Rice wine? No headache?" One of the passengers asked from the very front seat.

"Yes, there is, but not his special brand," Eun Hye laughed vivaciously for the first time and said, "Actually, his bottles are stocked up in every Mini Stop, GS25, and Family Mart along the way."

"..."

"You might need one of these grocery stores; local Korean meals are not the same as you might think; they don't eat everyday like a Mongol anymore, they nibble on Kimchi and rice... tell you more about this later. Back to business, your tour started the minute you stepped onto this coach. I will make sure you have the best treat, count on me—well, you have to, I am being paid to see you all have no regrets from this trip. You are under my loving tutelage; I am your tour nanny."

"..."

"One thing to bear in mind, always on the double, listen, and remember every word I say, then you will enjoy this trip more than you should have."

Sizzling sounds murmured throughout the coach cabin, with deliberate, but gentle hoo-hahs, and no one said anything out loud to inquire.

"I see that you all agree and understand," Eun Hye continued, "You get the best from my experience, I know this country in a hard way, and I am not asking for your praise or gratitude. The city wakes up in six hours... or I should say, you can only check into your hotel by then, and there is the unspoken rule to go five stars in Seoul. You can say South Koreans are perfectionist when in getting any job done without unexpected mistakes."

Her clients listened.

"One more thing," she added, "most citizens here do not speak or understand a word of English... they will turn their back on you if you do, so, best not to try. I will show you how to speak their language your way, simple words that are useful and needed for this trip. I will do that when all of you are sobered up from jet lag. On this trip, in case you have real problems, come to me, I am always here to help."

"You just stepped off of your flight," she carried on, "You have two hours rest on this coach before we arrive at the War Memorial of Korea, I will wake you up in an hour, before we are there, and tell you how to make worth of this visit; many visit this Memorial only once in a lifetime."

Two hours later... Only a handful of tour members stayed in the front seat when Eun Hye stood. A great number of the others moved to the far end of the coach, reclined their seats, and in a comfortable resting position to show they were careless, whatever their tour leader said.

"I see I have audience, and my job has to be done," She looked into the eyes of the person up front and said, "My pleasure in saying what I am about to say... it is a must to come to this War Memorial, and this is going to tell you everything about the Korean people... much more than from shopping on High Street. The ethic of this place is important for the Korean people, to remember how hard they tried to have peace, to be reunified with indifference... and is an important cause and mission for the next, or the next generation to accomplish building a nation without borders."

"Much like East and West Germany," The one from the very front seat spoke gently, "Please go on, you are making this more interesting than it seems to be."

"There is more than I can tell," Eun Hye said calmly, "I brought you here for you to understand as much as you can from this Memorial. If you can, you will see the Korean people have no intention to go to war. The film Taegukgi is a must, look for the film in the days we are here, if you want to go further. It speaks for Korea that there is no hatred between the Korean people from the two countries, and there is a hope for that promised day on re-unification. But by then, each South Korean might be carrying an albatross around the neck. South Korea is not as well off as West Germany, who could be able to throw money to unify East Germany. Even though, from my knowledge with the South Korean people, people here would still accept such a re-unification when the North is being abandoned."

"Have you met any Korean from the North?" Someone from the far back asked aloud, "How do they speak? are they really different from the South Korean?"

"I'd met one or two, just passersby," Eun Hye answered. "They speak the same language with different use of words, farmer-like, other than that, not much different from a South Korean."

"Have you been to North Korea?" Another person from the same far corner of this coach asked politely, but loud and significantly.

"Nope, I never have," Eun Hye said, " but I heard a story about someone who did. A well-educated lady was invited to visit North Korea for some sort of reason. On her way back to South Korea, she was received well by a North Korean Border Officer. She gave praise for her respect of this gentle military person to his commanding superior, and both of them ended up in prison with a charge on conspiracy and treason."

"…"

"Not just North," she said seriously, "Even when in South, the military persons are restricted to rules they born to live with, as a Korean soldier. North Koreans are more discreet by their doctrine, to such a state that modern South Koreans cannot understand or cope with, but this is not saying you can photograph South Korean military personnel with or without asking; keep this firmly in mind and not to try. Another thing to add, this could be important, their attitude towards elders applies to the social class in pre-modern societies, with solemn respect, and even a person just a few days older shall be the elder. For example, when the driver of this coach is older than you, he can speak louder, and he can choose not to talk to you. On the street, every person might bump into each other, there is no queuing rule, but they would never do that to a person who is older. Ladies are not an important accessory when they are out on the street with their men, so, never try to act like a Korean woman if you have a big ego in public, although it might seem convincing when the Korean women rule the house when their men are subjugated, with no third party around."

"Had any romance with a Korean man?" Someone shouted from the back.

"Yes," she sighed, "made one huge mistake with my first man, before I came to this country. After I sought advice from the local oracle, the prophecy on me was to have a fresh start in an icy country as my only alternative, so I ended up here. I made another huge mistake with my first Korean man, my ignorance in not knowing that Korean man prefers chicken bones more than chicken meat, and that was it with romance."

"We want to hear more, please!" Called a lady from somewhere near the back of the coach.

"Another time, maybe," Eun Hye replied, "now, get ready for your first Korean breakfast, breakfast buffet... Korean style. Everything is self-serve, and you have to clean up your table or you will be cussed. Please do not make this trip ugly, and please bring honor to every crew member working for your reminiscent joy from this trip."

...

The room gives Eun Hye a cleaver blade of shivers, a slit on her anguished passions, and she is weakening from not eating for a full day. The small room is the only place she can afford to live on her own, within a shady hostel for alien Pakistani workers. She has to fight against vehemence and hyperbole for friendliness from the others. One of them stole her only boiled egg. When there was no point in finding out who did it, Eun Hye curled up in a fetal position on the center of her bed, eyes closed tightly, and the tears came. Kyu Bong returned late in the evening, as usual, and he looked as though he lacked affection or enthusiasm for Eun Hye's hunger. Then, without a word, he went out and brought back a huge roasted chicken leg. In perfect silence, he stripped down the roasted meat from the chicken leg and gave all to Eun Hye. While she was devouring her tardy meal, solemnly, he fed on the bones at the other side of the bed. The silhouette from the scissor wall lamp paused her thoughts; she remembered Lewis Carroll, "'But I don't want to go among mad people,' said Alice. 'Oh, you can't help that,' said the cat. 'We're all mad here.'" Then feelings emerged to calm her conscience, "This man is real; his shadow is real; he gives his best; he must be mad; this strange country breeds mad people, because I do not even love him a tiny bit." But her fondness of him was building from the moment he gave her all of the chicken meat. Eun Hye had a shadowy, chaotic love in Hong Kong, her birth place, and she would not even dream of going back. She was stuck here in Korea, and at this moment, starting to have feelings of affection towards her first Korean man.

Mayhem In The Monashees

by Sheila Cano

Sweat stung my eyes as I batted mosquitoes and flies away from my face.

"Geez, do you think these suckers could be any bigger? I wonder what little trap door to Hell opened up to let them out."

I spat one into the steaming jungle-like vegetation beside the trail. My shirt stuck to my back and I thought about how good a shower would be right about then. Days of slogging through avalanche slopes and rockslides had worn me down. The exit march was not as much fun as the approach had been, a week before. The fifty-five pound backpack was only a little lighter than it had been on our first day, most of our provisions being freeze-dried imitation foods. I used my ice axe as a walking stick, steadying my loose rambling gait. Thoughts of a juicy hamburger and a cold milkshake propelled me downhill through the fern forest. It would be good to get back to the highway before the dark clouds let go on us.

We paused for a break. Glen, my husband, dipped his red bandanna in the water and tied it back on without wringing it out. I rinsed my glasses, and Pat, our friend and best mountaineering buddy, took off her boots to soak her moleskin-encrusted feet at the edge of the stream. Each of us hauled out the remains of our trail mix and nibbled silently, too tired to talk.

Just then a butterfly alighted on Glen's shoulder. It rested on his white shirt, a living epaulet in black, white and orange. Its wings opened and shut slowly, its coiled proboscis probing the salty fabric.

We stared, transfixed. I pulled the camera from my pack, moving cautiously to avoid disturbing the creature.

"Would you look at that," Pat whispered. "It's just staying there."

After several minutes and a lot of snapshots, our awe and wonder began to dissipate, and we prepared to get back on the trail. Glen got up, the butterfly still resting on his shirt. He shrugged to dislodge it, but its sticky feet clung fast. Even a little shove failed to budge it. Finally he plucked it off and flung it into the air, fine dust falling from its bruised wings. It fluttered away erratically and landed on a bush.

"No freeloaders," Glen said, hoisting his pack on.

A rifle shot split the silence. Around the next bend, we heard voices. Beside the trail were four young guys, three of them holding beers, the fourth with a half-quart of vodka and a .22 in his other hand. They looked generally as scruffy as we did, jeans and work shirts, lanky long hair, their packs lying in the dirt. They stared at us as we passed by.

"Oh, great, just what we need," Glen said when we were beyond them. "A bunch of drunken yahoos with guns."

"Yeah, not exactly the peaceful wilderness with them around," Pat said.

"Peaceful? You call fording the river yesterday peaceful?" I said. "I thought I was a goner when I slipped off that log."

"Ha! You were such a wimp, sitting down and scooting along on your bum. If you'd just walked across you wouldn't have had any trouble," Glen said.

"Oh, I guess I'm just not as well-coordinated as you are, huh?"

At our next rest stop, the sharpshooters passed us. Through the afternoon we kept leapfrogging each other, hearing their gunfire in the distance. Once we were some ways apart we relaxed, listening to the birds and the sound of the creek. As we neared a bridge, suddenly a shot rang out, too close.

"YAAAAA!"

Pat screamed, a terrified howl. A few feet farther on, we saw the guys lounging in a small open patch, bottles set up on stumps for their target practice. I strode into the middle of their firing range and yelled at them.

"What the fuck do you think you're doing?"

I raised my ice axe over my head and flung it ten yards into the clearing, landing it a few feet from one of them. They all turned pale and ran off into the woods as fast as their drunken legs would take them. I retrieved the axe and turned back to my companions, who looked stunned.

"Shelley, I've never seen you get mad before!" Pat said.

"Let's get ahead of these jerks," I said.

We swung into the mile-eating stride that had taken us up to the glacier a couple of days before, up to that beautiful other world where water and air bubbles percolated beneath our crampon-clad boots. I daydreamed the rest of the way back to the car, savouring the memories of climbing, the rhythm of breathing, stepping, planting the ice axe, exulting in the widening views and the sound of the wind in the clouds. We walked in silence, each of us decompressing inside and preparing to re-enter the social world.

At the parking area, we took our time unloading our packs and stowing the gear before our trip down the gravel road. A cabin at the

219

fish camp awaited us, rustic luxury after our wilderness camping. I eased into the driver's seat, amid the nest-like pile of stinking belongings.

"Hey, wait a minute! Ya got room for us, eh?"

The four musketeers shambled unsteadily towards us, so drunk they didn't notice who was driving.

"Sorry," I said. "We're full up."

I peeled out and left them in the dust. It was a twenty-five mile jaunt into Lumby, the nearest small town. We cruised the two-block strip for a place to get a hamburger. A little diner on the corner looked just right, and after sliding into a booth, Pat and I flipped through the selections on the tabletop juke box.

"Oh, perfect!"

Pat slipped a quarter into the slot and seconds later, "Surf City" blared out.

"Two girls for every boy…"

"You guys!" Glen laughed.

Bellies full, we ambled over to the car. As I opened the door, a butterfly drifted in, landing on the dashboard.

"Hey, get a load of this," I said. It was black and orange and white, missing a little bit of one wing. "We picked up a hitchhiker after all."

Where Would You Go?

by M Dawn Thacker

"Where would you travel, if you could go anywhere in the world right now?" I asked the group of women assembled at the Short Story Club meeting in the nursing home. We had just taken turns reading paragraphs from a travelogue written by twenty-two year old Lindsay, Mary's adopted granddaughter from the University of Virginia.

Lindsay graduated from college last year and is in Seoul, South Korea teaching English for a year. She sends us updates of her adventures through emails to Mary. Lindsay's latest exploits took her to Beijing, China. She made comparisons between the peoples, their food, how much they elbowed, made eye contact, and spit. The babies of China "are more rosy cheeked than those of Korea," she wrote, and are "bundled against the cold," looking like tiny Michelin men.

The elders enjoy reading Lindsay's travels. They recite her words with emotion, tone, and inflection. They laugh at the silliness of her Kindergarten students and put their hands to hearts at the kind gestures of her friends helping her maintain a sense of family in a foreign land. Today, we boarded the plane with Lindsay and her friend Elizabeth, traveled through the silk, pearl and jade markets of Beijing, and tasted a scorpion on a stick.

"I would go to Germany," Nancee said. "That's where my goose feathers come from." Nancee makes quill pens. She learned the craft and has sent sets to each President since Nixon and all the Justices of the Supreme Court since the sixties. They sign important documents with her creations. A goose farmer in Germany heard of

Nancee's project and sent her thousands of feathers at no charge. She washes them until they shine white, cuts them into quills, demonstrates how they work, and teaches her craft to others who want to learn. "I'd like to visit Reimer's farm and tell him thank you for his kindness," she said.

We moved onto Paulette. "I'd fly to Scotland. I've never been there. My ancestors were Scottish. I hear it's beautiful."

"I'd go to Hawaiia," Caroline mispronounced. I went once a long time ago and it's the prettiest place I ever saw. The flowers there are as big as your head and the people are so kind."

"Egypt," Shirley stated without hesitation. "I was there in the seventies and fell in love with the people and culture. It's hard to believe that civilization is as old as it is, but when you are there, you can feel the number of years. I watched the revolution on TV, watched that dictator fall. I would love to be right there in Tahrir Square, tasting freedom."

Mary was next. "I'd go to Seoul," she said, "to be with Lindsay."

Emma was last. She sat thinking for a long time. Finally, she looked up with watery blue eyes and said, "Home, I'd go home."

Journey To A Dead End Street

by Adrienne S Moody

My sister is a doctor and when she broke the news to me that dad had lung cancer, I knew he would not survive. The fear in her voice told me it was terminal; I booked a flight home. My parents picked me up at the airport and there wasn't any sign that anything was amiss. He was not yet in any physical pain. The grim prognosis had not been fully registered by anyone; it seemed so much easier to pretend nothing was wrong, that I was visiting like I often did. We'd play blackjack at the Casino, my dad and I, dodging household chores dictated by my mother. I would sit side by side with him on the couch while we watched David Suzuki and marvel at the man's ingenuity and love of the environment. I'd watch him read the newspaper in the morning and let him read to me, interesting bits of news or just be silly and make me laugh. We didn't have to do anything; we could just sit in silence and be content. We had a special relationship.

His cancer was an unwelcome guest and we refused to acknowledge him. I sat in the back seat of their white Honda Accord and my father drove while my mother chatted.

My mother, as usual, listed in order of importance, all the chores and errands she wanted done during my

three day stay. She was the one in control. I could tell by her determined tone of voice that this would not change, regardless of any change in my father's health. It sounded to me, half-listening, that the itinerary left me very little time to just be. This was all I wanted to do, be with him. I sighed hearing all the endless chores that she'd lined up, recycling, re-organizing, new blinds to choose and install, endless items off a list in her head. She interrupted herself with directions to the restaurant that she wanted us to have lunch.

I could feel my father's impatience and tried to distance myself from them by looking out the window and

disengaging from the conversation. An argument began about how to get there. My mother stopped talking; my father became very agitated.

"Which way, Janet? Left? Right? Tell me... come on! I'm just going to keep on driving straight till you tell me which way to turn!"

We were now off the main drag and heading deep into a residential area.

"Do we go straight? Left? Right? Which way, Janet?"

We passed children playing on the street and a dead-end street sign.

My mother stared straight ahead with her arms crossed.

"You have all the answers. Tell me...which way now?"

The road ended and our vehicle came to a stop. The three of us sat in silence.

Journey Through Locked Wards
by Adrienne S Moody

It's a pleasant enough place. I've been in worse facilities. The women at the front desk and the Director of Care rarely smile, and only occasionally speak to me. After the first month that my clients were admitted here, I became accustomed to the cold attidute at the front lines.

As one walks through the shiny, sterilized corridors, smiles from the cleaning and cooking staff greet you warmly. There is music and singing from the laundry room and laughter from the care aides at their lockers, starting or ending their shifts. I step into the elevator and press C 1.

The elevator door opens and I see the Recreational Aide is near the front of the room surrounded by elderly men and women, all in wheelchairs or slumped in institutional armchairs. Some are dozing with their heads to one side, but most are reasonably attentive and shout out the answers to her questions. Questions like,

"On what holiday would you send a card to a sweetheart?"

Ellen is not your typical 'inmate.' Her mind is sharp, but her body is failing. Walking is painful and difficult; she uses a wheelchair to get wherever she's going.

I knock loudly on her door; she is partially deaf. Upon entering, I see that she is immersed in a tennis match featuring her favorite player, Serena Williams. In her prime, Ellen played professional tennis and became a gifted painter. A couple of her best, framed paintings hang on the wall. I sit next to her and we cheer on Serena.

"How's Vincent?" she asks during a commercial.

"Haven't been up there yet. I hope better than yesterday."

"He was awful when you left last time… like a zombie," she says.

"I know. I'll take you up there in a few minutes."

"Did you find a roommate yet?"

"Yeah, I did," I answer.

"Don't get a man," she warns.

"Too late. He's moving in on Sunday."

"He is? Well, get a lock on your bedroom door. Ah well, probably better than a woman for a roommate. Women can be bitches, you know."

"I know." We smile at each other. "We should go up, Ellen, and see what's going on."

The elevator shuts and I press D-3. The elevator opens and we can see through the glass doors of the locked ward. Three Alzheimer's patients are hovering close to the door. We'll have to be careful not to allow them any chance of escape. I press the five digit code and hear the click, then I push us through quickly and lean against the door until I hear the bolt lock once again.

Vincent could be anywhere on this ward. We pass the shufflers, and the incapacitated. They're tipped back in reclining vinyl chairs. I don't see Neta—a tall, thin German woman who speaks in a thick accent. She walks with her back pressed against the wall and her head is tipped shyly. I always say, "Hello," and she always smiles.

We find Vincent in a room adjacent to his own. He is standing with his back to us, in front of Derek's dresser. The two men are rummaging in Derek's dresser drawer. I hear murmuring.

"What are you guys up to?" I ask.

They both turn, with blank looks on their faces. They ignore me. Vincent takes off his belt and passes it to Derek. Derek, in turn, gives him one of his own to Vincent.

"When you're done, Vincent, come into your room and watch some tennis with Ellen. Okay?"

"Okay, I'm coming now," he follows us doing his new shuffle, a head down gait that he has recently adopted.

They've been at this facility for over a year now. Vincent is moderately affected by Alzheimer's. The past month there has been a marked change in him. He's violently refusing any help by the staff and has broken two shower heads during bath time. He kicks, punches, and swears at the nursing staff and care aides.

It's obvious by his slurred speech and vacant eyes that the medication has been stepped up. This isn't something the family likes to see, but what are the choices?

Vincent was an ace golfer up until eight years ago; many hole-in-one trophies grace his mantle. He was a dental hygienist during the war and continued on with this profession until retirement.

I settle them in Vincent's sun-filled room that overlooks two towering oaks trees. They sit side-by-side; I click on the TV and pass the remote to Ellen.

"I'll stop by tomorrow. Take care you two." I wave at the door. Vincent does not look up, but Ellen waves and I leave.

My heels make a clicking sound on the immaculate green, tiled floors. I pass a man in a wheelchair and he calls out to me, "Hey, lady!" I ignore him. Yesterday he called out to me, "Hey, you stupid bitch, out of my way!"

I see Neta has befriended a newcomer and the two of them are moving slowly along with their backs to the wall.

"Don't speak to him," the newcomer says to me in a grave voice. 'He's trying to kill me."

"Well, you two stick together," I replied.

"Always!"

I press the code and leave the ward. I wait for the elevator and watch them—watching me leave.

From Saxis to Parksley and Back

by M Dawn Thacker

It was one of those days where everything you don't plan falls into place. The whole week had been windy and cold, stay in the car and see the sights from there kind of weather. We had missed lunch at Martha Jane's Restaurant yesterday by half an hour. A local had told us it was the best place around to eat. We pulled into the gravel parking lot at the end of an ugly cinderblock building on the edge of Saxis Island. Docks jutted out into the choppy Pocomoke Sound. Seagulls called out overhead. We assumed we were lost. A woman in a mini van opened her window and smiled at us.

"We're looking for Martha Jane's," I said.

"This is it," the woman said, sweeping her hand out toward the non-descript building. "We close at one o'clock though. I'm only here because I left my phone and had to come back for it."

"Thank you," I said. "We'll try again tomorrow.

"We open at five a.m.," she said. "The fisherman leave out of here early. Hope you come back. We'd love to have you."

We'd come back to the cottage last night and Mama had turned on the television before bed. She stumbled upon the Waltons, a family drama from my childhood. She was so excited to find a piece of her past. "Why can't things be like they used to be?" She asked no one in particular. "Everything has to change. Television shows these days don't make sense to me and everything is so fast paced and computerized. I miss the old days."

She's seventy-seven, and walks slowly now. She spends more time talking about her past than she looks to the future. She repeats my favorite stories for me no matter how many times I've heard them and we laugh like it's the first telling. We planned this trip together because we thought it would be fun for just the two of us to get away. I made time because I never know when it might be our last trip together.

Our start was earlier today and we headed straight for Martha Jane's. We arrived at nine-thirty, and found the place empty of diners, but half filled with old men, drinking coffee and discussing boats, nets, crabbing, oysters, and the week's weather. "Front's coming through tonight. Wind's gonna pick up, temperature's gonna drop. Rain's on the way," one of them said.

"Hey, you made it back," Martha greeted us. "I always worry that folks won't come back when they find out we close so early, or they make the trip and find the door locked."

"You came recommended as the best place to get home cooking," Mama said. "We're on vacation and needed a little taste of home."

"Come on in. Here's the menu. Let me know when you're ready to order, and I'll whip it up for you," Martha said. She went back to busying herself in the open kitchen. She had an array of skillets, electric frying pans, and griddles arranged behind the counter, just waiting for a fresh batch of breakfast.

I ordered sausage gravy over biscuits and two fried eggs. Mama wanted a western omelet and toast. We prepared our own coffee from the pots on the warmer. We sat down in the knotty pine booths, and read a story in the local town magazine about Martha Jane and her husband Kefford. She owns the restaurant. He is a waterman who carves and paints decoys and miniature boats.

Mama was in heaven. She kept offering tastes of her omelet to me, and sneaking tastes of my sausage gravy. "Your Grandma was a good cook," she said, "but I think this beats even her cooking. Don't you tell anyone I said that," she whispered through the hand over her mouth. I laughed and assured her I'd keep her secret. I could picture Grandma frowning down on us from her own perch in heaven.

Martha Jane walked us over to Kefford's studio to introduce us. "He's a shy man," she warned. "Doesn't have a whole lot to say, but he'll enjoy showing you his crafts."

His work was beautiful, finely crafted, carved, wood-burned, and painted in such life-like hues, you'd expect the duck to take flight before your eyes. Kefford's smile let us know he appreciated our compliments on his work. "How long you here for?" He asked.

"We leave tomorrow," Mama said.

"Be sure to take the opportunity to walk the shoreline here in Saxis before you leave," he said. "It's a nice day, not too windy, and the view is a good one."

We parked just outside of town and walked the short distance to the water's edge. Mama stood there, eyes fixed on the horizon. "This reminds me of when your sister was a baby," she said. "She'd cry and the motion of the car calmed her. We'd ride to the shore and she'd finally be sleeping in the back seat. I'd sit in the car and watch the ships come in. Look out there, it's a fishing troller."

We watched as the boat chugged past, then turned, and walked across the sand holding hands like we did when I was five years old. She told me stories I hadn't remembered, and we picked up pieces of colored sea glass to put in our pockets.

We were still full from breakfast when we got back in the car. I had planned to head back to the cottage, but Mama said, "You know I have a friend, Lou, who lives in Parksley. We're not far from there I think. Do you mind if we try to find it?"

I had seen the sign for Parksley on our way to the island. It was about fifteen miles to the South on Rt. 13. We passed the town limit sign and found ourselves in a quaint Victorian village. The streets were narrow and the main drag, Bennett Street sported 'Jaxon's' Five and Dime. A Railroad Museum, complete with dining, pullman, caboose, and passenger cars welcomed visitors just across the street. All around us were lovely old Victorian homes with gingerbread trim, wrap-around porches, and turret spires. Mama gasped. "It's like stepping back in time," she breathed out.

Jaxon's called, and we answered. Walking through its doors was like going into the old Woolworth's Dime Store Downtown when I was a little girl, only bigger and better. Each aisle displayed treasure after treasure, from sewing notions and embroidery thread to penny candy, from Johnson's Foot Soap to shaving brushes and homemade lye soap. The rear of the store housed the toys. Old fashioned cap guns, Slinkies, Hula Hoops, board games like Monopoly and Clue, metal trucks and china tea sets all vied for attention from the little girl in me. Jaxon's didn't stop with small items, they also carried canning kettles, baking pans, hammers, nails, Red Wing Boots, hard sole walking shoes for babies and suede Hush Puppies high tops. To the far right of the store, ladies and men's apparel graced the shelves and racks. Everything one could need for setting up housekeeping in the 1940's and 50's was right there. And, on the green and white linoleum tile floor stood a two cent weight/fortune scale and two twenty-five cent mechanical riding toys, a pink carousel horse, and a red train with billowing white smoke.

Mama walked the aisles and picked up item after item, remembering and telling stories about this and that. She mentioned to the sales ladies over and over again how much she loved the store and how she could spend her whole vacation right there among her memories. When we checked out, she loaded the counter with a vegetable peeler, two plastic combs, three quarter-yard pieces of gingham material, a spool of gold thread, two pairs of cotton underpants, a package of handkerchiefs and a white dress shirt wrapped in plastic to take home to my step-father, a box of stationery, some toenail clippers and a tube of red lipstick like she wore a long time ago. She grinned as she wrote out the last check in her checkbook. "I'm glad I saved this one," she said. "something told me to."

The ladies in Jaxon's gave us directions to Lou's house, a lovely white Victorian house on the corner just after crossing the railroad tracks. Mama walked up to the door and knocked. He wasn't home. She took out a piece of her new stationery and jotted him a note with my cell phone number.

The phone rang tonight and Lou was on the other end. Mama took the call in the other room so she could hear him. I couldn't help but listen, as her voice carries, and is louder due to the hearing loss. She told him all about our trip and how perfect our day had been today, how she felt like she had stepped back in time. The two of them reminisced, and I heard Mama laugh out loud more than once telling her stories.

She came back into the kitchen where I was after the call. "That was Lou," she said. "I haven't talked to him in years. He was so glad to hear from me." She beamed as she handed me my cell phone. "Good thing we're heading home tomorrow," she said. "There's no way we could top this day, absolutely no way."

I smiled up at her from my chair at the table. "I'm glad you had a good time. I did too," I said.

"I think I'll head off to bed now, I'm kinda tired," she said.

As she turned, she started singing a tune I remembered from my childhood, "Good night Irene, good night Irene, good night Irene, good night Irene, I'll see you in my dreams."

The Last Road Trip
by Adrienne S Moody

Ellen didn't want to go. Murray was becoming short-tempered lately and she found herself agreeing to things she never would have earlier in their marriage. Now he was insisting they go for a drive—on such a day! Raised on a farm, Ellen learned to read weather and she knew that snow was on its way. The clouds were grey and still; the air was crisp and cold, like biting into a Granny Smith apple. She sighed when she heard him open the front closet and pull his ski jacket off the hanger.

"Are you coming, Ellen? Come on! Get your coat and let's go."

"Why is it you are so hell bent on going out in this weather?"

She made one last attempt to try and discourage him.

"I'm tired of the frozen dinners Angela makes for us. She's a sweet daughter, but I'm sick of stringy meat and mushy rice. Let's hit the road… I'm taking you out for dinner."

Well, that made a little more sense, Ellen thought. She pulled on her beige lambswool coat and wrapped a new paisley scarf around her neck. She checked her hair in the bathroom mirror, touched it gently on the sides where the curls were still too tight from her recent perm. She pulled out her lipstick, opened her mouth into a large O, and painted expertly. She pressed her lips together onto a Kleenex, inspected herself in the mirror, and snapped her cosmetic case shut.

"Are you ever going to be ready?" Murray stood at the door jingling his keys, like he always did when his patience ran out.

Some things never change, she thought and turned off the bathroom light. Routines and habits engraved in their daily lives after forty years of marriage; it gave her a certain comfort. But Murray's health was sliding and she knew it. She hadn't told her daughter, Angela, because she knew if she said anything about Murray's increasing forgetfulness, Angela would insist they move into a facility. So instead, Ellen covered for him. If he got lost coming home from the grocery store and Angela called for him, Ellen lied and said he was laying down. She couldn't keep this act going forever; Angela was a smart girl and would soon see her father's confusion for what it was.

Alzheimer's is a scary word.

It became worrisome especially when he roamed throughout the house at night. Late one evening, she smelled something burning and leaped out of bed terrified of what she would discover. He was rummaging through a desk drawer in the study and had forgotten that he'd put a pan of water on the stove to boil an egg. The water had run out and the pot was smoldering hot. After that, she no longer slept until he came to bed and began his familiar snoring.

His speech began to remind her of the old 78 rpm records they used to play. They loved the Big Band era and Mitch Miller was a favorite of theirs. One of them had a scratch and skipped. She had to stop and think of the tune. Oh, yes, it was – Till We Meet Again. She thought of the song when he constantly repeated a phrase.

They sat together in silence as Murray revved the engine in a futile attempt to hurry the heater along. Another habit. She smiled thinking of the first vehicle they bought. It was a Chevy and had the sissy rope on the back of the front seat.

"Remember how we used to take Sunday drives, Murray?"

"Hmm."

"We'd just take to the country roads and drive. Remember that? Before the kids arrived and we had so little money, but we always managed to do that… didn't we, Murray? Oh, I loved those days. It seemed we had so few cares back then, but of course we must have had some… just thinking back now, the years, they seemed so carefree, didn't they, Murray?"

"Okay, here we go. She's warm enough," Murray reversed and backed the vehicle onto the street in one fluid motion.

"Where we going, Murray? You haven't said. Where we going for dinner?"

"Chinese food. That's what I'm wanting. Let's just drive down this road and see what we see."

"Oh, kind of like in the old days, then? Oh, Murray, what a fine idea. Just be spontaneous. Let's drive until we find the perfect place to have dinner. Kind of romantic, don't you think?"

"Yup. Romantic."

They were on the freeway and stayed in the slow lane. Murray didn't like going highway speeds anymore. They coasted along oblivious to the traffic speeding by, some drivers honking their annoyance.

"What's everyone in such a goddamn hurry for? Doesn't anyone just enjoy the scenery?"

"Pay no mind, Murray. But what's coming up ahead? Why, that looks like the border crossing. However did we get here? We're too late to turn around now, Murray. Good thing the passports are in the glove compartment."

"You see? Angela said don't leave them in the car and what would we do now if we'd listened to her? Here, pass them over here. And let me do the talking, Ellen. He don't want to hear all about your day. These men mean business and look 'em in the eyes if he does talk to you. Don't start getting all fluttery like you do when you're nervous. We don't want no dogs sniffing around looking for drugs. That's what they do if you act edgy. Okay. Quiet now."

But, there wasn't any problem crossing the border. The guard looked them over, entered their info into the computer and asked where they were going.

"Why, we're just going for a nice little drive and then turning around and heading on home," Murray answered his query.

"Well, Murray, you handled that very well, I must say," Ellen commented when they pulled away.

Ellen took out tissue from her purse and dabbed at her perspiring forehead. The elderly couple were on a country road which was devoid of any traffic. Murray kept his hands tight on the steering wheel, his eyes straight ahead. Ellen gave him a full account of all that she saw out her window. She pointed out the cattle in the fields, the goats, and the quaint farm houses that they passed. But after a couple of hours, she grew tired and her head dropped to her chest and she began to snore. Murray liked to tease her about her snoring. He said she sounded like a mad little dog. But, on this day his mind was vacant. He thought of nothing as he stared straight ahead at the endless stretch of road. Darkness fell and he continued to drive with only his running lights. His eyes felt fatigued from the strain, fluttering shut and then opening with a start.

The vehicle suddenly lost power and chugged slowly to a stop. Ellen woke abruptly and looked around in confusion.

"What? What's going on, Murray? Where are we? Why are we stopped here? In the middle of nowhere?"

Murray said nothing. His hands remained on the steering wheel. They were out of gas.

"It's snowing," he announced as the flakes gathered on the windshield.

"You're right, it is," Ellen unbuckled her seat belt and moved closer to her husband. "Brrrr…it's getting cold in here, Murray. Do you think we're lost?"

Murray said nothing and kept his hands on the steering wheel.

"It's snowing."

"Yes, yes it is. Put your arms around me, Murray. Let's keep each other warm. Do you think someone will come along on this road? It looks deserted, doesn't it?"

"It's snowing."

He put his arms around his wife and they sat together as the snow fell softly all around them. Ellen's feet began to feel numb and she wiggled her toes to keep the circulation going. She didn't feel afraid. She was where she wanted to be, next to her husband through everything life presented to them. Someone would surely happen by and see they were out of gas and would help them get back home. But in the meantime, she sat there, feeling her Murray's arms around her, and let herself be lulled to sleep.

Born To Ride

by M Dawn Thacker

"I can't do it without them," my cousin Annabelle whined, looking up into the face of her Daddy. He was holding the training wheels in one hand, the wrench in the other.

"Sure you can, Hoss. I'll be right behind you, holding onto you until you get your balance." Only her Daddy was allowed to call her "Hoss."

"You promise?" she asked, looking up at him.

"I promise," he said, smiling.

"Mariah, honey, you mind holding these while I give Annabelle a push?"

I took the training wheels and wrench and sat on the steps of the porch to watch Annabelle learn to ride her bike. She was from April to September older than me and she always reminded me of it. She was scared though, looking back over her shoulder instead of where she was going. Her handlebars wobbled.

"You have to look straight ahead and keep pedaling," Uncle Jeff said, as he huffed beside her, holding onto the seat, keeping her upright.

They stopped a few times for him to catch his breath, and then started again, him running, reminding her what to do as she forgot to steer or pedal, or both. When they stopped for the night, she still wasn't riding by herself and Uncle Jeff's face was red and sweaty.

"We'll try again tomorrow," he said patting her back. "I'm home all week."

I handed him the wheels and wrench, and followed Annabelle into the house for graham crackers and milk, our after-school snack.

Mama and I had moved to Hampshire Road during the summer so I could attend Burke Elementary School. It was within walking distance of my Aunt Kate and Uncle Jeff's house. I could go there after school until Mama got off work and came to pick me up. I could play with my cousin Annabelle.

She mostly bossed and I followed directives. We hunted salamanders and crayfish in the stream behind her house. When she found them, I had to pick them up to put them in the Mason jars of creek water. I climbed the tree to rescue the cat, and untangle the kite. She barked directions.

Her next door neighbor, Matt, liked me better than her though, and it made her scowl. He walked me home from school one day and she chased him with a stick all the way to his front door. I suffered a black eye for laughing.

It wasn't long before Annabelle mastered the bike and gloated. I didn't have a bike yet, but was going to ask for one for Christmas. Annabelle warned me away from her red, Western Flyer bicycle parked on the porch.

"Don't you dare touch it," Annabelle said to me. "You can't ride a two wheeler. You'll wreck it."

Annabelle took piano lessons on Tuesday afternoons from four to five o'clock. While she plinked the keys, I was on my own.

The piano was in Aunt Kate's living room and the big picture window faced the street in front of the house. Annabelle's bicycle was on the back porch. She couldn't see me as I went over and sat on the seat. I put my hands on the rubber grips, my feet on the pedals and pretended to ride up Burke Drive. I pedaled and coasted and even rode without hands. I felt the wind in my hair and never left the safety a kick stand provided.

The next week, I gathered my courage and pulled the kick stand up. My legs were longer than Annabelle's and I could sit on the seat with my feet planted on the ground. I looked out at the backyard. It had a slight slope, enough to let the bike roll. I sneaked around to the front of the house, peered into the big window to make sure Annabelle and her teacher were busy with their lesson, and ran back to the bicycle. I had a half hour before the bike had to be back on the porch.

I carefully walked it to the top of the slope, climbed aboard and dragged my feet behind the pedals as I rode to the bottom of the hill. I made three more runs before I parked the bike back where it was supposed to be. I was so excited I could have popped.

Every Tuesday, Annabelle's Western Flyer and I had a date. I graduated from dragging my feet, to lifting them and putting them back down again. When I could coast holding my feet up all the way, I put them on the pedals, but didn't push. I let the wheels do the work. Start at the top, coast down, walk back to the top of the hill.

"I told you not to touch my bike," Annabelle's voice screamed at my back from the porch.

I was caught. I looked at my watch. It was too early for her lesson to be finished.

"Why aren't you playing the piano?" I asked, walking the bike back up the hill.

"My teacher got called home. Her son is sick. Why are you on my bike?" she screamed at me, her face red, her hands on her hips.

"I didn't hurt your old bike," I said. "I was just trying it out. Look, not a scratch."

"I'm going to tell Mama," she said.

"Go ahead," I said.

"Mama!" Annabelle yelled. "Mariah was riding my bike without permission."

"Aren't you ashamed of yourself?" my Aunt said, walking out onto the porch wiping her hands on a dish towel.

I was waiting for a punishment.

Aunt Kate pointed her finger at Annabelle, "to think, young lady, as lucky as you are. Mariah doesn't even have a bike, or a daddy to teach her how to ride one. And you won't share yours? I thought I taught you better than that."

Annabelle frowned. "She didn't ask me," she said.

"That's alright," I said, dropping the kick stand. "I don't want to ride your stupid bike."

I went to the front steps and sat down, waiting for my mother to come pick me up. I thought about the blue bike I wanted for Christmas. At least if I got one, I knew how to ride without training wheels. I didn't need someone running beside me, holding me up, helping me balance, telling me to keep pedaling, or to hold my handlebars straight. I already knew how to do all that. I was born to ride.

They Gave The World

by Sarah Scott

Three U-Haul trucks, two vans, eighteen children, several adults, hundreds of boxes stacked in the back of the trucks, coolers in each of the vehicles, and hints of sadness in our eyes.

I was twelve, thirteen maybe. Colorado's summer wind kicked up dust as I dragged my feet around the back deck, waiting for that moment when the Cavalier would round the last bend and come into view. We were waiting on them, again. This time there was no leaving, not until they arrived. Fifteen minutes would come and go and still Dad wouldn't pull out of the parking lot, shaking his head. I wouldn't start crying because they'd stood me up, again. This time, we would wait as long as we had to—all of us.

The younger kids were getting antsy; the older kids were getting angry. I was giving up hope of my birth parents ever showing. "Let's just go," I told Mom and Dad. "They won't show up." He patted my head and pointed to the dust cloud around the curve.

"Don't be so sure kiddo." He smiled at me and loaded one more box onto the last U-Haul. Two more vehicles were parked in line, waiting for their drivers to crank the engines and roll on toward the Colorado border, headed east.

Finally, I could see the car through the dust cloud. A hesitant smile spread across my face. Sure, I was leaving them. Sure, they had 'given me away,' but I loved them, maybe even loved them more for it.

My mom climbed out of the car first and wrapped her arms around me. She gave me a bag of things from the house. "Thanks," I whispered into her auburn hair. It was long and soft. She hugged me tightly, tighter than she ever had before. For once her hands soothed me rather than bruised me. Her eyes shone with tears instead of hate and anger. I cried. Is this what it took for her to realize that she loved me?

My dad walked forward and hugged me next, tall and strong like a weathered pine, his bark a little rough around the eyes and mouth, but still alive. "I love you, kiddo. I know you'll be fine. Call anytime." He choked back a few tears. "We'll miss you." He turned away and got back in the car before I could see him cry, but I know he did, after I left. I can imagine him with tears pouring from his eyes, as he grips the steering wheel white-knuckled. I can see his shoulders shake, even now.

Lastly, my sister came and hugged me. She'd been crying too. Her carrot-top curly hair was a mess. Her blue eyes were bloodshot. I spoke first this time. "Take care of yourself, Rachel. I love you." I handed her a book from my shelf and in it I had written a poem for her. "Write me." I handed the stack of pre-addressed pre-stamped envelopes to my mom. She wiped a tear from my freckled face.

"I will," Rachel said, "every day." She hugged me tighter and then said what I was hoping not to hear. "Goodbye." I watched my ten-year-old sister walk back to the car. I saw her shoulders tremble and heard the sobs escape her throat. I knew her pain, felt it in my heart, but there was no future here. We all knew that.

"I love you." My mom turned and walked away, following the trail of tears my sister had shed. I gulped back my own; I had to be strong. I had to get in the van and leave. I knew that. They did too. I waved and headed for the open door, willed myself to get to my seat. Fifteen sets of arms hugged as I made my way into the passenger van. I took the very back seat—maybe so I couldn't bolt at the last minute? I turned around in my seat, waved, and cried the whole way down the road with my birth parents' car behind us, blurring and hazing more as the tears fell and the dust clouds rose.

As we hit the highway, my foster sister Jen started singing:

I'm carrying your love with me

Colorado east to Tennessee

I'll be moving with the good Lord's speed

Carrying your love with me

It's me strength for holding on

Every minute that I have to be gone

It's the only thing I'll ever need

I'm carrying your love with me.

There were two days of road stretched before us as we left our foster home in Colorado headed for the rolling hills of Knoxville, Tennessee. Two days… and a life of hope. I knew it then, just as I know it now: they gave me away because they loved me. It was their greatest gift; it cost them everything.

Sutter Buttes

by Sheila Cano

The shortest mountain range in the world rises like a mirage from the level Sacramento River valley near Yuba City. Mom drove us out there to show me a part of the county I had seen only from a distance. The hills were visible for a long way. She had been to a nearby school one day, and got a flat tire. It was such an adventure for her, she wrote a story about it. So she took me to the Sutter Buttes, and we saw amazing things.

All around the Buttes lay farmland. Tomatoes grew in long, green rows reaching to the foot of the dry, rocky little mountains. The farm-workers wore heavy boots and gloves, despite the intense heat, to ward off attacks by rattlesnakes. Crumbling rock walls demarcated some of the land, put there by the earliest immigrant settlers. Other fields had barbed-wire fences, hung at intervals with coyote skins to discourage the wild canines from culling the sheep. Paper signs nailed to the fence-posts informed us that the government paid a bounty of twenty-five cents per coyote skin turned in to their offices. I thought it was barbaric and cruel to do such a thing, but then I was a city kid unwise to the ways of farm folk.

We drove the narrow, winding road through the Buttes, emerging on the north side to a wide vista below. Continuing down the road, which became smooth, free of the potholes and ditches behind us, we suddenly found ourselves approaching an area of large, low modern buildings and high towers unlike any farm structures we had ever seen. The road came to an abrupt end at a guard-post gate with uniformed men carrying automatic weapons. We had inadvertently driven to the check-point of a NIKE missile base.

Stunned to find this encampment hidden on the other side of the hills, we turned around and rode home in silence. The coyote skins, the barbed wire, the workers breathing pesticides all day, the armed guards – all of this had shocked us. The dreamy flat world of the valley was only an illusion. The real truth was up there, secluded in the shortest mountain range in the world. It disappeared into the shimmering heat haze in the rear view mirror. We never visited it again.

Big Storm

by Steven Bird

The cat is cool. Their gray tabby is a smart little guy, and a remarkably good traveler for a cat. He is an unusual cat. He's been with them all of his life and he's made the long trip north and south for ten summers now. The cat knows the drill and recognizes that they are getting ready to leave when he sees them breaking down the fishing rods, the camp, and loading stuff onto the 4-Runner. Most cats would disappear at this point, necessitating a frenetic, cursing, last-minute search, but this one jumps into the rig an hour before they leave and makes himself comfortable. The existential cat has a pretty good feel for where he needs to be, a good grip on his overall position in the scheme of things.

The glaring blacktop approaches a molten state by late afternoon and the northern forest fades behind the travelers speeding south down the edge of a rolling plain quilted with lava beds and wheat fields and open stretches of pale sagebrush. The white sun blazes in the long, long sky, over the mountains, faraway at the edge of the seared brown plateau. The ribbon of highway alternately wanders and straightens over the skeletal plains and then, eventually, they glide imperceptibly down a gradual decline toward a mercury expanse of the Columbia River. The Toyota is a Spartan model with no air conditioner and the hot desert air blasts through the opened windows.

There is a promise of relief on the horizon, about 30 miles away, on the Oregon side of the river, where a bank of clouds assemble and advance like the risen dust of a distant army. Dark formations torn from the bank gallop ahead like charging horses, thin veils of rain falling from their hooves to evaporate in the furnace air before making it to the ground. He can see, there is a lot of wind in those clouds.

She rides slouched and languid, perspiring into the sheepskin seat cover. She's been quiet. She hasn't said a word for the last hundred miles. Frail ropes of wet hair cling to her temples. She'd removed the oppressive underwear miles ago and her light cotton summer dress clings to her. She rolls the dress up to her waist and settles with her legs slightly parted and glistening from the humidity. She leans her head back into the headrest and closes her eyes.

He wants to reach over and slide his hand between her legs and claim the heat. But his hand is frozen to the wheel. His hand is a rock. The storm has been building all summer, longer, maybe. There is something about the set of her jaw and the plane of her shoulders that discourages touch and stifles conversation. Separated by a short expanse of car seat, only the reaching of an arm away, he feels the gulf is too wide, too deep and perilous and beyond his ability to navigate.

Horse-cloud hoofs strike flint and lightning streaks to the ground in the distance. The cat emits a low yowl from the back seat.

"Subtropical front out of the south. Maybe we'll run into some rain down the road, cool us off," he says.

She doesn't reply. She turns her head toward the back seat and makes a kissing sound to the cat while patting her bare lap. The cat slips between the seats to accept the privileged spot, completes a few polite circles and curls himself over her thighs.

A far mountain consumes the cherry sun. In the distance, a tower of lightning rips the horizon. And then another, rippling out from under the massed and piling clouds of the swiftly advancing weather front. The atmosphere smells of metal and hot water. The travelers ride in silence while the relentless SUV tracks the yellow line, a hot grease and steel hound lined out on the distant bleeding storm. The Columbia River in the rearview mirror, they face a savage horizon. They wind up the bluffs at Umatilla, naked basin country prone and wide between the mountain ranges, closest, to the west, the volcanic spine of the Cascades, and far away to the east, mountain ranges belonging to the Rockies. The burgeoning electric storm fills the entire expanse laid open between the mountain ranges. Cloudbanks push and rise, stacking to regretful heights. Strange columns of lightning pulse straight to ground with rhythmic frequency. He imagines malignant angels hidden inside the black clouds – mad angels raining desolation, banging away at the hapless world, the planted fields, the car lots, mini-malls, RV trailer parks, the ancillary sprawl of new dream homes, the highway.

Raindrops dot the traveler's windshield, not enough to cool the stifling air, just enough to raise the humidity to a more intolerable level. He slows down to 60 and a semi hauling doubles roars up on them and hovers close to their rear bumper. He curses, "… Right on our ass." The trucker downshifts and the rig grinds past them like a berserk war elephant broken from the ranks and rushing to the fray. It's almost dark. Continuous lightning ahead of them ignites the cloud bottoms with a dangerous blue glow. Charged ions cling to forlorn particles. The cat lets go a loud, plaintive yowl, and, within the moment, they plunge through a curtain of rain and slam into the pounding red and black heart of the storm's rampaging trouble.

The rain sounds like rocks pelting the roof and windshield. He turns the wipers up to FULL and they clip back and forth at an irritating rate and don't do much good.

She rolls up her window. The cat roots for a better hold on her lap, panting in the heat, his face demonic, like an imp with pointed ears flattened and sticking out from the sides of his head, his short fur standing on end from static in the air. She strokes the cat with one hand while keeping a tight grasp on the safety handle over the door with the other. She looks straight ahead, a short section of her lower lip sucked between her teeth.

He backs off on the gas pedal some, and then a sudden sheet of heavy wind and rain forces him to slow a little more.

She turns to face him, her eyes are vulnerable and concerned.

Neon beanstalks flash and rise with spastic majesty on either side of the road, so close the lightning looks red – red blood veins straining from the black forearms of a furious god punching his fists into the imperfect clay of a botched creation. The acrid smell of burning grass fills the car and their throats constrict. Overlapping blasts of thunder punctuate waves of rain and hail hammering the roof and windshield. Drums of Apocalypse beat and foreboding coyote howls manifest from the storm. Raging voices, honey-thick with sex, hoarse with drink, promising the travelers strange pleasures, surging ecstasy, extravagant pain, prostrated and lush before the altar of annihilation inside the Burning Temple.

It is all too much for the cat. He pours from her lap and dives into the back seat to hide amid the luggage.

She squirms in her seat and rolls her dress back down to her knees.

He's never seen a storm like this, nothing even close. The wipers barely keep up with the rain enough to offer any visibility. He's in the slow lane, barely creeping along, straining to cipher the center line, and a truck hurtles by, blasting them with a wave of wind and water – they buffet sideways – a silver sheet of spray blacks out the windshield – the wipers slamming at a manic pace are useless against it – black sky and roadbed become one and all boundaries of safety dissolve – the sensation is like falling – he applies the brakes praying they don't get rear-ended by a semi – wonders how the truckers can even see to drive so fast in this – he barely starts to get some visibility, gets moving – and another truck plows by them sending out another wave of spray to black them out again – and they fall again. Rapid-fire lightning strobes crack and flash, and they can't tell the lightning from the headlights of speeding trucks bearing down on them.

She gasps, pressing her body into the seat back. "Why don't you pull off the road?" she says. A tear glints from the corner of her eye and courses down her cheek.

He can't see the road shoulder, if there is one, and he's afraid that if they pull off, somebody might follow thinking they're still on the road and plow into them. His fingers dig the steering wheel. "Baby I can't," he says, immediately regretting his dismissive tone, the despair in his voice.

They are barely moving, rain backs off some and he can see better and he accelerates a little. Suddenly a shape appears in the headlights and they bump over an object in the road – then swerve to avoid a nightmare entity sprawled on the highway in the flashing blue darkness – a bloody slick – ruined white fascia spewed and strung from obliterated flesh – and they barely miss hitting the carcass – and at the sight of it she cups her hands before her face and calls his name out loud.

Semi must've hit it. Bigger than a deer…Elk?… Cow?… Overweight motorist caught wandering on the side of the road after pulling off? He can't make it out.

They'd missed seeing the Elk Crossing sign a few miles back, an obscure yellow head lost in the storm's chaos.

The travelers hang on the accumulated assortment of weights and hooks of shared past, holding them together and set on the same destination, and the road rolls out ahead of them. And they roll. The man and the woman know little more of their future than does the cat. The rain decrease to a fine drizzle, and then it is gone. He turns the wipers off, rolls the window down. Good air fills the interior bringing the scent of washed sage and wet earth. A few stars beam cool between torn, straggling clouds. The cat has settled down and gone to sleep. And they all speed south through clean darkness.

She offers him a faint smile, her hands petrified doves on her lap. "My hero," she says. She turns her head away and amends her words to the stars over the black silhouette hills outside the window, in a whisper he can barely hear over the low thunder of road noise, "My ambiguous hero." She turns from the window to face him again, she is resigned and steady. "You are a hero in the end, aren't you?"

He wishes he could foretell the future. He wishes a lot of things were different. The question remains hanging between them, a thick exhalation of smoke in the car's dark interior, slowly dissipating out through the open windows to join the rushing slipstream emptying to the void outside. A simple yes or no. He can't say. The only thing he knows for certain is that they can't go back. Can never turn back. There is nothing behind them but the big storm.

The Foothills

by Sheila Cano

I

An iron spider spun a giant web to form the gate to Crystal Caverns in the Sierra foothills. Inside it was dark, with the sound of water trickling in a channel beside our feet. A blind cave fish patrolled an aquarium set into the rock wall. A blind newt waggled slowly along the bottom of its terrarium. Colored floodlights eerily illuminated the displays as we headed deeper into the cave. Sheets of rippled limestone hung resembling draperies or slabs of side bacon, translucent, glowing. Lumpy, bulbous shapes made a frozen rock waterfall, sparkling in the artificial light. Immense stone icicles dripped from the ceiling, meeting huge spires growing from below. A coolness pervaded the cave, respite from the glaring, dry heat of summer in the Mother Lode.

A spiral staircase descended one hundred feet down into Moaning Cave. When we reached the bottom, the guide turned off the lights. In the pitch blackness, the low howling of the wind did sound like moaning. The chirping of bats and shrieking of visitors echoed over and over until our ears rang. Human bones lay on the cave floor next to a fire-scorched rock circle. The cave provided shelter – and perhaps a last resting place – for aboriginal hunters in winters gone by.

II

Murphy's and Angel's Camp were two dusty little towns that boomed during the gold rush. Old wooden buildings, creaky rusting screen doors and ice-cold pop awaited us, tourists who came to see what was. We stayed at a cabin and campground area in Murphy's, played in the ponds created by concrete retaining walls along the stream. My brother was minding me one afternoon, when an older boy persuaded him to place me on a soggy wooden raft in the deep part of the pond. I slipped off and went down, down into a bright greenness, mica flakes glittering among flickering shafts of light. Someone dove in and brought me up, coughing and spluttering murky pond water.

III

Grass Valley and Nevada City were two more gold-rush towns becoming part of the tourist gold rush a hundred years later. Steep hilly streets, some still paved with stones, nineteenth-century architecture and fresh, piney air. The old brick jail house was now a library. Artisans and artists had begun to inhabit the area, opening funky small shops to compete with the antique and second-hand stores. An ice cream parlor had marble countertops and curved metal chairs. We stayed in an old hotel with balconies of wrought iron and brass beds that squeaked every time you moved.

We ate at the Blue Grotto, a diner with a neon sign, decorated outside with a cast-concrete grotto fountain, and fishnets and seashells inside on the walls. A candle, in a fat round colored glass with plastic mesh fitted over it, sat on every table. Far from the coast, most of the seafood was no doubt frozen, but it seemed like an exotic – and air-conditioned – spot on a roasting hot day.

IV

In Sonora we camped not far from the town's public swimming pool. We slept on the grass and looked up at a black sky full of stars that twinkled so brightly, you could almost hear them. Behind the campground was a reservoir, and I tramped around in the chaparral nearby. The Manzanita grew thickly on the furrowed hillsides and gulches, remnants of hydraulic gold mining. I looked down at the fine chalky powdered soil, and discovered a rainbow of colors: pale turquoise, green, rusty pink, ocher, grey-blue and cream swirled together like marblecake batter. The grey-green Manzanita leaves, edged with red, and the peeling, reddish bark revealed to me a landscape composed of glowing colors.

V

Columbia, another former mining town, was booming now with re-creations of pioneer life. Charles Surendorf had his artist's studio and shop open, showing the wood-block printing process. Miners and settlers populated his prints, and one modern family sitting in front of the TV, staring with hypnotized eyes. A few years later, we rode a stagecoach at full tilt through the streets, and the old opera house and theater were rebuilt new attractions. I imagined Surendorf being disgruntled by the development of the place. I imagine all these towns as having lost some of their charm due to commercialization. But we enjoyed them as places out of another time, another way of life from our own.

VI

I saw my first snowfall in Placerville when I was ten years old. We were staying at a motel at Easter time while Mom went for a job interview. We took pictures of the car, a DKW the color of mayonnaise, covered with snow in the motel parking lot. Mom was hired to do some testing in the schools, and so we lived there for about six weeks in the spring.

We moved into an attic apartment in a big old house in town. The yard was full of irises, of every color and type, and there was a swarm of bees attempting to locate in the eaves near the kitchen. After trying unsuccessfully to keep them out, we gave up and the landlord got someone to come in and eradicate them. We could open the windows again without fear of invasion. It rapidly grew warmer, hot upstairs in that little attic, and I remember being outdoors a lot.

The school was boring for me – I had already completed the years' worth of arithmetic, and here the class was still struggling with fractions and multiplication tables. I sat in the back of the room and was allowed to draw pictures. In fact, as open house night was coming up, the teacher asked if I would like to do portraits of all the kids in the class. We were only too happy to oblige: I, because it kept me from being bored; and the others, because they got out of classwork while posing for me.

I was given a set of pastel colors, which were pressed into powdery, square cakes similar to watercolor tins, with flat bristle brushes to take up the color. It was painting with chalk powder; there were so many colors, at least twenty-four of them. I did profile or three-quarter views of their faces. Most of the likenesses were easy for me, and admired later by the parents at open house – but one didn't come out convincingly. The boy was large and blond, with a thick neck that already had the appearance of a double chin. I tried not to represent his neck as seeming heavy, and the result was a slightly slimmer face. Nobody thought it was much like him, compared to the others. But he was pleased with it; he liked it. It was as if I had made him more pleasing to look at. Why did I do that? Perhaps that's how court portraiture got started.

One day we went to the nursery to see the irises. The field held an unimaginable profusion of colors, patterns and shapes. There were chocolate-brown flowers with mottled yellow throats; lavender and deep purple, burgundy velvet, orange, red, peach and cream, all with contrasting centers and sometimes darker edges, frilly or plain. Suddenly, along a patch of open ground, streaked a king snake, six feet long, black with white stripes ringed around it, trundling along in a bee-line for the brush. We stared, not moving, as it whipped by.

A girl in my class shared a discovery with me. She was freckle-faced and had light brown pigtails, a pudgy kid like I was becoming. Across the street was a vacant lot, overgrown with weeds and laced with bumpy, narrow trails. There in the grass lay a dead kitten, black and white and alive with maggots. We regarded it solemnly and then went back to my place to eat pickled hot peppers out of a jar in the kitchen. Looking back now, it was some kind of primitive child-rite of passage, encountering death and decay, followed by a ritual cleansing, or scouring, of the body.

Mom and I visited the cemetery uphill from our house. It was fallen-down looking, wooden crosses and markers with peeling paint giving way to grey splinters and insect holes. One grave had a picket fence around it, a tiny yard. The countryside was piles and piles of earth and rocks, left by the placer mining operations that gave the town its name. Like so many big mounds, these humps of soil were mostly bare, with small bushes clinging to dry sandy surfaces, deeply eroded. A strange, blasted terrain, the result of man's toil and greed. Hangtown, its nickname, came from a notorious incident of frontier justice in which several robbers were hanged at once: life and death in the foothills.

Red

by M Dawn Thacker

The only thing worse than going to Millington, is having to drive the 1987 four wheel drive red pickup truck to get there. I hate that truck and the feeling is mutual. Red teases me. I turn the key, her engine cranks up, but just let me try to put her in gear. She chokes, sputters and cuts off. I curse. I swear I hear her laughing, then, we start all over again. The truck and I usually ignore each other. She sits in the driveway, her back to me and I tip toe around her. Today we had to go together to rescue the only person who loves both of us, Bruce.

Millington is on the other side of White Hall, nearer to Free Union, but this side of Pea Vine Hollow. That's where Bruce's dump truck broke down. That's when Bruce called and said, "You need to bring the Four Wheel Drive to Millington."

"Can't I just bring the tool box in my car?"

"You can't pull the dump truck out of the ditch with your car."

"You didn't say you were in a ditch. You said you broke down. How'd you get in a ditch?"

"Steam was coming from under the hood and I was trying to get it home. I reached for the cell to call you because I didn't think I was going to get very far, and the road gave way under the front wheel. They're putting a culvert in up here and the dirt's soft. I think the dump truck blew a head gasket. I can't get it to cool down and hold water. It steams up and blows the water out. There are two cars behind me that can't get out and you're twenty five miles away. Can you just get in the truck and come on?"

"I hate that truck. I hate it. It won't run for me."

"If you drove it more often, you'd get used to it. Just crank it up, pump the accelerator three times, put it in gear and take off. It's easy," he says.

"It's easy for you." I grump. Where are the keys?"

"I think they're in the garage."

I stomp out to the garage and dig around in the desk until I find the key. I climb behind the wheel, turn the key, pump the accelerator three times, put the truck in gear, and she cuts off. I repeat the process, holding my breath, imagining people behind Bruce, blowing horns, cursing him, calling tow trucks or county cops. Red starts. I pump the gas, put her in gear and she sputters, then shuts off. I pound her steering wheel, then her dash.

"Dammit, you're going to start, and we're going to drive to Millington and pull Bruce out of a ditch. You need to listen to me and follow directions. I know you hate me, but this is important. Please start. I'm not asking for me. I'm asking for him."

It takes two more tries and when I finally get her in gear, we peel out of the driveway. Red runs on regular, as cheap-as-it-comes gas. When I'm driving her, I run on part fear and part adrenaline.

There are several ways to get to Millington. One is mostly straight, but longer. The other is on a winding road that runs past Beaver Creek Dam. Bruce is in trouble, so I choose the short cut. There's play in the steering of the truck, a lot of play. I don't consider the play until I turn onto the winding road leading to White Hall. Sweat breaks out on my forehead and I roll the window down. Red has no air conditioning and she blows hot air winter and summer. Her excellent heater, the curves in the road, the play in her steering, and my nervousness don't mix. My nausea as well as my hate for the truck grows.

This is a drive I would usually enjoy. The scenery is all old barns, blue mountains, split rail fences and wildflowers. I carry my camera with me all the time. Generally, I'd pull over to the side of the road several times and take photos. No time, no place wide enough to pull over, and no creative energy keep me driving.

Out of White Hall, Garth Road is a bit straighter and I'm more familiar with the route. I'm calming down and know that Millington is just up the road. I turn left toward Free Union and pass the old farm houses I recognize. A left onto Wesley Chapel Road leads me closer to Pea Vine Hollow. Bruce is almost close enough to touch now. The paved road changes to gravel and I get to a Y in the road. Not sure which way to go, I open the cell and call.

"Bear right at the Y and I'm about three quarters of a mile on the left. I'm walking down the driveway to meet you."

I breathe a sigh of relief when I see his blue clad figure walking toward me. I want to turn off the truck and jump out right then, but pull into the driveway and follow him to the dump truck. It's sitting precariously, the front passenger wheel at an odd angle. It almost looks like the axle is broken.

"No it's just way over in the ditch," Bruce says.

I crawl out of Red, my job done, walk to the shoulder, cross my arms over my chest and wait.

"What are you doing?" Bruce asks. "I can't pull it out by myself. Do you want to drive the pickup or the dump truck?"

"Neither," I say. "I've done my part."

Bruce shakes his head and chuckles at me. "Which one do you want to drive?" he asks again.

The dump truck looks too much like it will tip over, so I choose my enemy. I pull myself behind her wheel again. Bruce reaches in and turns the key in the ignition. She starts right up. Bruce looks at me and grins.

"See?" he says. "It starts just fine."

"Yeah," I say, "When it's your touch, not mine."

Bruce turns, hooks the chain to both trucks, locks the hubs on the four wheel drive, puts the pickup in gear for me, and pulls himself into the dump truck. He has much more confidence in me than I have in myself.

He points for me to pull off, and I put Red in drive. She behaves because he's watching. I push down on the accelerator. I feel the chain tighten and the truck groans. I push on the gas a little more and feel the tires grab. Red takes off and the dump truck follows. Bruce motions for me to stop. He unhooks the chain.

"Drive down to the church," he says. "Pull over and wait for me."

Wesley Chapel is about two miles down the road. I pull into the parking lot and Bruce pulls in beside me. The dump truck is smoking, dripping oil and water.

"Motor's gone," he says, dropping the hood. "Oil's all over the engine." He flips open his cell phone and calls my step-father who has a low boy trailer. He's not sure where to come, so Bruce offers to meet him at Free Union and lead him to the Chapel. There's a big sign in the parking lot warning owners of equipment and vehicles not to park there or towing will result.

"You comfortable staying here with the dump truck 'til we get back?" Bruce asks.

"Better the dump truck than that hussy," I say, pointing to Red.

As the sun sets, I watch it from the seat of the dump truck. The horizon turns shades of pink, orange, yellow and gold. With the Blue Ridge mountains in the distance, the sun paints an ever changing canvas with streaks of color brightening, fusing, spreading out again, fading and finally disappearing to shades of gray as the sun disappears.

I hear Red coming before I see her headlights. She takes my attention from the sky. I feel my shoulders tighten. The men pull up and load the dump truck onto the trailer. Bruce and I watch my step-father drive off, towing the load. We climb into Red's cab for the ride home. Bruce drives.

"You know, just beyond where we were tonight, there's a place called Fox Mountain. I've never been there until today," he says. "Before the truck broke down, I was thinking of bringing you there to take some pictures. You'd love it."

"We'll have to bring the car this weekend," I say.

"No, we'd have to bring the pickup. The road's too rough. We'd drag the bottom out of the car, gotta have four wheel drive."

I roll my eyes and sigh. "I hate this truck," I say.

"Sure served its purpose tonight."

"I guess," I say, crossing my arms over my chest again. "doesn't make it any more fun to drive. It just doesn't like me."

"Maybe the two of you should spend more time together, get to know each other," Bruce says. I can tell he's smiling, laughing at me.

"I'll go to Fox Mountain with you in the truck this weekend if you drive," I say.

Bruce chuckles, pats the seat for me to slide over closer to him, and says, "See, I told you the two of you would get used to each other."

I wonder if he's talking to Red, or me.

She Purrs Like A

by M Dawn Thacker

I hear chains rattle against metal and know some heavy piece of equipment is being hoisted. I cringe and run through the backdoor and out to the driveway. No matter how many times I preach, it doesn't seem to sink in. He never asks for a spotter. "One day…" I say, my voice trailing off as he dismisses my comment with a wave of his hand. He's too excited about this new truck to consider safety.

He pulls himself up onto the mechanic's body of the Ford F-450 truck and hooks the chain. He turns, grinning at me, showing a thumbs up, hops down and pulls himself back into the cab of the backhoe. The motor revs and the bucket lifts. Several pops and metal wrenching sounds later, the mechanic's body lifts and the truck is reduced to cab, metal frame and wheels.

It's his new love and to tell the truth, I'm a bit intimidated. Even naked she's sleeker than his old pickup, younger, with dual back wheels, and she purrs with that diesel engine of hers. Her exterior is shiny without a single blemish, her interior, supple tan leather, with automatic dimming lights that whisper romance.

His old love, the Red Pickup, finally died. She was the woman I could never be. She was tough, hard-bodied, enjoyed four-wheeling adventures through uncharted territories. She didn't have brains, but she did have brawn, get up and go, and a heavy-duty drive train. She hated me and I never liked her much either. Bruce was certain once we got to know one another, we'd be friends, but we ended up ignoring each other, our only commonality being Bruce. As long as he loved both of us, we tolerated each other from a distance.

Three weeks ago, Red choked and coughed when Bruce started her. She limped out of the driveway, sputtered to a stop on the road just past our house, wheezed one last time, and died. She sits in the lane now, tag-less, without insurance, and awaiting the Foxfield equipment auction. I'd have felt sorry for her if we didn't have such a volatile history.

Bruce didn't grieve long. He found the new white Ford diesel in an online Government auction in Buford, South Carolina. He bid, won, and took off the next morning to pick her up. He didn't ask me to accompany him. "I know you have a lot of work waiting for you this week," he said. "Ben's home for Spring Break. He can go with me."

Twenty hours later, I heard her distinct purr as Bruce coaxed her into the driveway. He walked straight past me, into the house, exhausted, and fell into bed without even a kiss hello. "Must have been a long, hard ride," I mumbled.

He's been with her ever since. He's outside now at the garage, welding and painting a flatbed body for her, all sleek and smooth with twelve inch treated pine board sides around the edge. She has a new trailer hitch and he's ordered one of those vanity plates for her. "FLATBDN" it says.

I went outside just a few minutes ago and wandered over to Old Red. Opening her driver's side door, I slipped inside and patted her dash. She wasn't looking so bad now. I wondered how much it would cost to get her running again. The two of us watched as Bruce backed his new love out of the stall and parked her under the huge oak tree. He got out and took a rag from his pocket, wiping a smudge from her fender. He stepped back and smiled.

"They're calling for high winds tonight Red, and that tree's leaning," I said, pulling up the door handle to warn Bruce.

Something stopped me. I let go of the handle, leaned back in the seat and smiled myself. For the first time ever, Red and I agreed.

Read This Please

Volume 2 Edition 11 – Doorways

November 11, 2011

Enter at your own risk. ReadThisPlease.com Edition 11 is all about doorways, the art of entry and exit, change, and realization. Doorways are special places where you can be there and still arriving. We invite you to read the passages and short stories by the wandering scribes at ReadThisPlease, in Doorways, Edition 11.

Junction

by Jac

I pass a place on my daily commute that I imagine is similar to places other people pass each day. It's a gorgeous spot, a natural junction; north and south meet east and west there.

Four or five times a week I wish I could stop and take pictures. Too bad it's an ugly highway bridge. The bridge carries I90 over the Hudson River through a natural gap in the hills. If I'm quick enough and traffic is light, I take a mental snapshot.

There's awe in the view, and depending on time of day and year the exposure could be almost anything; mist rising from the water, tugboat pushing barge, coastguard cutting through ice, crew teams practicing, freight train moving along the shore, riverfront park filled with walkers, sun rising or setting over the hills, snowstorms, thunderstorms, rainbows, trees turning green then shades of red, field of wild flowers, or simply the ribbon of river extending through the valley.

For me, the true awe of that place doesn't come from the gorgeous snapshots. I'm physically connected to that bridge no more than a few minutes a week, yet it inspires me. It's the junction of imagination, reality and emotion.

I see the travelers. Through my imagination, I see Iroquois, explorers, settlers, slaves, revolutionaries, immigrants. Through my car window, I see people moving through daily lives. Through my mind's eye, I see shadowy rippling threads of doubt and hope.

Past, present and possibility merge there. I almost see the millions of unknown thoughts and emotions that echo and will echo there. I wonder about the other travelers at that junction; were we, are we, will we be... them and I... their heart, my heart... their thought, my thought... different?

Deer Crossing

by Bruce Reisner

I'm half-out of this because I'm an atheist, but people are a religious animal. And they might be right. I could fry like a snack food for being a blasphemous little crumb. Disposed to Unitarian Universalism, though, diverse spiritualities are allowed to be their sweet selves in my camp. Again, it is the herds of deer that brought another worldview to mind.

I was returning from a ride on my electric scooter, coming up the steep dirt embankment behind the house. About eleven hundred tiny bungalows once filled the acres of wooded area behind my shanty. Left for decades to rot, most were demolished, leaving all the space needed for the animals that have been walking with a source of light. Deer are enlightened.

There was another chance meeting.

An eleven point buck lifted a hoof in a warning gesture, the way your Home Ec teacher used to indicate you need to be very quiet. The usual shunning behaviors the deer had been using on me like a social science were spared, and obviously this was not for lack of mistrust on their side our two worlds. The congregants silent, and still, a doe got up from the ground and paced easily among the group, speaking whispers to individual members of the flock as she did so. The buck turned to me, again with the please-just-contain-yourself attitude that I've grown used to. It said, "We're conducting a service."

Electric Avenue

by Adrienne S Moody

Don't wait outside there in the cold. Get in here before the lineups start. Have a seat, the music doesn't start until nine. Let me get you a drink and I'll tell you a bit about the place. I'm the piano man here at the King's Head Pub and I'm glad you found us on Electric Avenue. We're the hot spot right now—if you don't get in by seven you can forget it. The line up sometimes winds around the block.

I take credit for the popularity. The patrons like my voice and I can belt out the tunes. Piano Man by Billy Joel is a crowd favorite during the first set. Those were the Days always shuts the place down.

The pub is high class on a Friday night. We're situated here, downtown, a hot little number amongst the glass and steel towers. We get the oil tycoons and the stockbrokers. You can spot them with their thousand dollar suits and the women wearing their best dress-for-success Donna Karan outfits and their 'look but don't touch' attitude.

I don't want to brag, but I have taken many of these untouchables to the 'piano man's boudoir.' Maybe it's my voice or maybe it's my David Foster looks, but whatever it is, I can melt the ice off of most babes.

I'm not looking for anything permanent. I love women and I can't get enough of them. I don't bed down anyone under an eight. Yeah, I rate them and don't give me that look—most men do; they just won't admit it. I'll tell you a story of a 9.5 who graced one of the stools around my baby grand.

You want ice in that?

This happened only a few weeks ago, so it's still fresh in my mind. It still makes me hot thinking about her. Remember that snowstorm where half of the city lost power? It was a Friday nite and, of course, I was working. Around 11 p.m. she walks in. The bouncers make exceptions and she was the exception to any rule.

I was in the middle of What do you do With a Drunken Sailor? and I watched her scan the room. Then she walked through my bar like a thoroughbred. The crowd parted and the bartenders scrambled for whatever she ordered. It was some kind of shooter, because she tossed it back in one gulp and then headed for the door.

She smiled at me.

I have a trick and I take full advantage of it. If I see a babe about to leave before I can give her the piano man charm, I change the lyrics slightly. So when I got to the part "shave his belly with a rusty razor," instead I sang, "don't leave baby; do my heart a favor." I know, I know it's so corny, but I was desperate and that's what came to my mind. I nearly missed a note when she stopped and turned.

She sauntered towards me, put her delicate hands to the back of her head and pulled a rhinestone comb out of her hair. Auburn curls fell to her shoulders. She smiled a smile that told me she had secrets and her brown, fawn eyes burned into mine and I knew I would hear one of them.

I don't remember the last set; I only felt aware of this creature beside me and her Chanel # 5 perfume. I wondered if she wore silk stockings. I couldn't keep my eyes off her long legs which kept crossing and uncrossing.

We left together and by then, the snowstorm had been upgraded to a blizzard. You know the kind where the flakes are tiny in the wind and it stings your eyes. The temperature was so cold, I felt my nostrils stick.

She asked if I would drive her to her car, which was parked half a mile away. I let her into my BMW, started it up, and hit the switch to warm her seat. I swept off the snow that blanketed my car and finally sat down next to her.

"I'm going to call you Piano Man," she spoke with a husky cigarette and whiskey voice some chicks have. Drives me wild.

Let me light that for you. No, I don't mind if you smoke. So anyways, back to my story.

"Okay and what shall I call you?" I sensed the playfulness in her.

"Call me whatever you want, Piano Man," and she began running her hands through my hair.

I've got a pretty good routine with car sex. I reach over and tilt her seat back and I'm over there in two seconds flat. I knew with this one, however, that wouldn't go over so well. She was calling the shots.

The heater blasted out hot air and it was cooking in no time. She pulled her coat off and I put my hand on her bare neck and pressed my lips to her impossibly soft, fragrant skin. Her silk camisole strap fell off her shoulder and that has to be one of my favorite spots on a woman. I bit her there, gently, and she moaned.

Then she did something that in all my vast experience no one has ever done. She put her hand on the bottom of my shirt and her two fingers, moving like scissors, unbuttoned all my buttons faster than I could have under any emergency circumstance.

276

Can I do the buttons up fast? Ha! Very funny! You're right—in case the husband comes home.

So I'm feeling her hot breath on my bare chest and her hand caressing my skin is driving me wild, man.

My hands wanted to explore, but she put the Do Not Enter signs up and I didn't push. I couldn't go south of her neck nor could I trespass north of her thighs. I didn't care; I was happy to get whatever she was selling.

The windows were steamed up; the wind outside was howling and I knew we were covered in snow. The street was a one-way and no one had passed by during the time we were together. Needless to say, I lost track of time.

I heard her cell phone bleep.

"Just a minute, Piano Man," she whispered and dug through her black leather purse and pulled out her cell. She read what was obviously a text message. She responded back.

"What? Is something wrong?" I asked.

"No, nothing's wrong," she smiled this naughty smile at me. I wasn't getting it.

Suddenly I could see a vehicle with its high beams pull up behind me. At first, I thought it was a cop car and I began to button my shirt.

"Relax, Piano Man, it's my husband," she informed me as she pulled her coat on.

"Your husband?"

"You're not married are you?"

"No, never have been and probably never will."

"We've been married for ten years now and every once in a while we need a little oxygen to fuel the flames. You're sweet and I've had a lot of fun," she leaned forward and kissed my lips and then she left.

I couldn't see into their car when they passed, but I heard the short beep of the horn. Now maybe some guys might be pissed about this, but I'm not really. I'm kind of honored that she picked me.

Well, my break is over and the natives are getting restless. Do you see the wild looking blonde standing at the bar? That's Gwen. We have an on-again, off-again kind of relationship. She's jealous about the thoroughbred incident.

An hour ago she asked one of the bartenders for his t-shirt and when he said no, she whipped hers off and offered it to him. The crowd went wild to see her in a black, lacy, Victoria's Secret, push-up bra.

I love this place—you never know what's gonna happen next. Don't be a stranger. Our door is always open!

Doll Baby

by M Dawn Thacker

"Is this the garage sale edition?"

"No, it's about doorways."

"Well, I have a garage sale story."

Pause.

"Sure, why not? Garages have doors."

My Daddy picked me up and swung me around. "How's my doll baby?" he asked as I smiled up at him.

We sat together on the couch in the trailer. He and I watched cartoons, his arm was strong around my shoulders. A beer bottle dangled from his fingers. We shared a big bowl of popcorn and laughed at Bugs Bunny and Elmer Fudd. Mama watched us from the kitchen. When Daddy looked at her, she looked away.

I was nothing like my Mama. She was brave, and an adventurer. When she was a little girl, she rode horses bareback, shot tin cans with a gun, walked alone through the graveyard at night, and never played with dolls. She told me so.

I wanted to be like her, but never gathered courage for adventure. I cowered in fear of water too deep and trees too tall. I bit my fingernails to the quick, and slept with my sneakers on during thunderstorms because rubber repelled lightning. I refused to take

ReadThisPlease.com

the trash out after dark, even if it meant punishment. In my search for a likeness to her, I refused to play with dolls.

Mama and I left my Daddy one night; and we never came back.

In our new town, I found a friend named Charlotte. She had a room full of dolls, ones that cried, wet, burped, opened and closed their eyes, ones that walked, talked, and had heads full of hair to comb and brush. I loved playing at her house because I could hold, cuddle, feed and care for all those babies. I rocked them to sleep and tucked them in tight when I put them to bed. I kissed their foreheads and quieted their cries. I pretended they had daddies who came home and took them to the park.   When it came time to go home from Charlotte's house, I gathered my knapsack of plastic horses, cap guns, metal cars, coloring books, creepy crawlers; and I left the dolls behind.

Later that year we lived at my Grandma and Grandpa's house. On a trip to town one day without Mama, Grandma stopped at a garage sale. She went in search of new candy dishes and coffee mugs. I walked over to the toys on the table and stared at the most beautiful doll I had ever seen. She sat on the table staring at me with eyes that begged me to pick her up and hug her. I touched her cheek with my finger.

My grandma came up behind me and asked me if I wanted the doll. Grandma said at fifty cents, the toy was a bargain. I didn't answer; I just stood looking at that doll, wanting it so bad my heart hurt. Grandma paid the fifty cents and handed me the baby.

We walked into the house later that day. Grandpa smiled, took the doll's tiny hand into his big one, and shook it saying, "It's nice to make your acquaintance, young lady." He made me laugh.

I named her Doll Baby, and hid her in Grandma's walk-in closet. I told myself it was alright to have her since no one wanted her anymore. During the day, when Mama worked, I crawled into the closet, moving aside pairs of church shoes and hat boxes. Way back in the corner, under the hems of Grandma's soft dresses, I rocked Doll Baby to gentle lullabies. She didn't smell of baby powder, but the cedar that lined Grandma's closet.

Doll Baby fit perfectly, cradled in my arms. She had straight dark hair, like mine; and she wore a pink crocheted hat that tied under her chin. Her dress was solid white with tiny flowers embroidered around the neckline. She had clear blue eyes, and when she slept, her eyelids closed. Real lashes rested on her pink cheeks. She wore matching crocheted booties on her feet in winter; but in summer, I let her go barefoot.

Sometimes, when the coast was clear, we'd leave the closet and watch TV together on the sofa in Grandma's living room. Doll Baby loved cartoons.

At night, she slept in a cradle Grandpa made out of some scraps in his workshop. She dreamed under a quilt of cotton patches Grandma stitched together for her. Doll Baby felt safe in that closet, tucked away, where nobody knew about her but the people who loved her.

Ghosts and Truth

by Adrienne S Moody

All Mona wants is a spruce tree. It's her birthday today. So they came to visit, and there is quite the crew of people—in-laws, children—her beach front home rocks with noise. She welcomes the party at first, but after a few hours, Mona will disappear.

"Where's Mom?" someone will finally ask. And there she'll be, standing out on the oyster bed poking here and there with a stick. "Leave her be," the eldest will stop the children from dashing out the door to follow her.

Rene takes the ferry every few weeks to go see her mom, living alone by the sea, on an island with only a grocery store, and a missing letter on the sign so it reads, *ROCERY STORE*. The metal creaks and spins in the windstorms that hit the Island during fall. The store supplies the Islanders with everything from DVDs to wine for dinner to gasoline. Everyone knows everyone. Mona is the woman with the wide smile and freckles. She made the best blackberry jam and if she liked you, she'd give you a jar for your freezer. She wore those checked lumberjack coats during the winter. They all knew she had cancer and wasn't expected to survive it and they also knew the woman had pride and didn't want their sympathy.

"I am so sick of everyone coming up to me and asking how are you? I'm tired of it! It's like they see me dead already," she'd complain to her dog, Lady. Lady would slump down in front of the door and wait patiently for her while she picked up a few groceries, or a bottle of wine for her dinner.

When she lost her hair, the Islanders looked away red in the face. Either that or they clucked their tongues and rubbed her arm in sympathy. "It will grow back," they would soothe.

"Grow back?" she snapped at them. "What use do I have for hair anyways? Glad it's gone! Only thing is it's a bit cold now that the fall's come. But I've got toques. That will do me fine."

"I have an interesting face," she thought as she examined it in the bathroom mirror. Now, without any hair framing it, her eyes stood out bright ocean blue. She put her hand to the top of her smooth head and smiled. "All those years, coloring, streaking, cutting, primping and curling... it all comes down to this. The universe certainly teaches you what's important," she told Lady, while the cocker spaniel curled up in the heat of the wood stove. Lady stretched and yawned in response.

She looked forward to the storms coming. The wind cleared out all the deadwood in the forest around her. What isn't strong doesn't survive. It pulls down power lines and everyone is left in darkness. It's a time of filling the wood stove with wood stacked up against the cabin. The smell and the crackle comforts her. The sound of the waves crashing just outside her door reminds her of days spent at the beach when she was a child. There's a storm coming, Mom, we saw it on the weather station. Do you have everything you need? her children would call one by one their voices filled with concern and alarm. She smiled at Lady and patted her head and said to her if only they knew? The storms made her feel alive as nothing else did these days.

And now the spruce tree.

"Why can't she want what other moms want?" Rene aggravates, "A housecoat or slippers? Why not spa music to calm her? Bath oils?

No, she wants a stupid spruce tree. How can I carry a spruce tree on the ferry?"

Mona doesn't want a little one. No, she wants one that has some years on it, so that it will surely survive. And, Rene knows that a visit means hauling fire wood into the cabin and rearranging furniture. Her mother is not one to sit quietly or cook a meal together. Rene wants to please her mother, to be close to her. There have been opportunities, like the last visit, when they took a walk into town and sat at Brown's bench by the side of the road. The sun filtered through the Douglas Fir and onto their faces, that late autumn sun that holds just a little bit of heat, and you know it might be the last you feel till spring. They held their faces to it, mother and daughter, and just when Rene opened her mouth to say something like, "I love you." Mona slapped her daughter lightly on her knee and said, "Let's keep moving," and the moment was gone.

Mona knows why she's requesting a tree to plant in her front yard, but she won't let herself think it. In the middle of the night, that inky, lonely time when the house is so quiet, when ghosts and truth visit, she knows.

As Luck Would Have It

by M Dawn Thacker

I stand frowning at the old gas pump. I stopped to fill up the Honda at the Royal Mart convenience store in New Hope. Royal has cheaper gas than the service station over the mountain, closer to home. As luck would have it, they only take payment for gas inside, no credit at the pump. Oh well, I'm thirsty anyway, so I walk inside to pay for the gas and grab a cold soda. The temperature outside has topped ninety-eight and the humidity hangs on my shoulders. Even in the shade, taking breaths is like sucking in thick heat.

As I walk back to the drink cooler, a tall, thin man staggers past me on his way to the front of the store. He brushes my shoulder. "S'cuse me," he slurs. The smell of beer on his breath is almost as strong as his body odor. He grabs onto the display racks of cookies and potato chips, trying to balance on legs that are willing, but not able to hold him steady. He makes it to the front of the store, thumps the forty ounce bottle of cheap beer onto the wooden counter and asks for a pack of Marlboro Lights in a box. He leans against the counter for support.

I look into the glass display case of bottles and see the reflection of the man who passed me. His back is hunched a bit as he searches pockets. I see the cashier frown, hear the concern in her voice. "Is that all the money you have Jack? If that's all you have, you better take it easy. It's three more days 'til the first of the month."

I pick out my soda and press the cold bottle to my neck as I make my way to the cash register. Jack hasn't said anything to the cashier, but continues his search for money. He's a wiry man, mid-forties I'd guess, with long strings of wavy blond hair under a faded blue baseball cap. His hands shake. Jack wears a nylon windbreaker over his tee shirt, dark jeans and a pair of worn running shoes. I drip perspiration just looking at him.

I join the line at the front of the store.

Jack had put several crumpled dollar bills along with a wrinkled lottery scratch ticket and some gray lint onto the counter. He slides the bills and the lottery ticket up next to the glass beer bottle. He fishes in the front pocket of his jacket, finds some coins and scatters them across the counter top. A worn rabbit's foot key chain falls among the metal pieces. Its fur is rubbed off, its sharp nails prominent. It reminds me of a horror movie I'd once seen. From the other pocket, he pulls a worn paperback book. I'm surprised. It's a copy of Mark Twain's Huckleberry Finn. He lays it on the counter.

"Damn," Jack says. "I had another five here somewhere." He continues to reach into various pockets as the cashier removes a 'closed' sign from the other side of the register and motions the next customer to bypass Jack.

The man who was behind Jack sets his Red Bull and a bag of pork rinds down, reaches into the back pocket of his khakis for his wallet and pays with a twenty. The cashier counts his change back to him. He slips the ten and four ones into his billfold and lets the handful of coins drop into the plastic take-a-penny cup on the counter.

Jack keeps looking.

The whole line detours to the now open spot, and no one pays attention to Jack as he searches for more funds. The woman in a smart navy business suit and low heeled pumps swipes her credit card to pay for gas, a candy bar, and a pack of Newports. She signs the receipt and hurries out the door to the jangle of a bell.

I look at Jack. "A damn drunk," I hear my father's voice say inside my head.

When I was a little girl, we took walks on the downtown pedestrian mall close to my grandmother's house. Disheveled men leaned in doorways, sat with their backs against the walls of the tall brick buildings, and held their hands out for money. They had long hair and long fingernails. Most were quiet, but some spoke up, asking for change. Some said, "God Bless" when a passerby handed them coins.

I remember feeling a little scared of those men, their smell, slurred words, and whiskered faces, but mostly I felt bad for them. They looked sad.

"Never give bums money," Daddy said. "You can buy them a sandwich if you want, but if you give them money, they'll drink it away." My Daddy was a smart man. He knew what he was talking about. Before I was born, his father had been one of those men hunkered in a doorway, drunk, trying to keep warm.

Sometimes on those walks, I'd find pennies. "Take that home and put it in your bank," my Daddy said. "Pennies make dollars." Once, I found a quarter. I picked it up, excited about my luck, jumping up and down, showing off the shiny coin. Half a block away, I wanted to give the quarter to one of those old men. I held the treasure over his cupped palm only to have my Daddy jerk my hand away.

"Put that in your pocket," he said, pulling me away from the man. Daddy kept walking, tugging me with him. I looked back to the man and he smiled at me. I smiled back and mouthed "I'm sorry." He shrugged his shoulders, palms up, still smiling. I turned back and that's when my Daddy told me about buying and giving a sandwich.

We didn't buy that man a sandwich though; we walked on to the drug store where we sat at the counter and I picked at a grilled cheese sandwich. "I thought you were hungry," my Daddy said.

"Not enough for both Jack," I hear the cashier say, bringing me back to present. "Which do you want to put back?"

"Cigarettes I guess," Jack says. "I thought I had another five." Jack pats his pockets again, frowning.

"You ready?" the cashier says to me.

"Oh yeah," I say, placing my soda on the counter. "I need twenty in gas too."

She rings up the sale on the register. "Twenty-one, sixty-six," she says.

I hand her thirty in cash and she counts the eight thirty-four in change back to me. I stand with my wallet open, deposit the coins in the change purse and slide the bills behind my driver's license. I look at my picture. I look stern. They won't let you smile at the DMV anymore. I go to zip my wallet and stop. Opening it back up, I pull out the five dollar bill and hand it to Jack.

He takes the five, looks down at me, and says, "God Bless," just like the old men I remembered, only Jack is young. He pats my shoulder and smiles, showing even white teeth amidst more than a week's stubble of whiskers. "You're a good woman," he says.

"No problem," I say, pointing to his paperback on the counter. "I like Mark Twain too. Tom Sawyer was my favorite."

Jack picks up Huck Finn and thumbs through the pages. "Twain was a smart man," he says. Then he stops three quarters through the book and pulls out a five dollar bill. "Well I'll be damned," he says, smiling. "There it is. Must be my lucky day."

He looks at the two fives, then looks back at me. He offers the one I gave him back to me.

"No, you keep it," I say. "You need a bookmark."

"Thanks he says, placing the five back into his book.

I turn and walk toward the door.

"Give me back those cigarettes Shirley, and while you're at it, a computer pick mega millions ticket too," I hear him say as the bell jangles behind me.

La Petite Mort

by M Dawn Thacker

The doctor had said, "Come back when you feel uncomfortable." That was six o'clock in the morning and I spent the whole day walking outside, up and down the lane in front of the house, coaxing gravity to help my cause. My water hadn't broken completely. There was a slow leak. With every contraction, a small gush flowed. It was my Mother's birthday. I prayed for the gift of her first grandchild.

With the pain that doubled me over in the driveway, I said, "I think it's time to go back to the hospital."

Women were lined up on gurneys in the hallway. They were in various stages of labor. The moon was full. Wolves howled. Somewhere in the distance a baby cried. The doctor walked by me in a hurried clip, "Don't pay attention to the choir," he said.

I thought I was uncomfortable. Then, I thought I was going to die. I had practiced breathing, concentrating on puffs, and hisses lying on the floor of a Lamaze classroom.

I must focus on a fixed point, I told myself. There was a crack in the ceiling, two water spots, a dot of light. My vision darted from one to the other. The music I chose, George Winston on piano, my favorite, grated in my ears. Someone crumpled a potato chip bag. "Stop it," I yelled.

"She's going through transition," the nurse whispered to the man who had caused this.

"I'll show you transition," I hissed.

"Do you want to change positions?" my husband asked next to my ear.

"If we could, your butt would be right here instead of mine," I grunted.

"Turn on your side, see if that helps," he soothed.

"Let me stand on my head, see if that helps," I countered.

He wiped my brow and encouraged me to pant. "Concentrate on your breathing," he said. If I could have concentrated on anything in that moment, it would have been how to kill him.

Let's see where we are," the doctor said, raising the sheet at the foot of the bed, snapping on a pair of rubber gloves. I held my breath and gritted my teeth, again. Damn him. "Ten centimeters dilated," he said cheerily. "Time to push."

Sweat rolled down my forehead and pooled in my eyes. Someone stood behind me, pressing my shoulders forward. I pulled my knees back and pushed everything I owned uphill. I held my breath as someone counted to ten.

No sooner had I taken a breath then I had to start all over again, and again, and again.

"Here we go, here's the head," the doctor finally said. "Give me one last big push. You can do it."

I held my breath one more time, pulled my legs back and heaved.

"Stop," the doctor said. "Heads out."

"Gotta push," I grunted.

"Almost ready," he cautioned, "not quite yet."

What did he mean, not quite yet. They'd been yelling at me to push for hours. I didn't want to then. Now, I wanted to and couldn't.

OK, ready. Here come the shoulders. One last big—."

I grabbed my legs, closed my eyes, held my breath, gritted my teeth, hunched forward, and strained with every muscle. I screamed, and in that second, the Universe was altered. Then silence and a cry. Someone put the baby on my chest. We looked at each other in awe, our hair stuck wet to our heads, our hearts beating fast.

I felt a tug as the doctor stitched me up. "You know, giving birth is the closest feeling to an orgasm there is," his voice said from the foot of the bed.

"Really?" I asked. "How would you know?"

Doorways: 2012

by Gaboo

December 2012: The elections in the US have come and gone without fanfare. Nobody pays much attention because the revolt has already begun.

The trigger incident has been isolated to a moment in early July, when Noreen Klamus, aged 79, went to Spiff Foods to purchase staples for her modest cupboards in Winslaw, New Jersey. Apparently, she had neglected to realize the implications of a notice delivered a fortnight earlier. Social security payments normally directed to her bank card were withheld. Instead, the neck tattooed, Dubble-Bubble popping clerk named Randy informed her, that,

"Most people found out their money is at SuperBulk Foods… in food stamps… a public-private partnership."

"?"

Then she added, "Where's my money?"

"You don't have money anymore. You have SuperBulk food stamps."

Noreen thought briefly on her predicament and then uttered the now infamous words,

"Those bastards."

Noreen had enough. She grew up a product of the depression which launched her into an overbearing industrialized society. The parks and fields of her youth were slowly dug up and reshaped into towers of commerce. As she matured, Noreen learned to lurk under the overcast pall of nuclear threat. She'd seen political scandals and reprobates come and go. Through everything, she'd scrimped and saved, played her role, did her part, slaved and plodded in a menial capacity. "It's not your world," friends and family would console, when Noreen voiced her concerns.

In the end, she did it on her own: got an education, worked a job, purchased a meager home. She paid her taxes, volunteered where her taxes wouldn't stretch, voted, filled out the census, contributed to her pension, went to parades, waved her flag, picked up her garbage, fed her cat, and tried to get along. She is a model citizen who abides by the rules and fills out all the forms. And now they were jerking her chain. She had enough.

First, she went to Google. Noreen soon learned that most of her current problems started long before she was born. In 1913, exactly. She learned that the federal government contracted out the money supply to a bunch of guys with a lot of cash. She learned that the economy was designed to perpetuate debt, thus assuring a rate of return. The debt would be held by the people as they bought stuff. And if the money supply ever ran low, the guys with the cash print more of the paper stuff, while they jetted around buying oil and food to sell back to the people. She learned that at one time the people were allowed to keep real money, gold, silver, and their word. But those items were replaced by credit cards, mortgages and lawyers. She learned, essentially, that a bunch of testosterone sweating war mongers had hijacked the human species.

"Those bastards."

Little did she realize, the battle cry these two words would become.

What Noreen did next, we will leave with the annals of history to decide if her actions were just.

On July 23rd, a bright and breezy rush hour morning, Noreen Klamus went to the front offices of the Bank, walked into the middle of the street, and burned her bra.

Havoc immediately ensued.

She'd been a woman of conservative proportions with pear-shaped physique. However, as the years wore on, Noreen's struggles with gravity eventually lost out somewhere when her skin tone faded and Monocorp introduced genetically modified grains. Tube socks couldn't contain her. The bra was merely for theatrics.

Seventeen people were injured that morning as freight and commuter alike careened aghast at Noreen's public display. Pedestrians took flight, both suit and jogger, each scrambling, white-eyed, for visual haven. Police attended almost immediately, however, Noreen was adept, evading their demands that she "Cover those up!" Instead, she shook them.

"You bastards! Where's my money? All you guys have done is make war and machines and bombs and steel and garbage, and religion, and porn, violence and mayhem! And now, when women in American can almost stand on an equal footing, you've trashed the planet and left everyone in debt."

She railed, "I've worked all my life and you've tried to shut me up and put me down, but I'm done with you, boy. I want MY MONEY!"

Almost like leaves in a breeze, other women who heard Noreen's rant approached. They listened and nodded.

Noreen waved her bank card, "I want my pound of gold. I want my America." She threw her bank card with as much force as a seventy-nine year old can propel a two mil wedge of plastic.

Representatives from the large stone building approached, and then retreated, ushering forth Diane Retalia, concierge and client representative at the offices in question.

Retalia listened politely to Klamus' demands then returned to convey the elder's sentiments.

That was Day One of Noreen's encampment.

Within a month, a small city of bare-breasted pension-pressed retirees stood, or wheeled, alongside Noreen and her cause. And they could not be removed. What the Occupy Wall Street protesters had achieved, in terms of occupation standards, reaching 312 days consecutively, FemRage 2012 now exploited. (Sole remaining OWS occupier, Walt Tamerin, at behest of girlfriend Denise, wandered to Pappa Murphy's for Buck-a-Slice, and without a designated protestor on site, technically the 'occupation' was marked fini.)

They drew up a list of demands. Then they backed them up with a threat. Unless the government, which had been functionally male up to this time, stopped it's testosterone primed endorsement of gain, profit, exploitation, and penis envy empire building, they would take over the government.

At this point in the account, it should be mentioned that the FemRage 2012 movement had one strategy that the OWS protestors did not. They had a tactician, J. Bonny Lampurna. In a brilliant play of capital manipulation, Lampurna carefully worded a spectacularly motivating call-to-action by simply adding a single word to Noreen's popular catch-phrase and posted it on her blog. "Boycott Those Bastards"

And women did. They no longer purchased products from companies that didn't have a female CEO. Railways shut down. Airplanes couldn't take off. Freight no longer moved. The political country club schmooze fest ground to a halt. And women didn't care. The space program shut down. And women didn't care. Major league sporting events were cancelled, the sponsors left high on inventory and short on cash. Women didn't care.

Women already had the pragmatic fortitude to discount shop in advance. They knew instinctively how to tend and procure, and how to entertain without electricity using an age old custom called 'conversation'. They networked better than their male counterparts and rarely missed appointments. The cash flow stopped. Purchasing stopped. The industrial machine invested banking monopoly coughed and sputtered. And women didn't care.

But America was only one dominion, and women wanted the world. They infiltrated other cultures and quickly jumped borders disguised as wives and daughters, aunts and grandmothers. Their force seemed to pop up everywhere, in each household, where women demanded their spouses and mates refute violence and plunder. Males were forced to denounce guns and swords, and other cool stuff like exorbitant 4x4s and flame throwing jetskis, topless all you can eat baron of beef bars and movies that glorified harems. From now on, a man could only take from the earth what he put back into it. He could not buy or sell property. He could not exploit the future generations for profit. No more usury, no more intimidation, no more corrupt political leaders.

The events are a little foggy, but it was at this time a military coup took place. Rear Admiral Belinda T. Rasmussen embarked with the seventh fleet to repatriate women of the world. Taking from the quote by John Adams, Rasmussen spoke, "I am a soldier, so that my daughter may be media tycoon, and her daughter may be a golf pro," or thereabouts. In Persia, Asia, Africa and Europe, from traders in Indonesia to Matterhorn-haired hostesses under the noses of Swiss bankers. The battle was won before the forces in earnest arrived for each deployment. How do you go to war with your grandmother? In all nations, the laws of a male god were cast down. Divine will was considered logically unisex. No longer could a life be held subservient.

Men everywhere went into traumatic pout. However a growing realization began to occur in the male psyche. They acquiesced. They thought about it, and came to the conclusion that a male dominated society had basically failed. Under men, there would be no peace and no security. They too, wanted out. Then something strange happened. Men started asking women for their opinion. The movement had succeeded. From the two groups of cohabitants residing predominantly on planet earth, women assumed the seat of power.

Brother and son quickly chastised the old school gents who clung desperately to the patriarchal system of superiority, propriety, and duality. But women did not care, they went forward on a path of redemption and reclamation.

The wars ended and women did not care to start new ones. There was no space adventure to Mars and women did not care if we had to appreciate the red planet from afar. We did not dig a tunnel under the Pacific and women did not care. Super highways cracked and bridges failed. And women did not care. They were resilient and self sufficient and eager to repatriate with Mother Nature more than they valued economic progress. The paradigm had shifted and the change was underway. Food became plentiful. Boredom became a hazard. No more raping, no more pillaging. No more thinking you are the center of the universe. Everything's gone kind of omni. You see? That's what 2012 was about. Armageddon for some, not all.

(Subscribers ask me, what happened to Hillary Clinton? Daytime TV host with her husband Dwight. Cheerful, topical.)

November 11th, 2013: Where do we go now? No one is sure. But we won't be getting there anytime soon. During the last session of the Stewardship Bureau, women had the foresight to outlaw the muscle car.

Why have I been allowed to survive? Because I'm funny.

Garage

by Adrienne S Moody

It was an ordinary day, autumn, and about the time that if there's a harvest moon, it would be rising.

Jim shared a bedroom with his brother Andy, and he looked up to see Andy wander in. Andy was restless, home after a lengthy absence, and an absence that worried the family. Andy hadn't been feeling like himself the last year or so.

The change started with a head injury on the job. Andy worked as a heavy equipment operator. Along with a great paycheck came some risks. After an accident, he spent a week in the hospital where they did the usual tests to see if everything was normal. As far as they could tell, everything was. The parents were warned to watch for any unusual behavior. Beyond that, there wasn't anything the medical profession could do.

But Andy was different. Jim missed his brother's practical jokes and the whistle under his breath when he was concentrating. There were parts of his personality that had vanished. Often, Andy seemed really sad and when Jim asked him what was up, his brother looked blankly, like he didn't understand. There was an expression that Jim didn't recognize, like Andy wasn't there.

No one was certain. They only suspected that Andy purposely mixed pills and booze one night while the family was on vacation. By chance, his former girlfriend stopped in, to see if they could get back together. That's who saved him.

In an effort to figure what was going on in Andy's head, his parents took him to a psychologist. Andy was defiant during the session.

"Hey, I couldn't sleep. I took a few pills and I happened to be drinking. Buzz off. I'm no bridge jumper, okay?"

But the family knew something was wrong.

That night, the night of the harvest moon, when Andy wandered into the bedroom looking restless, Jim tried to look absorbed in a comic. He pulled the magazine a little higher, hiding his eyes.

"Hey, Bud."

"Hmmm…"

"Play me a game of chess?"

"Hmmm… busy. Later, maybe."

Over the cover of his comic, Jim could see Andy lift a rook from the chess board and twirl it in his fingers. Then his brother placed piece carefully where it belonged. He turned and walked out of the room. Jim could hear his steps trail towards the entry and out to the garage.

Jim knew what a gun sounded like when it went off; he hunted deer with his dad. Hearing a gun outdoors, and knowing it is going off, that's different than what he heard ten minutes later. The sound of the gun blast in the garage was a sound he would remember every day for the rest of his life. He ran downstairs missing a few steps along the way, then tripped on the last.

Before he opened the door, he knew.

Eleanor was upstairs drying her crystal. They'd had a party the night before, a few friends over for drinks and she'd pulled out the good glasses. She loved the way it caught the light and broke it into a colorful prism; it mesmerized her. She held the glass up, checking for spots, and wondered how something called 'lead' crystal could be so fragile. Eleanor was thinking on this when she heard the gunshot. The glass fell out of her hands and shards spread across the floor; a sight she would dream about for years after that day. The moment she heard that sound come up from the garage, she knew.

Despite the hangover from the last night's get together, Eleanor's husband, Craig managed to have one of his most profitable days. He secured a contract with the local hospital and that meant a bonus big enough to take his family on a cruise that winter. A dozen red roses and a card with the vacation surprise was propped on the front seat next to him. He wheeled his white Mercedes into the driveway and clicked the garage door opener on his key chain. He was about to find out.

Poe's Cabin

by M Dawn Thacker

"You know, Edgar Alan Poe once lived in a cabin on Ragged Mountain," our landlord tells us, a few months after we married and moved into our first rental. I am an English major in college and Bruce works for the Virginia Department of Forestry.

"Really?" I ask, intrigued. I'd studied a few of Poe's works, knew a little of his history. I'd not heard or read this.

"Yep, the foundation is still there, along the ridge line behind the house here," the owner says, pointing toward the mountains east of us. "Stories handed down in the family say that's where he got the inspiration for The Raven. You've seen them flying around here, haven't you?"

"I'm not sure," I say. "I've seen some big crows."

"Those are Ravens," our landlord corrects me. "They're bigger than crows and their call is different, more a croak than a caw. When crows fly, you can't hear 'em. Raven's wings make a 'swishing' sound."

After that, I watch and listen for the Ravens. I wonder about that cabin in the woods on Ragged Mountain.

I imagine a cabin unlike the chamber in Poe's poem The Raven. That chamber was fancy with purple curtains and velvet upholstery, a place fit for a woman named Lenore. Poe was thirty-six when he published The Raven. It was four years before he died. He wasn't the youngster he would have been when he lived near the Ragged

Mountains. His opulent chamber was only a dream when he lived in the Ragged Mountains.

The cabin I imagine is a primitive one-room dwelling crafted of hand-hewn white oak logs, chinked with Virginia's red clay. I picture Poe standing by a four-paned, wavy glass window, hands in pockets, his eyes fixed on the traces of sunlight filtering through the tall trees of Ragged Mountain. His front door, simple, made of unfinished wood plank, stands open, allowing the scent of pine and the sound of summer birds to reach into the cabin. I imagine him dreaming of Lenore, hearing her laughter in the warble of a goldfinch, her tears in the mournful cooing of a dove. The woman he loves lives in Richmond near Poe's foster parents. She may or may not wait for him.

Then, I stand on his threshold, feeling the cool of the place. Even in summer, the interior is cooler than other structures, a kind of cool where a sweater doesn't warm the body. Poe's hearth lays bare, scraped clean of ashes.

His cot in the corner is just large enough for him to stretch out his frame and throw his arm over closed eyes, making his vision darker than dark. A sturdy wooden table of straight lines serves his need for writing and repast. His papers, scratched with ink, lay scattered on the surface.

He turns from the window, sits at the table, picks up his pen and marks through the lines he's written that day. He begins again.

"Let's walk to the cabin," Bruce says one day. "I'd like to see it."

We decide to make a day of the adventure, pack a small lunch for a picnic. It's a perfect summer day for a hike, with low humidity. We call our landlord for directions.

"You go straight back behind the house to the old apple orchard, turn left at the fresh water spring, and head east toward 'Bear Rock', that's the big gray piece of limestone that juts out near the top of Ragged Mountain. The cabin's foundation is five hundred feet north-east of the outcropping. "You may have to kick around in the leaves a bit to find it," he tells us.

We make the trek. I think about Poe and his time in this area, how he'd come to the University, a smart man, ready to learn, but given less money than he needed for tuition and books by his foster father. He tried to make up the difference by gambling, and lost. He left the University, in debt and shamed.

As we walk, I talk about Poe's poem The Raven, the sadness of it, and then his story, The Tale of the Ragged Mountains. "Poe called them 'wild and dreary hills,'" I tell Bruce.

"They are wild," Bruce agrees as we beat down briars, and trip over fallen tree branches, "but I wouldn't describe Ragged Mountain as dreary." Bruce was born and raised a few miles from where we live. He's hiked the mountain's ridges, hunted in their stands of pine, and picked blackberries along their edges. This particular area is new to him, but the Ragged Mountains are his home. He's had a different experience than Poe.

The directions lead us to Bear Rock and beyond. I'm following Bruce's footsteps and admiring the wild violets, may apples and pipsisewa that grow under the tall trees.

"It should be here pretty close," Bruce says, stopping to look around, directions in hand.

I pause behind him and visually search for some sign of a dwelling, a clearing, partial walls, steps, anything. I see nothing that would hint at the history of a structure.

Bruce starts sweeping leaves away from the forest floor with is boots. I follow his lead. He moves in a straight line, I zigzag. He kicks a rock, moves to the right, and kicks another, and another, all of them in a row. We follow the line to a corner and sure enough, another line of rock extends at a ninety-degree angle to the one we've uncovered. When we finish, we expose a rock foundation measuring roughly ten feet by twelve feet. The logs of the cabin have long since rotted away and trees now grow within the confines of the former living space, but this is the spot we were searching for, Poe's cabin.

I sit down on one of the rocks and look to the west at a view that I've come to take for granted. The Blue Ridge Mountains rise in the distance in varying shades of azure, rolling hills, one in front of the other, with crests and gaps. The interstate winds through a pass. The sun winks off the chrome of cars and trucks making their way up the grade. Big puffy clouds throw shadows on the mountain's surface as they move with the wind.

I contemplate someone living way up on this ridge some hundred and seventy years ago. What road lead here? Who marked the foundation and lifted the rocks? Who felled the trees and carved their sides flat, then hoisted them for walls and roof? Who walked to spring for water and how far did he go? Who lived in this lonely place?

Bruce and I sit together, open our pack, and eat our sandwiches and slices of apple in silence.

"Do you think he really lived here?" I ask.

Before Bruce can answer, there's a rustle of leaves above us in the tree, then a swish of wing and the rough, throaty call of a Raven.

The Garden

by B G Lewis

Gladdy Phipps sets the keys on the counter, walks through the front door, closes it, and never returns again.

What compels people to change their lives? Is it when they can feel time draining and the opportunities becoming less, narrower? Gladdy is sixty-three years old, divorced, and suffers from schizophrenia. Diagnosed, she's running a balancing act between the doctor's modifications to her meds and the subsidized soap opera at Terrace Manor, where she's lived for nine years.

She has issues because she grew up believing in the lies that life could be butterflies and bunny rabbits. Ragged reality clicked in when she realized men could be dangerous alcoholics and strip you to the core. And in the pattern established by her parents and grandparents, she married one. He promptly moved her to a rural homestead in the middle of the plains and spent the next twenty years decimating her self-worth.

In an act of natural survival, she broke the psychological bond and fled to the coast, retrained for office work, and began a new life. However, the taunts and degrading insults returned, in phantoms and sideways glances. Gladdy was prone to spin out, talking herself into distress, circling in a groove of anxiety. A chance to patch a life was rent by a scarred self that could easily fixate and slide. She lost her job.

Social Services placed her in Terrace Manor, on the second floor of a ninety suite complex behind a shopping center. She soon discovered everyone in her world had issues. Dealers plied a profitable drug trade in the underground parking; their customers smoked and weaved in the elevators. Sane parents with children moved out, or cordoned off sections of the complex behind a tribal line of watchfulness. But those parents were also customers and had their own stories of neglect and self.

Crime was commonplace and Gladdy picked up quick---when to look and when to look away. In nine years she learned to yell, and she learned how to pray before a mugger. She made mistakes judging people, lending five or ten dollars to be kind, to make a friend and hedge her loneliness. 'One time' became an ongoing obligation, and when Gladdy's generosity left her own food budget short, she approached her most frequent borrower. She was informed that "if we borrow money and we have to pay it back, we beat the person up." Gladdy became increasingly dejected. She made a plea to her Social Worker.

On the seventh of February a miracle happened. Raymond Chan, a Hong Kong investor, bought a bungalow with a basement suite in the downtown district, sight unseen. He traveled to the area once. In forty-eight hours he purchased another apartment building and spent an evening with associates drinking and kicking himself in the ass for wasting money on the house. The residence in the urban core would never meet the easement qualifications for redevelopment. He was stuck with a real estate albatross.

A new North American adviser suggested Mr. Chan rent out the property and balance the loss against capital gains in his other purchases. The reasoning was, that if a tenant maintained the property, the value could remain intact. Offer low rent to a subsidized tenant and the lost opportunity could become an ongoing tax break. Raymond Chan considered the proposal on the flight home and phoned when he landed. The new adviser happened to be the spouse of Gladdy's Social worker.

For three months Gladdy has waited, parsing her possessions, remaining aloof in the halls of Terrace Manor. A smile has occasionally escaped, and her 'friends' have shown concern, telling her never to be too happy, or more often, "What are you hiding?" Gladdy has never let on that she's moving. She's wanted to, brag and gloat, let them know that she's not one of them, but she didn't want to jinx the chance. For once, she tried to appear solemn on purpose.

Today she goes forward and will never return. A man who advertises for odd jobs waits at the curb with her possessions in a pickup truck. Gladdy is shaking as she walks down the stained complex steps and crosses a broken patch of sidewalk. The man holds the truck door open and she climbs in, alongside her microwave and a replica wooden radio. Unlike Lot's wife, she does not turn and look back.

The social worker mentioned that Gladdy's new address had a small area in the back that once was a garden. A garden. It all sounded so mystical.

West 12th and Columbus is a busy intersection on a feeder route. The neighborhood is old, dilapidated, and cut through the middle by elevated train tracks. A ten block strip of eclectic coffee shops, music stores, and eco boutiques has slowly grown into a shopping destination. A farmers' market opens daily in a brownstone warehouse and the air tempts with wafting odors of fried foods, curries, and espresso. Patio chairs encroach the sidewalk and young entrepreneurs hock racks of t-shirts and sunglasses. The weather has brought out shorter skirts. For Gladdy, the area seems abuzz. She catches words of a community parade on a window poster.

Steve, her driver, curses and pumps his brakes, "Stupid traffic." The truck grinds and finds second gear, lurching left through a yellow light.

"If I get a ticket, you pay," he announces.

Gladdy's excitement keeps her mute. It's all alive and confusing. There's no depressing pall that blankets the people, like at Terrace Manor. She has no idea where she is. Steve glances frequently at a scribbled address on his dash.

"I don't get the numbering," he continues, "it's all screwed up. This should be your block." Another grind and the truck bounces forward. "Maybe if we go around to the alley---do they put the numbers on the garbage cans?"

"I don't know," Gladdy manages.

With two more loops of the block, they find the house. It's low slung, hidden by a hedge, and disguised with faded green trim and stucco. A rough walk leads past a broken shrub and up several crumbling steps. A crack in the front window greets them.

"What a dump---I can fix that glass," Steve offers, "for a hundred bucks."

Gladdy opens her purse and withdraws two shiny keys and fits them into a brand new lock, the only improvement to the property. Steve pushes past carrying a nightstand piled with cardboard boxes, "You go check the place out, I'll get ya moved in."

"Thank you so much" Gladdy is apprehensive and steps into the living room. It's carpeted in worn shag. The walls are painted off white and dim light from the door filters through unsettled dust. A mantle with a mirror stares back at her. She sees herself, a small, scared looking woman with short hair dyed jet black. Nothing special. Dowdy. Plain. Her winter jacket looks out of place. Gladdy looks out of place. She feels like crying.

"Watch yourself," Steve marches past and drops a sitting chair next to the window. "There, now you can watch the world."

Then his voice turns into echo as he trots down a short hallway past the kitchen, "Where's the can? I gotta take a pee so bad..."

Gladdy shakes away from the mirror and steps through the threshold into the kitchen. Yellow linoleum greets her. Yellow cupboards and yellow curtains above the sink overwhelm her. Next to the fridge, a side entrance beckons. She unbolts the slider and opens the door. Muffled traffic noises, children yelling, and the sound of urban birds flood into the kitchen, overpowering the draining urine down the hall. This place is alive, she thinks.

She tests the plywood porch gingerly with a step. Solid enough. Then she walks out into the sunshine and surveys her dominion.

The yard is tiny---and cramped further by a galvanized tool shed. Ivy and dandelions spring along a six foot slat fence that separates her new space from the neighbor's. She hears a splash, then a cry, then a yell, then another splash. Someone has a backyard pool. The alley runs directly south, beyond a chain link barrier. The other neighbor is a drab cinder block wall that belongs to a convenience store and marks the start of the commercial district. Mr. Chan had intended to tear down the house and build another enterprise. There was barely room for a hotdog vendor.

Instead, motley, untended dirt flourishes. A bent and gnarled tree stands as the only other tenant. Gladdy loves it instantly.

"Looks like you have a peach tree," Steve grabs the porch rail and shakes it. "This is pretty loose, too. Lotsa stuff wrong here. You should make a list and I'll stop back with some tools."

"I think I'll need a shovel..." Gladdy mentions, considering.

"Check that shed first, you never know. Lemme get the rest of your stuff---get out of your hair. Take your time---don't do it all in one day."

In a half an hour Steve is done. Gladdy offers him twenty, that she has tucked in her billfold, in case of emergency.

"Na, you keep it," Steve insists. "Bake me a pie when those peaches are ripe. I'll check back. You get yourself settled."

Steve leaves, wrenching the gears in his truck. Gladdy closes the front door and locks it. She doesn't stand for long---feeling small and insignificant. Through the open kitchen door noises and bird chatter call to her. Still clutching her purse, she steps onto the sod. Something happened today and it still confuses her. Today she has a garden.

"Seeds," she thinks to herself. "I need seeds."

In three weeks Gladdy is no longer clutching her purse. The small house has been cleaned and scrubbed. The shag carpet was vacuumed and raked. Steve returned and fixed the front window and the back rail. He informed Gladdy that the basement suite is uninhabitable and that if Mr. Chan intends to rent it, he's in for thousands more. Until the work is approved, she would be on her own.

Gladdy has not formally met her neighbors yet. They're a young Korean family, with two preschoolers. The kids have peeked through the slat fence and giggled, pointing out "the lady". The mother has waved meekly, bustling the children inside, and then into the car for an outing. The father looks tired, but smiles when he sees Gladdy. Perfect neighbors, she thinks.

However, night is not the same. At night the bars open and the pedestrians change. Out come the boisterous party-goers. Gladdy hears sirens often, and the yelling is in anger. By eight o'clock she's inside, puttering in her kitchen, or reading in the chair set at the front window. Sometimes she just watches.

One night a fight broke out at the end of the street and she awoke, creeping into the front room to peer past the curtains. A man had blood on his face and another was held against a police car. After the commotion quieted and the small crowd dispersed, she ventured out the backdoor and stood listening on the porch, clutching her robe around her shoulders. In her small plot new shoots grew in straight rows marked by jute twine.

"Peas and beans," she spoke softly, "and carrots."

Today, Gladdy begins weeding along the back chain link. She wears garden gloves and uses tongs to pluck food containers and soggy newspaper out of the wire. She also finds three syringes: one is broken and two contain a murky substance. She shudders and walks them each, at arm's length, directly to the garbage bin, making three trips. The mother next door greets her at the back gate and then scowls when she sees Gladdy's dangerous cargo. Gladdy understands why the mother is ever present, watching the children closely.

The tool shed yielded a meager allotment of implements. When she first entered, the smell of old gas, stale grass clippings, and peat gripped her by the throat. She remembered the smell in an instant, from her past on the plains, the grime and sour metal odor, her husband's tool shed. Gladdy recoiled. Eventually, she became determined to claim the space, and propped the shed door open to let the sun and air do their work. Today seemed a good day for an attempt.

With the trash picked up, Gladdy trowels along the chain fence, working below the weeds, churning gravel and dirt to loosen the roots. A car passes, leaving the back lot of the convenience store, and sometimes a pair of walkers saunter by on a shortcut. The store does brisk business selling cigarettes and pop, candy to the after-schoolers, and rolling papers to the pot smokers. No one bothers Gladdy, and few notice her toiling in the small yard. As she weeds, she can hear the back lot conversations. Young men converge on the corner, behind the cinder block wall and just beyond view.

"Twenty-five all the way up."

"C'mon, gimme a break on a half."

"No way, man, I ain't makin' nothin'... and this is primo. Totally get ya wrecked."

"Ya, ya, it better. Gimme two."

Gladdy peers up from her edging and catches the glance of a young adult, wearing a hoody and a scratched leather jacket. He has attractive features, short dark hair and a salesman's smile. She finds herself staring at him. When his customer suddenly departs, the young man looks directly at her and speaks.

"What the hell are you looking at?"

The statement doesn't match the face, and it takes Gladdy off guard. In second she is back at Terrace Manor and her own demeanor changes.

"I'm not looking at anything."

She gathers her gloves and trowel, briskly walks back to the house, enters, and closes the door. She remains inside for the rest of the day.

The next morning, she works the garden directly off the back porch. Twice she glances to catch the back of a leather jacket leaning against the store's back wall. Both times she looks away, avoiding another confrontation.

Steve arrives at lunch; he's carrying a water hose. "You'll need this. No sense packing water from the sink." Gladdy thanks him and casually mentions that strangers seem to congregate in the alley, behind the store. Steve marches to the back gate and leans over, looking side-to-side, up and down the alley. Then he strides back, in thought.

"Nobody there. Just dealers, probably. Don't pay them any attention. If you don't talk to them, they won't talk to you."

Gladdy tells him that Leather Jacket seemed threatening.

"Look, anybody bothers you, tell 'em..." he rolls up his sleeve an shows Gladdy a dark tattoo inked into his skin. "I did a stint in jail... you tell them I'm around."

"Thank you, and thanks for the garden hose." Gladdy smiles showing relief. She waits to close the door until she hears his truck pull away and clatter down the street.

By two in the afternoon the alley is quiet and the sun turns the tiny back lot tropical. The peach tree, dense with leaves, offers the only shade, but it overhangs the alley. Between the shed and the back gate, Gladdy makes a discovery.

An old folding lawn chair is wedged tightly. The settling ground has pinned the chair, probably long forgotten, but it looks in fair shape. Yanking the aluminum frame causes creaks and rattles. Gladdy struggles trying to extract the find. Suddenly, a shadow looms over her and she looks up to see a stern expression on the face of Leather Jacket. He lunges forward, and Gladdy whimpers a short cry, but his arm moves past her and grabs the chair. In one maneuver, he frees the frame and pulls it up, and over the fence. He flicks it outward, like a rag, and the chair snaps open. Then he hoists it back over the fence and sets it upright in front of Gladdy. Startled, she watches him strut behind the store and beyond view.

Gladdy can't remember how she returned to the house, but remains there for the rest of the day. The chair sits where Leather Jacket left it.

The routine plays out again the following morning. Gladdy weeds in the garden, tentatively, watchful. Leather Jacket is back in position and disappears during the afternoon. Just before supper, he returns. Gladdy is in the kitchen, with the window open, when she hears yelling.

"Screw you!"

"I don't owe him nothing."

The voices are tense, combative. More yelling, then cursing. Then the squeal of tires on asphalt behind the store. When she looks again, Leather Jacket is muttering to himself and kicking at the chain link fence, her fence.

Compelled by impulse, Gladdy steps on to the porch, turns on the outdoor tap, and walks with the garden hose toward the gate. Leather Jacket glances at her, but turns away, looking anxiously for someone who isn't there.

Gladdy approaches and tries to speak clearly, assertively, against her better judgement and the advice of Steve.

"Thank you," she says.

"'Thank you' for what?"

"For helping me get out the lawn chair."

"Yeh, like you used it."

"I will use it, that's why I'm saying thank you. That was very kind."

"Forget it."

Gladdy sets down the hose and turns to her rows of vegetables, now showing color, and the protruding orange carrot roots bulging from beneath the soil. The stocks are young and tender. She pulls out half a dozen and washes them with the hose.

She offers them over the fence to Leather Jacket, "Try some. They're good."

"Na... I mean, no thanks." He avoids her, turning to case the parking lot again.

"They're very healthy... good for you. Just try one." Gladdy smiles, the sun reflects in her eyes and sparkles back, faintly.

Leather Jacket begins to wave his hand down, passing her off, then he hesitates. "OK, I'll try one."

He plucks a root from her hand and examines it against the light. He blows away imperceptible dust and takes a chomp.

Halfway through, he's talking at her, "Hey, these are pretty good. They taste like carrots."

Gladdy can't help laughing out loud, "They are carrots."

Leather Jacket lowers a look back at her, like she's offended him. "My name is Mike," he says.

"Hi Mike. My name is Gladdy."

Gladdy knew better than to ask Mike his business. She comments on the weather, and how pleasant the neighborhood is---in the daytime. Mike nods and munches, then excuses himself, "Hey, look, thanks for the snack. They were good. See ya around."

Gladdy smiles and withdraws, walking slowly to the house and carrying back the hose.

Mike calls to her, hesitating, and then speaks directly, "Hey, uh, lady---Gladdy---that's the first carrot I ever ate---like from the ground."

"Really?"

"Yeah, no kidding. Thanks."

"No kidding." Gladdy wonders about his statement. It seems profound to her. Something felt right in offering the harvest, she decides, and turns back to the porch. That's when she catches sight of the watchful mother next door. The woman is peering through the slat fence and frowning.

Gladdy feels an overwhelming urge to talk, to connect with this foreign mother living a normal suburban life in the tumult of a big city, but she decides not, opting for a nap instead.

Over the week, Mike's presence in alley and behind the store becomes commonplace. Gladdy has her own routine: puttering, weeding, watering, hanging freshly washed towels and sheets on the line. Mike nods to her in passing, even stopping to ask the condition of the garden and how the different crops are doing.

Gladdy points out the peas, beans, explains how runners climb up the twine to reach more sun. She starts a row of radishes and begins a compost next to the shed, mulching her leftovers into the soil and sprinkling squash and pumpkin seeds. By the end of the week, Mike is hanging over the fence with a coffee in his hand, gossiping about the neighborhood.

"It's decent around here, steady customers, good people, not the same crap on Eastside."

"Do you have another job?"

"Can't get one, but even if I could, the money sucks---hold on, be right back." Mike balances his coffee on a gate post, then trots behind the store and attends a car driver lowering his window. The transaction takes moments, a brisk clasp of hands and the driver peels away. Mike saunters back, flipping bills low in his hand.

Gladdy has no opinion. She's learned not to have an opinion. She learned that trick long ago. She crouches on her knees plucking weeds.

"They never stop." Mike comments.

"Yes, you look quite busy."

"No, I mean the weeds. They never stop growing. I've seen you weed that garden ten times now."

"I like to chat. The weeding is just an excuse." Gladdy grins. She actually feels more comfortable than she has in years. Her medication hasn't been adjusted in weeks. Even keel, her doctor was impressed at her last appointment. And Mike had become a welcome acquaintance.

She enjoys his banter, and he samples the fare. He tried fresh peas, radishes, carrots, early tomatoes, and strawberries that sprang first from the compost. The soil is good.

He watches her pluck and tend, periodically excusing himself, but always returning. Once he bought her a coffee, fumbling with creamers and sugar stuffed in his leather pocket. She declined, but then sipped it to be polite.

Today, he blurts out a question.

"Do you need any help?"

Gladdy leans back and looks at Mike, studying him, "Are you offering?"

"Sure, why not?" Mike walks to the gate and reaches over to unlatch it.

The words of Steve crash in front of Gladdy---"Don't talk to them..." She remembers her friends at the Terrace Manor, using her, sizing her up.

Mike is different, she thinks. "OK," Gladdy agrees and stands, brushing her slacks.

Mike shrugs off his jacket and hangs it on the slat fence. Someone giggles, followed by a splash.

"I'll show you what to do," instructs Gladdy and she points out which sprouts are weeds and which are a new crop of vegetables. Their conversation lapses and the methodical rhythm of planet and sun replicates in their motions, hands touching the earth and renewing an age old endeavor. In half an hour, their labor is done. Mike rises and stretches, "That was fun. Ya get lost in your head. Hard on the back, though."

"You did well," Gladdy praises him, nodding, "there's a farmer in you yet."

"Not likely. Hey, I gotta go... bidnez." He says, grabbing his jacket, and then vaults the fence to the alley. Gladdy suspects a degree of embarrassment, helping an old lady weed her garden. She chuckles, "He'll be back."

Three o'clock in the morning, fighting breaks out again. Gladdy no longer bolts awake. Sirens blend into the orchestra of night and she even congratulates herself for not being scared anymore. The voices are loud, shouting obscenities. They're just behind the store.

There's a yelp. Someone is injured. More shouting and Gladdy hears muffled thumps of punching. Police should be here soon, she predicts, and drifts, waiting for the sirens to approach.

An hour later she startles again. Someone is groaning out back, in her yard. Gladdy rises slowly, reaching for her robe, then she pads to the kitchen. She hesitates turning on a light, and checks the latch on the door, peering past the porch through the glass.

There's a moan.

"You go home!" Gladdy calls, then stops mid-breath. What if someone is lurking? She retreats into the kitchen.

Then a voice. "Gladdy..."

"Who is it?"

"It's Mike."

"Mike? What are you doing?"

Gladdy opens the door and steps forward, brushing a shape slumped against the porch. The young man is bent forward. Shadows distort and a ruddy sheen covers his face. He's been beaten.

"Oh, Mike, what happened?"

"They rolled me."

"Oh my gosh, you're bleeding---you're bleeding a lot."

"I got stabbed." Mike coughs and moans again.

"I'm calling an ambulance," Gladdy turns, but Mike's arm thrusts forward, grabbing her leg. Sticky, cold blood smears down her robe. "Don't," he says.

"I have to. I'm calling the police."

"Don't, please, don't." Mike winces and looks up to her.

"Mike, you're hurt. God knows I should have woke up---that was you! The fighting--"

"Gladdy, don't. If you're my friend, don't tell anyone. Rat these guys and they'll kill me---the cops will make me talk."

"I don't know what to do, Mike. I don't know what to do." Gladdy trails off, staring at Mike, broken and hiding in the dark. Wind rushes in her ears and her head feels dizzy. She's slipping; hands grip her from the past and drag her down, force her down. She can feel the boot coming. She knows the boot is coming.

And then she's back, grasping Mike, falling beside him and clutching him in her arms. He is crying and she is crying. She holds his head to her shoulder.

"Let's get you inside."

"Steve?"

"Who is this?"

"It's Gladdy, Steve?"

"Gladdy? I was dead asleep... what time is it?"

"I don't know, four o'clock. Steve, I hate to ask, I just don't know what to do."

"What's wrong? Are you alright?" Steve glances to his alarm, focusing on the numbers.

"Do you know first aid?"

"Gladdy, what's wrong? What happened?"

"It's Mike, he's been injured."

"Who's Mike? Why are you calling me? Call an ambulance."

"I can't---he won't let me."

"Oh, geez Louise, are you talking about one of those kids out by your place?"

"He's a friend---"

"Call the cops, Gladdy, it's not your problem."

"He says they'll kill him, the people who did this."

"Just call the cops, Gladdy, and do your friend a favor, call the ambulance first."

"Please Steve..."

Moments pass and Steve speaks again.

"Where is he hurt?"

"He has a wound, a knife wound, on his left side, his ribs."

"Is he breathing? Wheezing?"

"He's in pain---I think they cracked his ribs."

"Oh Gladdy, I'll be there in ten minutes. Don't let him in the house."

"He's in the kitchen."

"Great. If I fix this jerk up, I'm gonna kick his ass afterwards."

"Please hurry, Steve, please..."

In ten minutes Gladdy hears the rattle and grind of Steve's truck pull in front. A door slams in the early dawn and then a sharp rap sounds on the front door. Gladdy rushes to open it and catches herself in the mirror above the mantle. Blood is smeared across her cheek, where Mike rested his head. Her robe looks like a crime scene. She shakes herself out of fixation and unbolts the door.

"Where is he? I had to stop for gauze--- that's a little hard to find right now."

"He's in the kitchen. I couldn't move him any further. I put a pillow under his head."

Steve moves like a cat to prey and stands over Mike. "What happened to you, jerk?"

"Somebody doesn't like me."

"Nobody likes you."

"Gladdy likes me."

"Shut up---this will go quicker."

Steve pulls off Mike's jacket and tears the t-shirt in half, exposing blood smeared gash on Mike's side.

"Nice one. Any of it still in there?"

"The knife?"

"No, the idiot."

Steve runs his fingers tenderly over Mike's ribs. The younger man winces.

"Yeah, you cracked two. Can't fix it. You just have to lie still for six weeks."

Then he pulls sterile wipes from a bag and sops up the blood around the wound. Clotting has begun.

"You're frikking lucky. It hit bone and bounced off." Steve dumps out a small plastic kit and retrieves a long stitch needle. "I sew like shit, heh."

In five minutes, the gash is clean and closed. Steve applies half a dozen butterfly bandages and wraps enough gauze to compress Mike's ribs. Then he stands. "I'm gonna wash up, Gladdy. Watch this fool. I want to talk to him."

Mike tries to pull himself up against the stove, but Gladdy gently eases him back to the floor. "You're not going anywhere. I'm putting you in the bedroom. You have to rest."

"No, no, Gladdy you're great and all, but I gotta go right now."

"Enough. She's right," Steve returns, calmer, but firm. "You can't move. If your rib splits and punctures your lung, you're done. You should go get a tetanus shot."

Mike couldn't move on his own anyway. Bruises were turning dark over his face and torso. Gladdy and Steve hoisted their patient between them and stumbled him into Gladdy's bed. She insisted Steve help take off his boots, but left him in jeans. She covered him in a thick comforter and stole back to the kitchen with Steve.

"Get him out of here as fast as you can, Gladdy. Tomorrow. He'll probably slink out on his own. Give him water if asks, not too much. And a couple aspirins. I've got no pain killers---he's a practically a pharmacist, anyway."

"Will they come back for him?"

"Na, they just want him out of action for awhile---no competition. If he was supposed to be dead, he'd be dead."

"Oh gosh."

"Stay out of it. They're like cats---feed 'em once and they spray on everything."

"Thank you, Steve. How can I---"

"Peach pie, Gladdy, a big slice of pie."

Over the next four days Gladdy busies herself between tending garden outside and minding Mike. She prepares him healthy meals---Spartan, but fresh and homemade. She helps him into the washroom, letting him lean on her until he's comfortable, then excusing herself and waiting outside the door. His mood wavers, sometimes grouchy and other times almost cheerful. They talk for hours. He tells her of his life, the mistakes he's made, and she speaks at length about her own history.

On the fifth day, Mike makes his way to the porch and ventures outside. Gladdy brings the lawn chair close, and positions Mike to watch her work in the garden. The vegetables have grown in abundance, and she pulls samples to display, holding them proudly as Mike laughs and shows her a thumbs up. Slowly he heals. Slowly, their friendship grows.

On the weekend they prepare a feast, Mike steadies himself against the sink, scrubbing the harvest, while Gladdy minces onions and dices carrots. Two pies simmer in homemade crust.

"Steve is coming over, too."

"How is the old boy? Have to thank him when I see him. He didn't do too bad---under pressure---but he was right. He sews like shit."

"You be nice. He did us a wonderful favor."

"I will, Ma."

Mike catches himself, and blushes. Gladdy blushes too, and then beams. "You can call me whatever you want."

Glasses clink and silver ware clatters. Food passes from bowl to plate.

When they finish, Steve invites them to the porch and they recline. Gladdy and Mike sitting; Steve leaning on the slat fence.

"Do you want your pie now, or later?" Gladdy asks.

"In a minute---a little toast though, everybody gotta glass?"

"What shall we toast?" Gladdy ponders, the past weeks a whirlwind. She turns to Mike.

His eyes catch sun and he smiles, "I know---garden fresh."

"To the garden," Steve chimes.

"To the garden," Gladdy sighs.

Read This Please

Volume 2 Edition 12 – Firsts

February 1, 2012

Remember our first? ReadThisPlease.com Edition 12 is all about firsts. Some experiences happen upon us and we acknowledge that this was a personal first, first chances, first disappointments, first moments. We all have opportunities to travel into the unknown and experience a first. Even if a road is traveled a thousand times, the first journey is special. We invite you to read the draft passages, short tales, and compilations as is. Brought to you by the wandering scribes at ReadThisPlease, in Firsts, Edition 12, first draft.

First Memory

by M Dawn Thacker

I was playing under the house trailer. I know I was under it because I saw the long black axles lying across cinderblock, and I smelled the dirt. I was too tall to stand up straight, so I was on my knees. It felt cozy. I looked out from the shade around me and saw the other mobile homes on either side. The yard had patches of green and brown grass. My feet were bare.

The girl from next door was with me. She was older than me and had two Barbies. She showed me one of the dolls. She let me hold it. The girl had yellow hair and she was wearing a white dress. She smiled at me. She took the Barbie dolls and sat them side by side on one of the cinderblocks. Their dresses were fancy like hers, their feet were bare like mine. They were friends.

I saw a woman's feet and legs. Her high heeled shoes were black and shiny. She bent over and frowned at us. "Come out from under there this minute in that nice white dress," she said to the girl.

My friend scurried out from under the trailer and left the dolls sitting there with me.

Writer's Firsts

by Sarah Scott

I remember my first poem—about a cat—and I can recite it by heart. I have it scrawled in grade-school letters, in a notebook in a box in my house somewhere. It's there.

I remember my first A-earning essay, and the joy I felt at a job well done. I floated all the way home to show my parents. The next morning, I dug the paper out of the trash, ink smeared, pages reminiscent of stale ale. I saved it, neatly tucked in a once eggshell-now-dingy faded manila envelope.

I remember my first award for English, my first written short story, my first novel manuscript, penned in old ratty notebooks, smudged with tears. I remember a lifetime of moments, standing on the bridge, overlooking the valley. And I remember all the doors that had to open, to bring me here.

I hold the book in my hand, with its polished cover and glossy words. I am mere months away from my first college degree, and but a few years beyond I'll have another certificate to hang on the wall. But it's not about the certificates. It's about the words on these pages in my hand. It's about what that piece of paper gives me, the confidence to stretch my arms up to the sky and throw my head back, to scream into the valley below: "I made it to the mountain top!"

First Real Friend

by Adrienne S Moody

Eternal Friend and Soul Sista

Those were the words she wrote me before she died: eternal friend and soul sista. This friend since primary school is gone and she's taken a part of me with her. No one shares these memories that we have and no more will I be able to call her on a whim just because I need to hear her laughter. There for me when first my dad died and then my mother. She rode in the funeral car both times as she was considered part of the family. She was more my sister than my own. And my family knew it.

She was my tennis partner in high school and we would still, as adults, laugh at the coach, Mr. Wood and his ridiculous loping gait. She was the one who instigated me sassing the Math teacher, Mr. Denny, and snickered as he ridiculed me. We spent one year not speaking to each other for some girlish unspeakable crime against each other. On the last day of school before the freedom of summer we walked parallel on opposite sides of the street and I remember looking at her and wishing we were friends again to spend the summer together. I said to her 'do you wanna be friends?' and how we both burst out laughing and back together we were.

Over the years, I have dreamed of the back alley that leads to her home. She lived only two blocks away. When you're a child you notice things, like the color of the brick on a home, the black dog that races up to the fence when you walk by, the shape of the trees that line the lane. I remember the back of Linda's house and how she always had rabbits there that she loved and tended to. Her dog

Goldie would be sleeping in the sun and would raise her head at me. A cat or two lazed in the hot prairie sun.

She sang at my wedding. She put a flower and a little gift on my bed when I stayed with her for my father's funeral.

She would leave a happy birthday greeting and song on my answering machine. Whenever she missed, which wasn't often, I would call feeling a little hurt and saying , "What's up? No birthday song?"

I don't think I can fly home for her funeral. I can't bear to even imagine her in that coffin. It would surely tear me apart to see it lowered to the ground.

She died on Friday afternoon and I had talked to her on the phone on Thursday evening. I received her email the following morning, just hours before she collapsed to the ground at the golf course. The paramedics could not revive her.

I dreamed last night of being in the hallways of our old high school. I stopped a mutual friend and said, 'did you hear that…. Sharon died?' a sister of another friend. I knew that was wrong. 'no, it was Sharon's mother,' I amended, but knew again that was wrong. And then I remembered it was Linda and I woke and listened to the rain.

Chime Music

I always look for signs. Ever since my dad died and I connected with him many times afterwards, I feel and know that strong connections can stay intact even after death. Linda died on Friday early afternoon. Suddenly. Her pain must have been very very short. And of this I am grateful. She died on a golf course. What better place than that especially if you love golf and she did. No one contacted me that day. I went to bed that night knowing nothing. I had received her email that morning just hours before she dropped to the ground. I smiled at her ending, the words, eternal and soul. I didn't know then that these words would be like a parting hug from her.

I woke up in the early hours; I lifted my head off the pillow to look outside as I sensed the moon would be visible and it was. I marveled at the beauty of the eyelash moon in the autumn sky. I whispered to no one, 'how beautiful.' And put my head back down and went to sleep.

The next day after work I arrived home to see two messages flashing on my machine and heard this woman's voice saying that she had something to tell me about Linda. I knew it couldn't be good. But dead? No, I did not think that. My mind wouldn't go there, but I knew it was something serious. And so that evening was spent calling mutual friends from back home, telling them the awful news. I called my brother in Indiana. As I told him my voice broke up. I couldn't get the words out easily. It just didn't make sense to put the words Linda and dead together.

I felt grateful my roommate was still out on the Sunshine Coast and I had the place to myself. I finally fell asleep, heaviness in my heart and feeling so very exhausted. I drifted off thinking, 'who will know these stories that she and I have? I can no longer phone her and say, *'remember when we were in the funeral car at mom's burial and you whispered to me... now I know why you can't stand your sister, she's driving me crazy?' No one laughs like she and I do. No one laughs at my jokes like she does. No one gets me like she does.'*

Again I woke in the middle of the night. Something roused me. The wind. Chimes. That lovely tinkling of chimes in the wind. I lifted my head and listened intently. Music. And then, suddenly, like someone put on a tap of water full force, the rain. Such force and I laid awake and listened to it and could sleep no more.

What's Around the Next Corner?

I thought maybe, three days after her death, that the slip of a moon, the chimes in the middle of the night or the downpour of rain was her speaking to me somehow. But, I'm not convinced and I feel that I will know if and when she connects with me. At least I think I will. I did with my with dad. It was with certainty that he alerted me.

This is my first.

My first close friend to die. It's different from my parents, or relatives. Our friends bring death closer to us. We expect our parents will go first and it is an alien thought, our own demise. At least for me. While she waits wherever a body waits for the relatives to retrieve and begin the process of burial, I could feel the cold of the steel that surely is there for her. I tried not to think of this, but I cannot help it. I wish her body was kept warm by the fireside with her friends all around and not in a steel environment awaiting an autopsy.

Her brothers have arrived now and someone would be tending to her and preparing her for public display at her funeral.

During these few days since she died, I've thought of many things. I've thought about what our friends mean to us. Now I'm thinking, that could be her last email. I think that could be the last phone call. I know this will fade and I will take everything for granted once more, as that is the way we are designed. How else to live day to day doing such mundane tasks to keep everything moving? Work to pay bills to take vacation to keep the heat on and gas in our cars. It is all so mind-numbingly mundane; it is best to live without mindfulness.

Easier that way.

I thought she and I would still be comparing notes well into our 80's. I really did. So now I reminisce about her and how much she meant to me.

Our last phone conversation, we talked at great length about our health. I told her how I have never felt so good; I have boundless energy. I feel and look great. But I can't take stress and anxiety. I'm seeing a counselor for that. I'm tired of sleepless nights worrying about work related issues, work run by drone-like idiots who pass out letters of expectations with an evil grin on their faces. She told me that she wasn't feeling well the past few months. She'd spoken of this before.

She spoke of a boil that appeared suddenly on her left breast near her heart. The doctor lanced it and tried to drain it. It hurt terribly. There was a lump under this and he booked an appointment for her a week later. There, he said, was a triage and a mammogram would be done and that there was a surgeon right there if he was needed for any other treatment.

"I will call you on Wednesday, Linda," I said as I wrote this on my calendar. She scoffed. "It's probably nothing. I'm just gonna call to see how it went."

"Strange, Adrienne, how when he did this procedure, my breast became very very hot and was so red. He put me on antibiotics."

Maybe this is what did it. An infection so close to her heart.

If one sentence could be used to sum up a person's personality, heart and soul, then the following is Linda.

When she was only twelve years old her parents took her and her younger brother to Ireland. Once there they stopped at a pub in the middle of Belfast. The parents warned the two of them to 'stay in the car, or else!'

Linda watched them disappear into the drinking establishment.

"Stay here or else!" she warned her brother and left the rent-a-car.

She wandered down the busy grey-looking city sidewalk and turned the corner.

A car bomb went off across the street from her.

She ran back to the car as fast as she could, more concerned that her parents would see she disobeyed them than her near brush with violence.

"Whatever motivated you to do this, Linda? Why would you just wander into a strange city like you did?" I asked, shocked at this detail of her life that she'd never disclosed before.

"I just had to see what was around the corner," was her simple answer.

And I see she has done this once more.

First Vacation

by Gaboo

Scene 1

The scene opens in a scullery. Cooks in aprons whirl to prepare a feast. One sits alone in a corner, peeling and having a conversation with himself.

Bellow, bellow, bellow. The sire's in a rage. Boo hoo. Mind yourself, hush, or you'll be summoned and whipped, or worse, dipped. I could use a good dipping this time of year. Don't jest, you almost went without noggin last night. Oh you… whine, whine, whine. Bellow, bellow, bellow. Two dongs loose from their bells. I won't warn you again.

Promise?

A bucketful of slop flies over the head of the lone peeler and douses him.

Oh, thanks. Thanks a lot. Now look what you've done… why are you even here? Hiding out?

Whine.

You're in trouble again.

Whimper.

Just remember, don't drag me into your complications.

Scene 2

Enter the ante room of a palace. High ceilings filter light through stone archways. Various guards, and servants loiter and pace. A booming voice yells off stage—there's anger in the words and the entourage turns nervously. Some shirk and withdraw.

Where's my fool! Where's my fool! Bring me that cursed fool!

A page nervously approaches the voice, stage right, and stoops lower, timidly.

Your fool is peeling eggs, sire... in the kitchens, sire... causing a mess, sire.

The voice yells louder.

He's doing what?!

A diminutive, but rotund man struts commandingly to center stage. He's shod in fancy open shoes, cloth leggings, ribbed vest and a thick open robe. A wobbly crown perches on his head. Two servants follow frantically with fishing rod contraptions to correct the crown's position. The regal man looks left and right, then to the audience, searching with his eyes. He whirls and struts, the two servants following desperately to balance the crown.

A taller, snakelike servant dressed in flowing gray robes appears from a shadowy alcove. He approaches and takes a position behind the crowned man's ear.

My wonderful king, do not be overcome with disappointment. I will advise you in any way possible. Ask of me, and I will do my utmost to fulfill your greatnesses requestesses.

The king peers at him, annoyed.

Oh bother, go find my fool, you lurker. Did you hear me summon my Royal Speculator? Oh Royal Speculator, Royal Speculator, where could be my Royal Speculator?

The king mocks the man, wiggling the royal fingers in the air as if distraught. Then the king scowls.

Bring me advice on the Whereabouts Of My Royal Fool! Seeeek him!

("Seek him, seek him, seek the fool" whisper and mutter the panicked servants as they flee off stage.)

At the thunder of the king's command, the entourage disperses hither and fro. The Royal Speculator evaporates fearfully into the shadows. The two servants balancing the crown become entangled. They fall in collision, lying prostrate in failure. The crown tumbles to the floor. The scene ends.

Scene 3

The king is on a turret balcony, overlooking the moat. He leans forlorn against a stone window sill, staring despondently at the setting sun. He speaks.

Why do you leave me in my time of need?

The egg peeler in Scene 1 approaches from off stage, standing opposite the window frame so that both men can view the sunset. The egg peeler speaks.

You have to learn how to get on with things. I'm not going to affect the outcome much. You know that.

The king sighs and speaks.

Yes, I know. But it's hard taking those steps alone, without someone to offer a realistic opinion.

The egg peeler bodychecks the king affectionately, making room for himself along the window ledge. Both men gaze at the horizon. The two crown balancers appear from off stage and make subtle, manual adjustments to the position of the king's crown. Eventually, the egg peeler speaks.

Hey, thanks for the vote of confidence. I mean it.

The king clasps his own hands together and peers at the moat below.

Well, you deserve it. I know I've been pretty demanding lately... with all my conquering and pillaging and all that. It takes it out of one, trust me.

The egg peeler pulls a crumpled jester's cap out of his vest and sets it upon his own head.

Same here, I've been running out of material. It gets old and I just want to be fresh, get some new perspectives.

The king looks at his servant.

I hear you, buddy.

The egg peeler, now court jester, gives the king a friendly punch in the bicep. The two crown balancers again appear with hasty adjustment. The jester speaks.

You'll do okay.

The jester stoops and plucks a rucksack, and a walking staff leaning against the wall. Then he turns to the king and speaks, smiling.

Hey, don't be sad... I have one more for you... how does a poor man wipe his nose?

The jester wipes his nose on his own sleeve. The king chuckles. The jester continues.

How does a gentleman wipe his nose?

The jester tugs open the top of his own dusty vest and wipes his nose on the collar, discreetly. The king guffaws, smiles. The jester continues.

How does the King wipe his nose?

The king looks on curiously as the jester leans forward and wipes his nose on the king's sleeve.

That's how. I'll send a pigeon with a postcard when I get there.

The king roars as the jester departs. The curtains close.

First Time

by Gaboo

It's not all that glimmery.

"Is this your first time?" she seemed incredulous. Of course it wasn't my first time! I knew how this worked. I read all those porn mags the welders tossed in the dust bin behind Wrenchrite Manufacturing. We discovered them together, me and my two best buddies. What a glorious summer, sitting by the creek in a ramshackle fort, paging through days of glossy butts and breasts. We read all the articles, and compared all the information gleaned— cartoons, Dear Editor letters—and we labeled all the prettiest faces and the perfect bodies. Kids today have the internet. Back then we had to use mental imagery. We had a gold mine. I remember the exotic model photo, with the banner, "The Russians are Coming". She was gorgeous, a four by six inch goddess. I clipped the picture and saved it in a buckskin wallet. Until the fear of being discovered led me to kiss the scrap goodbye and toss her, folded to the wind.

I remember scrambling along the creek that same fall, late for school. Someone else was rooting through the cache, so I crept up quietly and peered through the twigs. Robert Nash, my arch nemesis, was engrossed in a tattered, soggy pin-up book. I'm sure he had his hands down his pants, giving it.

"Robert Nash looks at nudie magazines!"

Oh, I made sure he was busted, embarrassed royally. I ran and laughed. What a good laugh…

But of course it wasn't my first time—how could it be my first time? I was a worldly guy; I knew how the plumbing worked. Just the motion was screwing me up.

"Lie back."

And there it was. I was doing it, or I was being done. It was not really as scary as they say, most of the fear was in my head, because something was happening, my body was taking over. It was like a separation of wills. The skin, the hair, the sweaty heat combining two living forms together. I was getting too excited, letting too much go. I couldn't stop. So this was it…

The door kicked in and The Hag stumbled through the threshold, with a couple of sneering drunks in tow. I couldn't make them out, the street light shone past them and hit me like a deer. My eyes were bleary, almost teared up. We had been talking for hours, my belle and I, kissing, fondling, touching, playing dating games, closer, closer, and somehow here we were fully engaged and DOING IT— for real, and then her roommate had to crash in, the neanderwoman, the boor.

The Hag slopped herself next to the cluttered kitchen table, pushed against the wall of the one room shack and plunked in a chair. Her dates stood chuckling in the doorway.

"For frick sakes, I'm drunk," she slurred.

"Just go take a walk," my wondergirl scolded.

"You take a walk," the beast defied, and then perked, "Hey, who's that?"

"Nobody."

"Hey, were you guys having sex?" she cackled.

"Just go, please."

"Well, ha, ha, ha, serves you right. I'm watching TV."

The Hag's two escorts stood debating, then promptly stumbled off.

"F you, too." Deb snorted.

Well, I was almost there, half way there. I could have been there, the first time, but I got robbed.

My First Bad Boy

by Adrienne S Moody

Our communication started with a simple line sent via email.

Have you seen the film, 'The Notebook?'

An odd question, I thought. I looked at his profile and although his picture posted was somewhat fuzzy, out of focus, I could see a man with strong features and a smile that looked self-conscious. Not a guy who liked his picture taken. He was in construction work, a working stiff, is how he described himself. What a strange question from such a macho looking kind of guy.

Yes, I did and I loved it.

I responded and waited for his reply. We messaged back and forth for the next few days, getting to know each other. I finally asked him what possessed him to watch a film known to be a classic 'chick flick.' Did someone push it on him? Yes, he replied. My son who knows me beyond the tough guy exterior. There is this soft romantic in me that I don't usually show anyone.

He said that he was drowning in a loveless marriage at the time and that the film brought him to tears when he realized the truth. He'd not felt that kind of love depicted in the film, since he was a teenager. The kind of love that makes it so you can't eat.

I wrote that I loved the part of the film where the mother takes the daughter to this rock quarry and points out a worker in a hard hat as a man she used to be crazy about as a young girl. He had nothing materially to offer her and she'd turned him down in favor of someone who could give her the lifestyle she desired. This man in the hard hat suddenly looked up and saw the woman from his past and the expression on his face said it all. That look is what chemistry and unrequited love is all about. He wrote:

That look said, 'It was good.'

I do remember love that made it impossible to eat. He lived across the street from me when I was only 14. His name was Kelly and he had a chipped front tooth making him look reckless and wild. His white blonde hair was too long and a lock of it kept falling into his eyes.

"Do not put one foot into his yard, young lady," my father warned me, sensing something was brewing in the neighborhood and it involved his eldest daughter.

Children spilled like marbles out of a jar from the homes of my old neighborhood. So many of us, jumping, screaming, conspiring, challenging. Baseball played in the field across from our bungalow, touch football on the dead end street. The street lights flickered on bringing the moths out of hiding, twenty or so of us congregating by the telephone pole playing potato man to see who would be 'it' in a game of hide-and-go-seek.

Kelly and I dashed away together holding hands. We climbed fences, trespassed through darkened yards, smelling the musky damp earth and the sweet peas in the late summer. Together we hid under a lilac bush, both of us on our backs looking up at the stars in the sky. His lips were moist, and tasted like licorice, and he smelled like the wheat fields at my Uncle's farm.

He professed his love for me there, on that night. Told me he was only trying to make me jealous when he would call out to my sister as we walked home from school. Kelly and I hid so well that everyone just gave up on us and continued on with the summer game. I remember my mom calling me in the distance and heard the sound of the screen door slamming. I knew I had time until my dad would stand on the front porch and whistle his Three Short signal, which meant "Get in… or else!"

Kelly was always in trouble for something. He was the oldest of eight kids and his parents didn't seem to know how to look after them all. None of them were ever dressed properly for the season and whenever there was a break-in or thefts committed in the neighborhood, fingers pointed at Kelly's house. My father reported at the dinner table one night that he saw Kelly's father asleep in his truck down by the river early that morning. I asked one of Kelly's sisters why they never seemed to get called in for meals like we did. She answered that usually their mother cooked up things like pancakes and left them on a big plate on the cupboard and everyone just grabbed as they walked through the house.

Kelly disappeared from the neighborhood the following year. As my high school years dragged on, his face faded from my memory. One day, my girlfriend and I were walking towards town, to hang around, and a car slowed beside us. We looked over and saw Kelly in the passenger seat with a known trouble maker, Maurice, driving.

"Wanta ride, Adrienne?" my childhood love asked.

We jumped into the back of the car, always up for some excitement. Kelly asked if I wanted to sit with him in the front, so I climbed over and sat next to him. There was that same wheat smell, and when he kissed me, the unmistakable odor of liquor. But it was a warm feeling that emanated from him. And I didn't mind. I felt lost in that kiss and didn't want it to end. It wasn't a demanding sort of kiss that some are. No, his was soft and lingering and sad.

I moved away shortly after that incident. Around my 18th birthday I traveled around with a friend, aimlessly. Neither one of us knew what we wanted to do in life and taking a bus here and there around the west coast seemed as good an idea as any. We did odd jobs like chamber maid work to finance our adventure and one day while we waited to board a greyhound bus I saw him. Like putting a finger into a light socket, his eyes met mine above the crowd and it stopped my breath. The look on his face said, 'You're never gonna forget me.'

"Who is that?" Cathe asked, noticing the electric charge in the air.

"Oh, someone I used to know," I answered in a far-away voice.

My mind wandered back to when I felt his hand in mine as we raced through yards and hopped over fences in the moonlight. I remembered the taste of his mouth.

A decade later, I was married, and settled into a very normal sort of life; I received a call from an old neighbor. She regretted to tell me that Kelly was dead. It was a drug deal gone wrong, she informed me. Dead. He never had a chance in life. I know that I couldn't have saved him from his destiny and I had to let him go. But a part of him still lingers in me.

A wise friend I know said this:

'You want my take on why some women like bad boys? Validation. Cause the bad boy can choose anything, take anything. And he takes you.'

Memorable Firsts

by Adrienne S Moody

My friend said it right: first anything usually isn't at all what we expect. First sexual experience? How many can report back with rave reviews?

First scouting for a job?

I was with a gaggle of giggling girls; we were all of 13 years of age. We bounced into the local meat market and asked the butcher if he needed someone to sweep up all that 'sawdust,' to which he responded with, 'Get outta here allofya!'

First time getting fired?

I decided to moonlight and work a second job across the street at this hotel working as a waitress serving drinks at a nightclub. I've never done this kind of work but it looked kinda easy to me. I loved music and the music there was loud enough to hear across the street. So off I went for my first shift. I knew I wasn't cut out for the position when a young guy about my age walked up to me as I stood at the bar tapping my foot to the music, slammed a full drink down on the counter and said, 'You got it wrong for the fourth time. You owe me one!' I believe I just walked off the job before they put the axe down.

First break up?

Oh yeah. That would be Lyle. Grade 11 I was and wearing his black Alaskan ring on my left hand, looking very important, indeed. The first date was memorable as he didn't show due to his negligence in turning the heater on in the chicken coop and killing all the chickens. Things improved from there. I remember his hands, long slender fingers, but strong due to all the farm chores he had to do. His cheeks flamed red like firelight. Wasn't meant to be, however. He just faded away and after a few weeks I passed my ring to a friend who passed it to his friend and that was the end. He was a dismal kisser, so no great loss. It wasn't heartbreak for me, at least.

First betrayal?

Not a man, no, but a female friend taught me what it is like to have someone leave you at a time when they are needed most. And she did this more than once. Rumors abounded about me in my late 20's. Slander of my character. She called me and hinted that it was going on. And that's okay but what wasn't is I could tell by her voice that she believed what was being said. Ouch! And then this same woman decided that I was fabricating or at best I was delusional in thinking a man was criminally harassing me. I no longer speak to her. I saw her profile on Facebook and it saddened me.

First kiss?

Won't ever forget it. Kelly, the bad boy from my youth. We were at a movie held at an elementary school up the hill from where we lived. I would be about ten years old, maybe eleven. My sister and I were walking home afterwards, in the pitch blackness of the night. I remember the sound of our shoes on the wooden sidewalk and the sound of running behind us. I turned, startled and felt his lips press

352

on mine like seagull wings. And then his excited laugh as he kept on running. I touched my fingers to my mouth. And smiled. Now that was everything and more than what I expected a first kiss to be.

First Girl Friend

by Casimirr Rexregys

"You are going to a party."

Stan spoke then picked up Val's laptop and headed toward the exit gate.

"Yes? Mr. Rexregys," asked the airline attendant, trying to act normal, while Val held the ticket in mid-air staring amazed at Stan.

"Well, yes," Val said with an informative smile, "not this flight, thanks."

"My pleasure, Mr. Rexregys," The attendant replied smoothly.

"Five years since London… how have you been?" Val asked when he caught up with Stan.

Val spoke again, "Now, what's wrong with London?"

"Everything was wrong," Stan said, eyes fixed on Val, "Do you see Sarah around? You didn't even ask."

"Why should I ask?" Val laughed, "Sarah only knew that she was your spokesmodel and what else?"

"Yes," Stan said, "I did not shag her, that's what is wrong with London. Answer your question?"

"Getting laid and London are two different things," Val responded, "If Sarah was not expecting both, that's your fault."

"Respect," Stan said, "and you know why, right?"

"Yes," Val said, "she is related. Hardly your fault."

"She is like a sister," Stan said, "the same blood that goes with the entire lineage."

"Please don't," Val interrupted, "we've discussed this from the first day you wanted me to know, we've been through it all, the opinions of learned men, but it does not go that way. You are you. You don't have any birth defects or syndromes. You didn't inherit any on the way up, and will not give any going down the line either. All this worry is not doing any good, except to make your life miserable… and those who know you. Being an ascetic monk is not helping to improve your chances, either."

"Sarah is history," Stan said, "She got married last week and is expecting in the next few weeks."

"You'll be the Godfather, right?" Val said lightly.

"Yes, Val," Stan answered in a low voice, "she is Roman Catholic, you do remember?"

"Sure. And now," Val said, "what party?"

"Call your chauffeur," Stan said, " the party just started."

"A party, you say," Val grinned and talked to his chauffeur on the cell phone, "Come back to airport and pick us up… where I was."

Stan smiled with a grin.

"Where's the party?" Val looked to Stan.

"The Police Officer Training School, in the Officers' Mess" Stan said, "Chief Inspector Lee."

"Kat," Val had his secretary on the phone, "a regular party hamper to Chief Inspector Lee."

"Yes, Boss," Kat's voice came through the phone.

"The Police Officer Training School, Officers' Mess" Val repeated, and said, "after I have arrived."

"I will arrange this with your chauffeur," Kat said over the phone, "Anything you want me to write on the card, Boss?"

"Just write 'From Stan'," Val answered. "That's all. Thanks Kat."

"Sure, Mr. Rexregys," Kat replied.

Stan regarded Val as the quintessential representative of charity—with a selfless desire to help. This should be a moment of joy, seeing Val at the airport, but Stan would never forget the day they first met at the London National Gallery several years ago. Val and his friend Alex were ribbing Stan's exhibits, and he decided to spy on them, serving them drinks without telling he was the host of the show. Stan sensed they were not small calibers, that they were not carping. Alex was bent on showing off his superiority or good breeding. Stan felt that he made the right decision choosing Val as a friend. Now they'd been friends for years.

Stan imaged how Val would handle such a weird situation, how Val would handle these obnoxious police officers at the party. Stan wondered what Val would think of this Chief Inspector Lee.

"You are not...," Val sounded seriously but broke off.

"Yes," Stan said, "intending to seed one of his sisters."

"But a cop? Chief Inspector Lee?" Val asked. "Why him?"

"Lee was on almost every front page after they smashed that big vice ring before he was demoted to take charge of this officer training school—this will be good for me," Stan said in one breath. "The party we are going to is a Singles Party hosted by Lee and other inspectors... for their single sisters."

"Hey Stan," Val exclaimed, "you are a film producer... you own two of the best restaurants in London... is this time going to be for real?"

"For this girl," Stan said, "yes."

"Why involve me?" Val asked.

"Because I know you," Stan said calmly.

"So?" Val said.

"You are an attraction," Stan said.

Val laughed, "I asked my last girl friend to find a better man. This is wrong, bringing me into it, Stan."

"Do this for me, Val," Stan said, "They will be pleased that I brought you."

"Promise me this," Val spoke sternly, "I will catch the next flight, tomorrow morning."

"Anything you say, Val," Stan said with a grin, "We will talk about that after the party."

Val sighed.

"This could be my first girlfriend," Stan murmured.

At the party...

"Rich or poor, high or low," Chief Inspector Lee was trying to break the ice at the table with debate, "such nonsense inventing differences of opinion, when people can do without all that. Everyone has an angle."

Lee was using his latest studies in sociology to impress Val. Other inspectors at the table remained quiet, as if embarrassed.

"Yes, pretty interesting," Stan said, "But I think I am wanted in the ladies' corner. I'll leave you gentlemen to entertain Val."

From experience, Stan knew Val would always be the focus of attention. Stan himself wanted to be like Val. Val had a refreshing sense of purity; he never knew Sin City, but Stan understood all those rules from the dark world like the back of his hand. Val had no idea how much organized crime had become recognized and respected.

"Sure," Inspector Lee replied, "will do."

"Your father was a prominent man, Val, very wealthy," one of the police inspectors commented. "I'm James, James Harris."

"Thanks, James, yes he was," Val replied.

"I never would dream you are a friend of Stan," Chief Inspector Lee smiled, "We are thrilled to have you with us tonight, Val."

"But you are here because of Stan," spoke an Inspector from the far end of the table.

"And I have your invitation," Val said with a smile, "that's one of the reasons why I am here."

"Yes, right," The man spoke again, "I'm Brian, my pleasure to meet you, Val."

"Brian was in charge of Human Resources, Val," laughed Chief Inspector Lee, "he thinks he still is."

"He was the one who hired that recruiting officer… the one who sent all those piglets here, to keep us busy," spoke the inspector seated next to Brian.

"Let me introduce Mark," Lee said, "the most hated PT instructor on campus."

"PT? Piglets?" Val said.

"Physical Training, " Mark laughed and said, "All freshers are piglets."

"Don't mind the language, Val," Lee said, "All of us were once piglets."

"They have a different title with the Fire Brigade," Val said, "One of my classmates was in charge, on my last visit, he demanded the entire force to perform a formation in the training yard just to demonstrate obedience."

"Yes, the Fire Brigade has more privilege than us," another inspector spoke, "we can only move a patrol."

They laughed.

"Meet Andrew. He was once an Internal Affairs Officer," Lee said. "He was sent here because he sympathizes with the police force."

"Now, I know what Stan meant by 'interesting'," Val said, " I would miss all this vital information if I was with the ladies."

"Stan?" Lee said, "He could never stay more than a minute with us, even when I didn't say a thing."

All the Inspectors laughed intentionally, to encourage the Chief Inspector, and his pride.

"Well, war and peace are just a matter of opinion," Val said. "You mention my father respectfully, and as high ranking police officers, you should be able to say anything, as freely as you prefer, but I made you hesitate. I am glad to know you all, for such respect, and that you accepted me despite your opinion of my father. I am sure we have an understanding and we can enjoy ourselves. Very best to you all, and until the next time we meet…"

The Inspectors at the table nodded their agreement in silence.

"See how thoughtful Stan was," Mrs. Lee approached in her shoulder dress with sequin panels. She walked around the table and said, "spicy soft drinks from Burton-on-Trent, with oatcakes and cheese for you gentlemen. The rest of the hamper, chocolate, is going to entertain the ladies."

"Stan has never done this before," Lee spoke aloud, "time can change a person into someone better."

The other inspectors pondered Stan and then Val.

"You were holding a one way ticket," Stan asked after the party, "You were heading to Canada."

"Yes," Val sighed and continued, "my sister asked me to join her, she thinks Canada suits me better."

"What about your father's business?" Stan asked. "You put in so many years of effort after his death."

"Yes, but it's time for me to go, Stan. My father's money is too big an attraction for everyone—it would make things ugly if I join in for the fight."

"Then the Canadian trip is not a rush," Stan said, "stay for one more day. We have not seen each other for five years; we have so much to talk about, for old time's sake."

"Very well," Val responded, "I suppose so. See you at breakfast?"

"Breakfast it is," Stan smiled.

During breakfast...

"Val," Stan said, "you must come out with me tonight."

"With you?" Val asked, "Where?"

"To a dinner for three," Stan said, "You have to be there—you were invited."

"That girl full of sunshine at the party?"

"Yes," Stan said, "She will not go if you are not going."

"Hey," Val said, "I am not going to get between you and your date? That wouldn't be right."

"If you are not going," Stan spoke, "there will not be any date."

"Are you sure about this woman, Stan?" Val said.

"Yes, I am, Val, but I would feel better if you were there to catch me if I make a mistake."

"You traveled thousands of miles to date this girl, you risk our friendship by involving me," Val said, "I really hope you are right this time."

After dinner…

Stan decided to go back London, to forget this girl who showed more interest in Val. She adorned Val all through dinner. She was not meant to be Stan's first girl friend.

My First Honest Thoughts About Mice

by Jac

I'd never really thought about mice and never needed to search for an exterminator. So, when I did and saw the number of websites, I was positive that today, now, this very moment, many of us have mice in our homes. Prior to the two days before Christmas this year, my only experience was twelve years ago.

Back then, I lived in a two family house converted into four apartments. The landlord roughly finished part of the basement as a laundry room for his student tenants. Our accommodations: unpainted sheetrock, no windows, one light bulb in the ceiling, semi-new washer and dryer, some wooden shelves, cold concrete floor and a beat up old couch.

I'm not complaining, this was luxury compared to going to the Laundromat, but I smiled every time I saw the couch. The room was dim, loud and claustrophobic. An eight by eight by seven room, with a washer and dryer running; was he thinking we would sit and read? Weren't our apartments just steps away? The four of us wished it was an ironing board.

We only used the couch as a table for laundry baskets and folded clothes. I shouldn't say only, because there's an exception. One day three of us ended up there at the same time and started chatting. As I moved my basket to sit, I knocked over a pillow and revealed a thick pile of dust, lint, hair, fur, shredded pieces of upholstery fabric and foam with little black specks scattered about, like grains of black rice.

Let me tell you, when I realized I was looking at a mouse nest, my skin crawled. The specks turned out not to be black rice. It was mouse scat, dropped wherever the creatures felt the urge. Mice are dirty rodents... I could remember folding towels and tee-shirts and laying them over the arm of the couch and the top of that pillow every time I did laundry ...and I was disgusted. My only experience with mice ended, the semester was over and I was moving out.

That experience scrambled out of my memory the day before Christmas Eve. I moved a dish near the sink and saw a grain of black rice. It only took a second or two to understand what it was. My mind started working over-time. I began scanning the counter and floor, imagining five or six of the little animals running around and I was grateful to have shoes on. It wasn't too long before reason returned. I realized that had a mouse been in the kitchen the two dogs and I entering surely scared it away.

I'm not squeamish about mice; I didn't scream and jump on a chair. It's just that I'd rather not have them running across my bare feet. I'm not compulsive about cleanliness either. Growing up with four brothers and living with two dogs proves that messes are inevitable. The history of mouse dirtiness, on the other hand, is almost mythological.

What upsets me about those littler critters is that they're small and stealthy, as are the messes they leave behind. Would you notice mouse scat every time you encountered it? If you're familiar with mouse poop, do you know what mouse urine looks like? Do mice pooh every time they pee? Do you ever plop your bread down on what you think is a clean counter top while getting the plate for your sandwich? GROSS!

I'd much rather deal with the dogs playing keep away with a piece of frozen poop, or bringing me that special turkey carcass from the neighbor's garbage, or my sometimes unsanitary brothers. What I'm trying to say is; I'd have a better opinion of mice if they were the size of dogs or brothers. Then, I'd have a better idea of where they were and where they'd been.

Okay... fifty pound mice in the house... not such a good idea. But, neither are three ounce mice in the house. Just the thought of that stealthy mouse sitting behind my head on the back of the couch, watching me watch TV, all the while leaving me little black presents, was making my skin crawl... again. And, that's when I thought; game on mouse. You've picked the wrong single woman to mess with... you're soon to be history... dead!

Ever try to kill a mouse?

I remember the time a farmer brought produce to the store I managed. As he opened his box truck, he saw a mouse inside. He quickly climbed on the truck, closed the door and for the next thirty minutes I heard his quick steps as he moved around the inside of the truck, his elaborate and imaginative swearing about the damned mouse wasting twelve boxes of leaf lettuce and his unforgettable stomping. When it was over, he opened the door with a proud smile and a rather moist flat mouse by the tail.

This method had no chance of working for me. I needed a different plan.

After calling the landlord, I went to the computer and researched which exterminator to hire. Next, I researched what to do about the one rodent currently running around my kitchen. I found that there are tons of products that catch or kill mice, but it became clear; the best, most humane way was the old-fashioned mousetrap. Then, it was off to the hardware store. I bought a package of three.

Peanut butter, one of the websites explained, is culinary heaven to mice, which made me wonder if I had anything else in common with them. Also, I learned that setting a mousetrap takes patience. Nothing about that in the trap's instructions. I guess the manufacturers don't think it's important.

Ever try to set a trap?

Are you kidding me? My best guess is the hands of surgeons and watchmakers have lost patience trying to set a mousetrap. After being very careful not to snap my fingers and who knows how many tries, it was finally set. Only to have one of my less than surgeon like hands carelessly bang into the trap. The collision startled me but, nothing happened. Still set, the trap sat there a few inches from where it'd been.

It seems these mousetraps can be set to not work unless Bigfoot steps on them, which means that mice can eat the bait worry free. Or so delicately that exhaled breath can make them pop, which makes setting and moving them irritating. Three times in the next one hundred-fifty attempts to set this marvelous invention the jaw snapped and caused my heart to stop. Each time as the trap flipped across the counter I wasn't sure it would restart.

I was learning. Good thing I had nothing really important to do that Friday morning; this was going to take some time. I'll skip over the part where I tell you setting a mouse trap while standing comfortably at the counter is an altogether different talent than setting one while kneeling on the floor near the hole you discovered chewed through three-eighths of an inch of pine molding. It's enough to say, the learning continued.

The mouse that I'm almost sure was watching, listening at a minimum, must've had limited intelligence, because the two dogs who were very interested when this all began, lost interest after experiencing the amount of time and frustration it took me to teach myself the tricks. My dogs would pull a sled over hundreds of miles of snow-covered tundra in a blizzard, just for the opportunity to lick a fingertip covered in peanut butter and they couldn't be bothered with the trap but, no sooner than I had set and placed the third trap, the first snapped and I'd killed a mouse.

Now what do I do?

The scene was horrible. The jaw of death had cleanly snapped the mouse's neck. Actually, it was more like a complete flattening of a very narrow strip of fur, flesh, blood vessels and bone somewhere between its shoulders and head, like a dull guillotine blade might. I probably didn't need to be that graphic, as if I haven't been graphic enough thus far, but for the first time my interactions with mice were becoming more complicated than I'd anticipated.

I'd never watched a mouse living its life, never imagined mouse life. As I said earlier, I never really thought about mice, except as disease carrying rodents whose only place in the grand scheme was as a food source well removed from the chain that sustains me. Now, because it was obviously alive minutes ago, I began to contemplate what its life might be like. Light pondering, nothing that would cost me time from sleep, but I was experiencing a thing that had earlier only been thought... I'd ended a life.

Friday ended uneventfully and Christmas Eve morning I woke up refreshed and ready for anything. Well, almost anything. The dogs and I went for a run, we played some Frisbee in the yard and by about 8:30, I was in my office reading emails. I had completely forgotten about mice and the other two traps I set, when I heard the snap of a trap. One was in the closet with the brooms and the door to the cellar and I placed the other near the hole I discovered in the baseboard behind my desk.

Having a trap slam shut unexpectedly while trying to set it, is one thing. Having one snap that you'd kind of forgotten three feet from your feet, is worse than heart pounding. After jumping straight up, banging my knee on the desk and startling my pups, I looked...

There behind the desk, in the corner, near the hole in the baseboard, sitting half on and half off the trap was a mouse. It looked plump, bigger by half than its dead relative, totally healthy and was staring back at me. How odd that was, I thought... surreal actually. The mouse just sat there; why didn't it run away?

While I was pondering that question the dogs came to investigate and the scene quickly changed. I remember those few seconds being like a Saturday morning cartoon; the mouse jumped and the trap jumped with it. I jumped when the mouse jumped and compounding everything the two dogs were trying to find any possible route to behind the desk for a closer look.

Just... and I mean with the squeals of my two yanked handfuls of their fur... before I was chasing one of them around the house with a live mouse and a mousetrap hanging out of her mouth, I got control and locked them in their crate.

Immediate problem solved... now what to do with an otherwise normal mouse that has its back leg caught in a trap? I picked this kind of trap to avoid this. I'd read that the sticky glue traps sometimes didn't kill the mouse and its only avenue of escape is to chew off its own leg. This wasn't supposed to be happening. I was in tears imagining the unimaginable. I had to do something.

Aside from its cousin the day before and that was different, I'd never killed anything bigger than a fly or a spider and certainly not something like this relatively cute little mammal with huge and beautiful brown eyes. I was frantic, and stunned. It was clear that I had to kill it, but knowing that certainly wasn't going to make it easier.

And, to make the situation more difficult for my emotional self, Ebenezer Scrooge and Jacob Marley came to mind. On my honor, between thoughts of what to do next, that pair was all I could think about. I'm certain it was because I watched Patrick Stewart play Scrooge the night before on TV, but now I felt like the worst kind of Scrooge and that the poor mouse was carrying Marley's chains.

It must have been half an hour I stood there and thought. There was no way I could stomp it like the farmer. And worse, it was amazing to me how many forms of torturous death I was able to contemplate. Just flushing the whole thing down the toilet, like I'd done with the body of the other mouse, wouldn't work because of the trap. My mind didn't carry that thought to conclusion until later when I realized how awful it would be to drown that way. And, only after that thought did it finally dawn on me that there isn't any such thing as a good way to drown. The same goes for suffocating it in a bag or a glass jar or tossing it trap and all to the neighborhood cats.

I know… I couldn't believe these thoughts were occurring to me. It's no defense but, I wanted badly to be detached from the act of killing the mouse. I was kidding myself, there was no way I could kill it. I was having a hard enough time gathering the courage to pick up the trap with a live mouse attached, let alone finding the courage to end its life quickly, humanely, in real-time, with my hands.

If only one of my brothers had been close, I was sure each of them would know and be able to do exactly what was needed. They weren't close and I was paralyzed, unable to do anything.

Finally and only because I knew that doing nothing was the worst kind of torture for the poor mouse, I forced myself to act and put it out of its misery. My plan… With gloved hands, armed with my stainless steel pasta strainer and a small garden spade; I would pick up the mouse with the strainer, keep it from scrambling out with the spade, take it outside the backdoor and with the shovel kill it.

Does anything ever happen as we envision it? Each step was nearly impossible for me.

Through all of its effort to get out of the strainer and through the deafening sound of its little feet scratching the mesh, I was able to get it out the backdoor and on the ground. It just sat there looking at me, same as it had in the house.

I thought about it… maybe too much. I knew I had to hit it hard and didn't think I could. I'm ashamed to say, I almost just left it there. Contemplating that cruelty helped me muster my courage. I wound up and swung down with all the weight of the tool, only to watch helplessly as the mouse jumped at the last fraction of a second. It moved just enough to have the force of the blow land on the trap, not its head. The shock severed the trapped foot and the mouse jumped away out of sight.

The intent was definitely there but, I'm thankful I didn't kill the mouse. At first, considering the alternative, I thought the mouse was lucky. I've had time to think about it in more detail and it wasn't lucky. The mouse took survival to a level I'd never understood and did it with grace. I don't wish to face life or death any time soon, but I hope that if I'm ever in a similar situation I can deport myself as gracefully.

This ordeal started with me as the proud wannabe huntress annoyed at these small mammals for ruining my day. By the end, I was the inept huntress, guilty of torturing and maiming a critter that was, same as me, only trying to get through the day.

As I ponder it, I feel just as and probably more trapped and handicapped by instinct, over confidence and lack of thought as any seemingly unintelligent mouse. Though, I don't plan on sharing my peanut butter sandwiches with the resident mice, I can't believe how much I learned from that Christmas Eve mouse.

The First Church

by Gaboo

To find the first church, you must destroy all the beasts and insects that are a nuisance, or annoying, or dangerous. To ensure these life forms do not return, salt and pave the earth. Build walls and fences. When you are satisfied that you have disposed of all this competing life, then kill all the plants. Use saws and shovels, and combinations of chemicals to eradicate any flora. When you are satisfied that you have eliminated all these beings, then begin to build.

As you build, surround yourself with things. Make your own tools and use nothing without burning it, hammering it, or cutting it first. Build high and wide. Break the earth open and spill the waters. Adorn your buildings with lights and jewels. These are prizes of your work.

Begin to see yourself as a god. Walk upon the earth as a ruler. Control all. Decide who lives and who dies. Decide who is good and who is bad. Judge all things and judge yourself to be good.

Enter the tallest, largest building which you have made. This is the sanctum. Within, find isolation amid your creation. Find satisfaction in your ability to attain and control. Find solace in your ability to kill all that might intrude upon your creation. Call yourself a god.

Next, seek the quietest, most secluded space within this building. Enter into this space. Kneel before a statue which you have made of yourself and listen. When you realize that all you have done was for nothing, ask for forgiveness. You have found the first church.

First Fear of Death

by B G Lewis

I remember a lonely night in the bottom bunk, age five, I think. My younger brother was asleep and oblivious to my turmoil. A stone turned in my mind and I realized then that my parents, my beloved mother and father, would one day die. I could not envision them getting old and gray, or lying still. I just knew that they would leave us and enter into dark and nothingness. The fear gripped me and I called out. My mother attended.

I explained my fear, that she would die. The woes of her young child must have blindsided her, because she was unprepared for such philosophies.

"You don't have to worry about that. I won't die until I've lived a long time and then death doesn't seem so scary."

Her ambiguity soothed me. Her words, led or not, sufficed and the anxiety faded. Play returned, as my vocation.

I also remember the time I lost my fear of death, when the lie was proven. The whisper came and said, "turn, look." I did and the smile I found was timeless.

First Crack in a Marriage

by Adrienne S Moody

A woman knows when her lover is interested in someone else. Kyra didn't worry too much about the sexy neighbor living next door. In the beginning. Even her penchant for mowing the lawn in heels, short shorts and halter tops that barely covered her ampleness. Her husband of three years merely averted his eyes from the scantily clad blonde smiling and waving in their direction as they parked their vehicle. She did notice that the woman, Myrna, seemed to spend a lot of time sitting on her front step whenever her husband Jacob did his yard work. Still, she was wary of this siren, but not worried.

It was the end of October and in the middle of a glorious Indian Summer when Jacob decided to wash their car while the sun still held some heat. Kyra had the windows open and could hear the sound of the water on the car, the music playing on the car stereo. She glimpsed Lynn smoking on the porch wearing her usual uniform: short shorts, heels and plunging top. The scene changed suddenly and just when Kyra walked past the open front door. She saw Lynn running up to Jacob and attempt to grab the hose from his hands.

"Don't embarrass me, Lynn…" she heard her husband mutter to the giggling woman.

It wasn't what he said, so much, but how he said it. Like he knew her intimately. It was like lightning struck Kyra. She turned away from the door and felt the blood leave her face and she felt faint. Her heart pounded fiercely in her chest. She felt ill. She no longer felt safe there, in the tiny wartime home, with her husband whom she knew everything about. There were no secrets. But were there? How could she possibly know everything?

She heard Lynn ask him to come over for a beer and he agreed. The situation was growing more and more dangerous for Kyra. She was asked by Jacob to come along. She disagreed and sat in the house listening to the music pouring out of the windows next door. And the laughter. There was another woman there, Lynn's friend. He returned home in an hour or so and they never spoke of it. But the sense of betrayal that Kyra felt was like a crack tearing at the very foundation of her life, her marriage, her relationship. She had nothing but this, him and this life so recently constructed.

A couple months passed and there was a distinct change between the couple, but nothing anyone could really point out and say, 'this is what is different here.' Their usual gentle playfulness was gone. She recoiled when he tried to tickle her into humor. He soon stopped. She found fault in most everything he did, even the way he shifted their five speed Camaro. Winter arrived bringing the typical prairie bitter cold. They had taken to playing Bingo at the community centre.

They were the only 20 somethings there. They went every Sunday and sat amongst the chain-smoking senior ladies with thinning blue hair. They giggled afterwards at the seriousness of the senior crowd and the women with their arthritic knuckled hands showcasing what appeared to be Shopping Channel special rings. Boiled hot dogs in soft white buns were on the menu along with stale black coffee in Styrofoam cups. Kyra was on a winning streak and her winnings in a month topped over a thousand dollars. They looked forward to picking their cards and settling in side by side, nudging each other from time to time, "What number was that?" But both of them were aware of the change and they knew not what to do about it. They picked their cards in silence.

Kyra decided she wanted to go home for a weekend and thought she'd leave Jacob on his own and if he wanted an opportunity to be alone with the blonde next door, then fine, she'd give it to him. He didn't put up any argument about her going, but mentioned that the fuel gauge wasn't working and maybe they ought to get it fixed before she went out solo on the three hour highway drive. Kyra insisted there wasn't time, but decided to bring her lassie dog, Doug, with her for protection and company.

Her marriage didn't feel like home and she thought going to her parents' place would give her that feeling of security and comfort she was missing. They were worried about her making the trip alone but happy she was coming for a visit. Kyra packed up the vehicle and gave Jacob a squeeze around the neck and waved goodbye. Did she see Lynn in the side bedroom window watching her leave? She couldn't be sure. She pulled away from the curb and couldn't help herself watching in her rear-view mirror, until she turned the corner and then she heaved a huge sigh.

Halfway there her car suddenly sputtered to a stop. There they were, on a two lane divided highway, deserted due to the wicked weather. It was now a blizzard and visibility wasn't great. Desolate. The wind picked up particles of snow and created little whirlwinds. Fear. Having grown up in the North, she knew immediately what to do. No hesitation. Being a prairie girl they were taught young that if ever you are out in this kind of deadly element – move! Often she and her friends were in the position walking home without proper dress and had their feet, hands or facial features freeze. They knew of people who became very tired and would just lay down and go to sleep and freeze to death.

She bundled up in her warm jacket, scarf around her face, mitts on. She and her dog left the vehicle and stood at the edge of the highway waiting for a vehicle to pass. Ten long frightening minutes ticked by. The wind swirled white around them. Headlights. She waved her arms frantically. To her amazement it was a tow truck. Two guys sat in it and called out to her. In no time they hooked up the vehicle and one of them sat in the car with her dog as there wasn't any room in the tow truck for all of them.

The guys were drinking beer. She was very leery of both of them. They were rough looking and she was afraid, but more afraid of being left at the side of the road and meeting an icy death. She drank two bottles of beer to take the edge off and it did. Also, she felt this urge to be buddy buddy with these men. She chatted about how her family punctuated that they knew where she was and would be very worried, maybe sending the police looking for her. She knew it was important to say this and let them know that she was a woman alone, but with strong connections.

She kept turning around in her seat looking for her car. She couldn't see it. It was really dark but still...it didn't appear to be there. She told the driver. He shrugged it off ... nah it's there you just can't see it in the dark. She insisted. Finally he pulled over. Sure enough the connection broke and the car was in the ditch somewhere. They circled back but couldn't find it. Now he was low on gas. He decided they would carry on and his buddy would get hold of him the next day and don't worry about it. It'll all work out.

Her dog! Her car! She had to go to the bathroom. Bad! She told the scruffy driver he had to pull over as she could not wait until they arrived in the city. She didn't care for his smile as he pulled over to the snowy shoulder; Kyra bounded down the snowy ditch and relieved herself. What a predicament! She was tense and distrustful of the guy. They were still a good hour away from the city, her parents, her safety.

She kept up with this mindless chatter: "We're buds! You're like my brother. You're such a good guy!" She praised him, "My brothers will really be happy you found me and saved me and my dog!"

Finally she recognized the lights of her hometown city in the distance. She began to breathe easier. She called her family from a pay phone and agreed to meet them at a hotel on the outskirts of the city. When Kyra saw them looking bewildered but like home, she ran to them, embraced her mother, and broke into sobs. Her mother pulled away and looked at her grown daughter in disapproval "What brought this on?" she asked. Her set features and and narrow eyes told Kyra all she needed to know. Her mother thought she was acting inappropriately and as usual, over-reacting. The tow truck driver gave them his number and told them he was sure his buddy found his way into the city and they could contact him the following day and figure out how to get the dog to her.

Kyra let her mother's arms go and walked beside her outside towards their car. She wanted to tell them of her fear of the men who picked her up and how she handled it, but they'd already gotten into a discussion about how to pick up the car and her dog the following day. She wanted to tell them that she feared her marriage was in trouble and felt like she had nowhere to go. Kyra looked out into the dark winter sky and knew it was a mistake to come home.

It wasn't safe here either.

First Man

by M Dawn Thacker

At seventeen, I picked the man I would marry. He met my criteria:

1.   He was my height. At six feet, we saw eye to eye. I hadn't known too many boys in my life who came close to that.

2.   He had beautiful legs. I'd never seen a man with more beautiful legs in my life. Watching his calf muscles from behind made me turn all shades of red.

3.   He could drive in the snow. I'd watched him play on the hill leading to my house, car window down, grinning at me with his arm resting nonchalantly out the door. He mashed on the gas and the car pulled sideways up the hill under his direction. He was having fun in conditions that terrified me.

4.   He wasn't a talker. He was a doer. He fixed things: cars, trucks, and bulldozers, cut and split wood, built fences and caught and cooked fish over an open fire. When he did talk and said he was going to do something, he did it.

5. He had a car, and a truck. The truck was a 1976 Ford pickup with a camper shell. He hunted, and knew all the places to hide that truck, especially after dark. He also knew all the right moves.

Yep, at seventeen I picked my man. My first, and my last.

First Time I Saw Her
by Trularin

An excerpt from A Window Box of Roses

There is a moment in any person's life when the sight of someone or something becomes captivating. For those who think they are at the moment, they stare and either catch the eye of that person or get run over in a street – makes no difference, they are captivated.

Cheryl stood for several minutes at the first sight of Phyllis. Her flowing auburn hair, her shapely figure and tight jeans drew Cheryl to stare. She had never seen such a woman.

People walked past, maneuvering around her as she stood captivated. A sudden quiver in her abdomen followed and should it have not been for traffic, she might have had gone over to Phyllis and said something.

She was suddenly interrupted by people passing, their looks and bumping jarred her from the trance. She had never felt this way. Her husband had satisfied her; he knew all the right things to do to give her those feels, but she had never had them simply from looking at someone.

The worry and conflict of discovery quickly followed and Cheryl began to check herself mentally. She looked up again at Phyllis. It took a moment, but there was no mistaken the sensation, she was captivated by the sight of Phyllis.

She stood and stared again. Minutes passed and without a further thought, Cheryl walked to the cart that Phylis was working around.

There was an overwhelming desire to immediately reach out and kiss her. Cheryl could not believe what she was experiencing – a desire to be with another woman. Yet, in her mind the conflict was not that Phyllis was a she, but whether she would be able to kiss Phyllis.

Strong was the urge and her body language overflowed with expression. Cheryl began a conversation as her gaze swam in Phyllis' eyes of cool blue. She asked a few questions, testing the water, to see if there was a possibility. Cheryl was in uncharted territory; she knew not what to ask, only that she felt tingling as Phyllis took her arm to show her something.

There is always a first time.

First Time For Real

by B G Lewis

It had to be our seventh year, which is typical. We'd been at odds for months, and compatibility was at best, strained. I was not who I wanted to be and she was not who I wanted her to be. We were in a lie with all the blame and wasted time. I think we both pushed away too hard.

Despite the fog of inexperience, something was cracking, through the hard exterior, the fact that we were individuals was breaking. There was a force greater than the two of us, and it dropped and shuffled like little magnets in between us. Melancholy to stay. Wasteland to leave. We were caught in relationship purgatory, and neither mature enough to give in willingly.

But we did give in. I couldn't live without her; she pined for our love, to be what it could. I was better off to stay, she was better off to try. Like how I imagined her before we met, did I tell you that? I used to have these fantasies where I was welcoming her into my world, letting her in my head, showing her what was important to me, revealing. And then I met her, though I didn't recognize her until much later. She was that vision in my mind.

Still misery does come, and I remember her eyes, all red and soured with heartbreak, pleading for some kind of halfway. She looked at me, the anguished one, torn between duty and our bond. We would collide together or wither apart. So we fell together.

Letting go is easy when you collapse in a heap. Tears and slobber, strands of hair and clutching hands, when you can't get close enough, can't hold tight enough. And there was that dream about her—I remember her standing on porch, walking out of a country cabin, her arms laden with plates for family and friends. She was smiling, greeting her guests who loved her, adored her, beckoning her from tables on the lawn. She was entertaining. I walked up the steps and her smile widened. She looked right into me, and I knew that she recognized a deep and soothing love in her life. She was old and gray, wrinkled and frumpy, but I loved her more. I loved her because I knew we'd journeyed so far and we'd seen what needed together. In the dream, I think I was dead.

And in waking, she became part of me, still young and the future ahead, and I became part of her. For hours we bathed in each other's presence, the intimate coil, swaying. No her or me, just the shared entwine as one. So it is real, two versus the world and the bond ever ours to grow, to nurture every day, every way.

There is a lake in heaven, and for the willing, we enter and touch love.

First Time Alone

by Casimirr Rexregys

"You've never been to an art studio before?" Celine asked, "It's my dad's pride."

"Every time when we came this far," Val said as the chauffeur cast a quick look in the rear view mirror, "this is the only shop that attracted our attention."

"Your brother said the same thing," Celine added, "the day we first met."

Ken, the resident chauffeur, was aware Arthur stalked Celine almost every day for weeks, before arranging to bump into her 'accidentally'. Ken couldn't forget how Arthur's entourage, Karma and Wallace, made a plan in this very same car. Ken didn't like Arthur's friends and he told Val when Arthur was away in London.

"A cup of tea?" Celine asked. "Dad and mom shouldn't be back for another hour."

"I don't mind meeting your parents," Val responded, "would be nice to meet them in person."

"Another day, maybe," Celine said. "I need time with you in private."

"Very well, Celine," Val replied and then looked to his driver, "Ken…"

"Five hours from now? Master Val," Ken answered softly, "Maryann's place?"

"Yes, Ken, thanks."

"You take me home because of Maryann?" Celine complained, "I should have known."

Stepping into the small photography studio...

"It is like one of my sisters' doll houses," Val spoke, "and the color is comforting."

"Father is an artist, he paints and sculpts," Celine pointed to several works, "and Mother is a professional choreographer."

"They make a perfect pair, and you?"

"I am working for your father, a junior secretary," Celine announced, "you know Arthur and I went to the same school, don't you?"

"Yes, you were one of the prettiest girls," Val said, "you still are, if I may say so?"

"Thanks, Val," Celine laughed, "yes, you may."

In the living room at the back of the studio...

"I have not heard from Arthur," Celine wondered aloud.

"Other than that," Val relaxed, "do you have other worries?"

"Yes, I have," Celine said, "my parents, they are getting old."

"Your parents are artists. They sent you to an exclusive school," Val paused, then added, "so they have rich parents."

"That is exactly the problem, " Celine told him, "they don't."

"And you understand what it's like to be wealthy and spoiled," Val said. "You should."

"Yes," Celine said, "I should."

"You did not answer my question, Celine," Val said.

"I am not attracted to your father's money, if that is the question" Celine smiled defiantly, "I used to think money is evil. Am I wrong, Val?"

"I am taught to think nothing is evil," Val answered, "No, that is not what I was asking, Celine."

"Then!" Celine smiled with an expression intending she wanted to kiss, "What was the question? You are a very attractive person, Val, I can hear nothing wrong."

"You should understand Arthur before you bring your parents into this," Val sat back with a smile, "That is the answer to my question."

"I cannot stop my parents from peeping at that lovely car," Celine said, "They were flabbergasted at first sight."

"You work for my father," Val looked at her, "and your parents agreed?

"Yes," Celine said, "but if Arthur…"

Val interrupted, "I know Arthur less than anyone else, the same as he knows me."

"You're a spoiled kid?" Celine asked.

"I am," Val said, "that was why they kicked me out of school."

"But you are very well educated," Celine said, "unlike Arthur."

"That was the last school. I got smarter." Val continued, "Father hired all the best tutors when he saw I was willing."

"I am sure you are good," Celine purred, "You are the dream man for all the ladies in your father's empire, they admire both your talent and your charisma."

"One of those ladies made my father very angry," Val said, "I did not realize."

"Yes," Celine said, "I cannot see that passion between Arthur and I, my parents would be shocked to know."

"Shocked to know what? Celine," Val made a gesture of dismay.

"Arthur is not going out with me," Celine said, "they thought…"

"Did Arthur come to your parents and ask for their daughter?"

"No, Arthur never did ask," answered Celine. "He never met my parents."

"My father treated you like one of his daughters." Val sounded like he was interrogating, "and that makes your parents think you are going out with Arthur."

"I was going out with Arthur," Celine retorted, "I spent more time with Arthur than with my parents. Every day after work, I went to your father's house and stayed until late. It was like my second home."

"Did you go out with anyone before Arthur?" Val asked.

"Nope," Celine just shrugged, reclining on the couch.

"I see," Val smiled and continued, "that is why you are so important to my father."

"Did I sleep with anyone? Is what you want to know?" Celine sank further into the couch and grinned, "No, not even with Arthur, if you want to be sure."

"You parents would understand," Val offered, "they know what love is, and they know how to keep things in order."

"Thanks, Val, those are wise words."

"I will be in London early next week, staying with Arthur for a while, before I go off to the States."

"Actually," Celine said, "you don't have to go to London, right?"

"Father asked me," Val answered, "a change of plans."

"I am your concern," Celine smiled, "that makes me feel better."

"By all means," Val said, "you deserve every concern, you deserve the best."

"Maryann should be proud," Celine said, "she has your heart."

"The one who can keep yours," Val grinned, "will hear music even when there is silence."

"Yes," Celine said, "I will hear music when you are gone, even in a year without summer. A woman falls in love through her ears."

In the car...

"Celine is not some expensive toy... to your brother," Ken said.

"You think the worst, Ken" Val responded, "You know Arthur more than I."

"Arthur is not a bad person," Ken continued, "he is confused."

"I am a stranger to my own family," Val looked out the window, "I need to catch up for all those years."

"Yes and no, Master Val," Ken advised, "there is nothing you can do about the past. Some things can never be mended, not in your father's life time."

"Yes for stranger," Val asked, "and no, not to try?"

"Correct," Ken answered, "Master Arthur had a serious crush on one of the house staff while you were away, and Celine was his substitute of choice. But I wonder if he could forget that maid, the affair went on for years and then she was fired. Until now, she has been trying to keep in contact."

"My parents knew about this?"

"Only your mother and your aunt," Ken said, "everything is covered up perfectly. Maybe your father knew a few details."

"What details?" Val asked.

"The maid carried a baby," Ken announced, "She refused to speak of the father."

At Maryann's place...

"Your mother is beautiful," Val commented, looking at a photo.

"Because she is French," Maryann asked, "or because she is my mother?"

"Because she is your mother," Val pulled Maryann closer and said.

"I will not see you again," Maryann kissed Val and said, "if you go to London."

"Write me," Val said, "I have to."

"I will not write you," Maryann said and tears in her eyes, "don't ever think I will."

On the plane...

"Welcome aboard, Mr. Rexregys," greeted the attendant.

"Yes," Val smiled, tired, and said, "In my cabin?"

"Yes sir," She replied, "I will."

Inside the first class cabin...

"Not with the ground crew, Sophie?" Val asked, smiling.

"I lost a few pounds, so they let me on here," Sophie pulled down the sliding door and leaned over to give Val a friendly peck, "and because you are alone on this flight."

First Spat

by Gaboo

"So you want to crawl around in this city? Figure how it ticks? Forget it. Most don't know squat except for hand to mouth. Even the planners. How much time do you want to put in this zoo, anyway?"

"Long enough to get what I need." Max wraps her knuckles to her forehead like she's trying to remember. I think she's been doing that a lot. Or she has weird headaches that she's not talking about.

She's still rubbing her head as the hem on her frayed sweater sleeve tangles in her sunglasses. Here we are again, hurry and wait. Max is a hyper-chondriat, you see, always running into things, with bumps and fractures everywhere, and then she complains about it. Boating? Never again. She's a real shark, finely tuned to her environment. Ha.

"Well, I flipped the page, Max (I'm letting her know what my intentions are) It's not getting any better. I'm just stringing you and everybody else along, wasting hours until I can make a move, make the jump."

"Jump where?" Max is pulling yarn in a triangle from her frames to her wrist.

"Take your glasses off—I want to go somewhere different. (I'm the one who's usually good at being reassuring) Don't worry, you'll wind up with the right person. It'll work out. How long have we known each other? Being inseparable is just a big cliche anyway— bumper cars, that's what we are. And we've been on the same circuit a long time, one big, happy carnival. You crash into someone and they're never gonna be the same—right? We got dents, Maxine. How many times did I bump you around?"

"Millions." Max gives up and starts over. She sets her glasses on the dash and begins looping the snagged sleeve, trying to look attentive. She always avoids squinting to prevent crow's feet. There's these evergreen eyes flashing between blinks.

"And how many times did you bump me around? (She won't answer that one.) Don't bother counting, it was lots."

Then I catch this look at her, and she's different, legitimately concerned, like she's not supposed to be here.

"Hey, you're alright," I tell her.

"Please don't coach me, not today."

"Okay, you're a mess. The ability to not get noticed makes you a good observer," I say.

"Thanks, you're a real sight for yourself." She is ornery.

"I was just trying to be funny. I worry about you," I say.

"It's a little chilly today, and if we have to go running… Reid, just let me fix this."

"You are oddly extraordinary (I have to be honest with her) or extraordinarily odd. You appear hard-assed, but I think you are just determined—"

Was that a laugh?

"I don't have time," she mutters. She doesn't have time. Sure. Max is yanking her stupid wool, a feeble attempt to snap it. Then the sleeve cinches. Three feet of fuzz comes flying off in her hand.

"Oh, my."

I admire her subtle restraint. She's good at that, standing blissfully headlong. What do I do when she is flailing around? I grimace, "That's not the way."

"That's not the way to what, Reid? Can't you see what I'm doing?"

I don't mind a snotty attitude, but when somebody brings it… "Eventually, Max, you're gonna make me wanna square breathe, you know that?"

And then she stops, looks right at me, and I think she's listening to herself pronounce. This is good, finally a sign of compassion. She looks directly at me and says, "Reid, I am sorry. I am not myself today. I don't feel well, and I don't really know how to keep up with you agonizing about leaving. Please forgive me."

It can be really hard to figure out if she's being patronizing or not.

"C'mere, you clumsy, little brain."

I fake her out like I'm gonna rub her head. Then show the appropriate level of concern… "I think I want to take you to lunch on a patio. Not today, but soon. Just me and you, no work, no yakking. You can just sit there with your mind off and feel the sunshine."

"That would be nice. I appreciate that."

I can almost see her little walnut heart get jiggly.

"Anything for a buddy," I say.

Well? She is.

"We're close friends," she says—nice, I'm in Max's books.

"And partners."

"Check."

Discussion settled. We're rolling. I put on my best cheerful face, "Can we go bust this creep?"

"We're on it," she smiles.

I always drive.

Siren and fade.

First Lover

by Adrienne S Moody

I had every intention to hold off until I met the man I would marry. That is until my brother and I sat together on top the Grotto behind the Catholic Church and he revealed to me that his girlfriend of five years put out completely when she was just a babe of 14 years.

"You're joking? Melissa? You and Melissa did it? And she puts on to be such a little angel. Is this why you hooked up that electric current to your doorknob?"

He nodded.

"Kept you out, didn't it? If you tell anyone, Adrienne, I'll kill you," he threatened. "Shhh!"

He pointed down below where a lone priest walked looking ghostly in the moonlight.

"She put out? She isn't a virgin, then?" I whispered.

"No. No she's not. So what. And like I warned you A, if you tell anyone I won't hesitate to kill you and you know I will. I convinced her to go along telling her no one would ever know."

I changed my mind about the value of virginity that night. If Melissa gave it away then maybe a little experimenting before marriage wasn't such a big sin after all. The following day my best friend and I took a train out to her family home on the coast. She came back to her home town to pick me up and off we went on this perceived big adventure. And it was, for me, not having ever been away from my family for any length of time.

Freedom. It was the 70's, the tail end of the era of free love, drugs and rock and roll.

Rob was the first young man I met and went steady with. He had long red hair and beard and wore these wire framed eye glasses. He was tall and thin, kind of looked like an anorexic Santa Claus. I still remember his belly laugh. And his kisses. He brought me to his home for a family dinner and his parents looked disapprovingly at me. My hair was long, straight and parted in the middle. I wore a micro-mini skirt and not at all the kind of girl they'd hoped for their only son. I was told afterwards that I shouldn't eat one item at a time off the dinner plate. I had never heard of such a rule. I would eat all the potatoes, then the meat and pick at the vegetables. Rob's family seemed to have rules for everything. Their home looked like no one ever really lived in it. Everything neat and tidy and sterile. There was no music and everyone talked in low monotone voices. I heard disapproval whispered in every corner of that home.

He brought me to this new sub-division and took my hand. I followed him up the stairs of this one home with only the framing done. I remember the smell of fresh cut lumber. We stood at an open doorway and he held his hand out and said that this is what he wanted. He looked questioningly at me. I pretended I didn't know what he meant. I was afraid of his certainty. I felt life with him would be like his parents with rules I would never get the grasp of.

Then I met Kevin. He was as injured an individual as I was. I somehow knew he would never cheat on me and that he would always treat me like I was special. I don't know why I thought that and it certainly didn't turn out to be true. But, it was with him that I lost my virginity.

We were in a tent at the beach and it was so incredibly hot in there. The temperature soared to close to 100 degrees Fahrenheit that day and the night cooled only a few degrees. It was like a sweat lodge.

He was very considerate and very careful, using two condoms. It was over almost as soon as it started.

I remember sitting up afterwards bewildered that such an insignificant experience inspired the most beautiful poetry and music! What was I missing?

One thing that this experience did cause me to do, was feel committed to this man. We ending up marrying and I guess as hard as I tried to shrug off my upbringing, I felt compelled to walk down the aisle with him.

Of course the letter that arrived soon after this sexual experience, from my father threatening to disown me if I didn't marry Kevin, kind of influenced me. I believe the letter started out something like, 'No daughter of mine is going to shack up...' Yes, definitely influenced me.

That First Step

by M Dawn Thacker

I light the last cigarette and step back from the group. My stomach rolls, my head aches already and I feel myself slipping to that dark place. The nursing home patio is usually bright. Five times a day, a handful of old folks gather in this place for their cigarette break. Today, my charge is to monitor them, to make sure they don't catch fire. That means I keep the lighter. For the most part, I love my summer job; but I hate this task. I watch the curls of gray smoke form a cloud under the porch roof. Folding my arms over my chest as it tightens, I fight the shadows. I wonder if given enough breath, I could blow all the smoke, and the memories attached to it, away. Would the feelings disappear? Could I be normal?

Teresa waves her arm and captures my attention. She's stuck. I know how it happened. She went out earlier to bathe her arthritic shoulders in the morning sun and time slipped away. The smokers storm the door at eleven o'clock and Teresa got caught on the wrong side of their exhaust.

I cross the divide to help her.

"Thank you for rescuing me," she says. "I need to get away from those cigarettes. I can't stand the smell of it."

"I don't like it either," I say as much to myself as I do to Teresa. "It makes me sick to my stomach—always has." I maneuver the old woman's wheelchair to the edge of the path and open the patio door to take her inside.

"You OK now?" I ask.

"Sure, thank you honey," she says.

"I have to get back out there," I tell her, opening the door to face my nemesis again.

I collect the cigarette packs and lock them in the metal box used for storage, then help the elders back into the building, but I notice Teresa is still where I left her. She's staring out the window transfixed.

"Are you alright?" I ask.

Teresa shakes her head like she's clearing cobwebs and shivers. "My father smoked," she says. "The stench of it always reminds me of him."

I look down at the top of Teresa's head as she sits in the wheelchair. I imagine myself where she is in sixty years. "My father smoked too," I lower my voice.

"What's that honey? I didn't catch it," she says.

"Never mind," I say, "It's not important. Can you make it back to your room alright, or do you need me to help you?"

"If you can spare the time, I'd love a little help," Teresa says. "These shoulders of mine are hurting something terrible. Feels like I've been carrying a load on them bigger than I am."

I have several phone messages to return and an exercise class to lead, but I wheel the old woman down the hall to her room. Teresa's door is around the corner, the second on the right. She invites me in. Her room is cozy with family photos decorating the walls, and a handmade quilt on her bed. Her little table top is crowded with powders, lipsticks, lotions, perfumes and a hand mirror. I catch a whiff of White Shoulders, the perfume my grandma used to wear. It comforts me. Teresa's surroundings don't shout 'nursing home' like so many other rooms do.

"My absentee ballot came in the mail today," Teresa says, pointing to the envelope on her dresser. "Do you have time to help me with it?"

"Sure," I say.

Simple chores are hard for Teresa. She was born right handed but has to use her left due to the stroke. In the time it took the clot to travel to her brain, the once fiercely independent woman was reduced to what she says, is half her former self. Her entire right side is useless. She's a survivor though. She can rip open little pink packets of artificial sweetener with her teeth, pull her wheelchair along the hallway rail using one good hand, and applies her makeup meticulously, adjusting her lipstick to hide the side of her mouth that droops. Teresa tells stories of her stubborn determination, and how she was a 'Mama Bear' when it came to protecting her children.

I tear open the envelope from the Office of Voter Registration. There are papers and instructions. I read them to Teresa and hand her the ballot.

"I've been a Democrat since I got married. Democrats look out for the little people. Jeffrey taught me that." Teresa said. "Just point out the Democrat and I'll check it off."

I locate the candidate of choice, point his name out to her, then turn my attention to Teresa's family photographs on the bedside table.

I lift one of the pictures carefully and stare at the people smiling back at me. They look so happy.

"That's Shelby, my daughter," Teresa says pointing to the one I'm holding. "You've met her, and that's her husband, Frank, standing beside her. He's a nice boy. I liked him from the beginning. Those beauties in that white frame are their girls. The oldest is a senior in college. The boy on the wall over there is my son, Jeffrey. He was named for my husband. He teaches school. My husband's picture is right there beside the bed." Teresa's eyes mist. "I was married to that man for fifty-six years. Couldn't have found any better," she says, her voice catching.

I pick up the picture of Jeffrey and touch his face with a finger. "He was handsome," I say.

"Yep, he sure was," Teresa says smiling. "Better yet, he was a kind man, the kindest I ever met. You got any prospects? How old are you now child?"

Before this summer job, I volunteered at the nursing home starting in seventh grade. "I'm sixteen," I say. "I don't have a boyfriend."

"You've got all the time in the world," Teresa says. "Be picky, though." Her brow furrows. "When you choose a man, you're picking a father for your children. Remember that. Children need a decent father."

"Yes they do," I say.

Teresa gets that far away look on her face again. She stares off into her past. "My father and step-mother taught me what a family shouldn't be," Teresa says. "Long before I ever got married, I made up my mind what I wanted in a family, and it wouldn't be what I grew up in."

I look up from the picture of Jeffrey. Teresa's tone startles me. I'm not used to hearing anger in her voice. I'm not used to hearing elders speak about their parents with anything less than reverence.

"Don't look at me like that. It's the truth," she chastises.

"N-no," I stammer. "I didn't think you were lying. It's just that I've never seen you angry before."

Teresa's face softens. She smiles at me. "Oh, I can spew it, honey. For a long time I buried it so deep, no one saw it. I've learned to let it out over the years though. Can't hide it or sugar coat it. Bottling that poison up only makes you bitter. Anyway, that man you're holding in your hands right there helped me through it."

"It sounds like you lucked out," I say, my eyes going back to the picture of Jeffrey. "Your husband really loved you."

Teresa smiles, and reaches out to squeeze my hand. "One part luck, maybe, but nine parts careful honey. I first met him at a dance in Midford County," she says. "My friend Stella pointed him out to me. 'Tessa,' she said, 'he's the best looking thing out there tonight.' "

"He was good looking." I say.

"At that time I didn't think any man was good looking," Teresa says. "And from a distance, he looked rough. His blue pants were two inches too short. He wore a green shirt, black socks, and brown shoes. I wondered if he was color blind or dressed in the dark. Thought maybe his mama was color blind too. Why would she let him out of the house looking like that? His hair hung over his collar too."

I laugh. "Something made you change your mind," I say.

"It's good to hear you laugh child. I seldom see you smile. You remind me of myself when I was your age. I wanted to hide, wore my clothes too big, didn't wear makeup."

I look down at my long denim jumper. I touch my naked face.

"I was shy too," Teresa says. "I didn't think I was pretty enough to be at that dance, didn't really even want to be there. Stella pushed me to go. 'Come on Tessa,' she wheedled, 'just this once. You'll see how fun it is.'

I listen to Teresa's story.

"I stood off in the corner drinking punch while Stella had all the fun. She danced and laughed with all the boys. I was miserable."

"I don't like crowds either," I say.

"Then Jeffrey came by to get a cup of punch. He was shy too, stood there with his head down, staring into that cup. I'd peek over at him and when he looked up, I'd glance away. He did the same thing, until we both giggled. He finally got the courage to say hello."

"You were alike," I say.

"We were. He said he wasn't much of a dancer either. We stood there talking for a while, until Stella and Jeffrey's friend came to the punch bowl, all out of breath from dancing. We all took a table together. Jeffrey and I talked and talked. We met at the dance hall every Saturday night for a month after that. Never did dance, but got to know each other better," she remembers.

I'm listening to Teresa, but I'm thinking of the activities at my school. I've never been to a dance, never been on a date. I go to school, make good grades, and have a few girlfriends; we eat lunch together. And I work with old people. I lock myself in my room at night. My cat, Crenshaw, is the only male interested in me. I'm not interested in any male other than him either.

"Then you got married," I say.

Teresa puts her hand up like a traffic cop to stop me. "Oh no, not that fast. I put Jeffrey through his paces, didn't let him too close. He was persistent though, wouldn't stay away. He didn't push too hard, but he didn't let me too far out of his sight."

"So he pursued you?"

"Yep, he showed up at the dances, found his way to the movies Stella and I went to see, and turned up at the pencil factory where I worked to walk me home. My father didn't like him. That's what made my mind up about Jeffrey."

Teresa's mouth sets in a straight line that droops on the right side from the stroke. Her eyebrows come together again. Her left hand becomes a fist, and she says, "He wasn't a thing like my father. That was the meanest, hatefulest man there ever was."

"He was?" I ask.

Teresa's jaw clenches. A muscle twitches in her cheek. "I hope he's burning in hell," she spits. "God might not like me saying it, but I hope he burns over and over again. Even that's too good for him."

I've never heard Teresa talk like this. In a group of nursing home residents, she's the upbeat one, finds the good in those around her and in most every situation. She laughs at her own mistakes and forgives easily. I watch her anger grow, and her emotions overtake her. I pull a chair from across the room and sit facing my friend. I reach out and take her shaking left hand into my own. I look into her eyes and see my reflection there.

"He married my mama when she was young, too young... fifteen, I think. Then, he forced six children on her, one right after the other, two girls and four boys. My mama died giving birth to the seventh and within a few months my father found someone else to marry, my step-mother. I don't see how either woman could stand him. He'd go after anything in a skirt."

"Oh no," I say.

"That wasn't the half of it. He went after his own daughters. You know, that's just plain wrong. How can a father not know any better?" Teresa asked, looking directly at me.

I cover my mouth with my hand, and close my eyes. "I don't know," I whisper.

We sit there together in silence for a long time.

"Give me one of those tissues," Teresa finally says, pointing to the box of Kleenex on the dresser. I try to find my legs, but they don't want to work. My stomach is tied in knots. My head hurts. I let go of her hand and reach for the box. I hold it out to her.

Teresa pulls out one of the tissues and wipes her eyes. "You know, I didn't cry when he died, not one tear. I stood over his grave, spit on the dirt, and told him that I hoped he burned in Hell."

I'd never heard this story, not from Teresa, not from her family.

"I was the lucky one," Teresa said.

My eyes shot up. I couldn't imagine how she could be lucky. "What do you mean?" I ask.

"My little sister Darlene got pregnant by him."

"Oh no," I say, feeling the bile rise into my throat and burn. I jump out of the chair, open the door to Teresa's bathroom and heave the contents of my stomach into her toilet. I stay on my knees for what seems like hours, waiting for my head to clear, trying to figure out what I'll say to her, embarrassed by my reaction.

I come out with my head down. "I'm sorry," I say.

"Don't you apologize for that," she says. "I've lost my supper more than once over it. He was a monster." She holds her hand out to me and I sit back down.

"My step-mother treated Darlene like a dog after that, kept saying if she had kept her legs together, the boys down the road wouldn't have gotten her in trouble."

"Darlene didn't tell your step-mother about your father," I state.

"No, of course not. Neither of us said anything. We were too scared of him. He was mean, and an even meaner drunk. Sometimes, we thought maybe our step-mother knew, because of the way she looked at us and then at him, but if she did know, she didn't let on."

My voice drops, along with my eyes. "She should have protected you."

"I thought so too for a long time. Oh how I blamed that woman. Still do sometimes, but her life wasn't easy either, seven kids that weren't hers, four others that were, and a hateful man on top of it all. She had her own Hell."

"It wasn't easy for anyone," I say.

"Nope, sure wasn't. I always felt bad that I couldn't keep him away from my little sister, like I should have protected her. Then she got pregnant. They made her give the baby up you know. Strange thing was, she didn't want to, said she wanted someone who loved her just for her."

"I understand why you'd want to get away from home," I say.

Teresa takes a deep, shaky breath. Then she sighs. "Like I said, Jeffrey was my saving grace. He asked me to marry him after our third real date."

"And you said yes?" I ask.

"Nope, the thought scared me silly. I turned him down over and over again. But like I said, he was persistent. When I finally realized he wasn't going away, I sat him down and told him I wasn't pure. Men expected that when I was a girl, and I didn't want him to feel like he got saddled with damaged goods."

I look down at my hands in my lap, fingers intertwined, knuckles white. "What did he do?" I ask.

Teresa sits up straighter, her eyes shine. "He got fighting mad, that's what. He stomped around the room with his fists balled up. I'd had enough of that in my life. I stood up to leave. I was sad though, almost wished I'd lied, because I thought he was a good catch, but I had to tell him the truth. He caught up with me before I got out the door, grabbed my shoulders and turned me around. Then I got scared and started fighting him, telling him not to touch me, to leave me alone. He dropped his hands and apologized. I was breathing hard and glaring at him. Then he did something I didn't expect. He looked me right in my eyes and said, 'It wasn't your fault Tessa.'"

"He did?"

"Just like that, yes he did," Teresa says. Then, she raises her eyes and looks into mine. "You know, until today, Jeffrey was the only person I ever told about my father. After he passed away, the secret was going to die with me. That seemed like what I should do until today."

"You changed your mind." I say.

"Yes," she says. "Of course Darlene knew, but she would never talk about it. Poor thing, went from one man to another and finally drank herself to death. She held it all inside and let it kill her."

"Oh, I'm so sorry," I say.

"Everybody has to deal with things the best way they know how. I was blessed."

"Yes," I say. "Yes, we do have to deal with things the best way we know how."

I hear my name paged overhead. I look at my watch. "Oh my, I've let time slip away. I've got to run," I say.

"Sorry I kept you so long honey. You go do what you need to do. We'll talk more later. You come to see me anytime." Teresa smiles and hugs me with her good arm.

"Thank you," I say, opening the door to the hallway.

Sally passes me. "They've been paging you," she says. The smokers are waiting for you."

"I turn toward the patio, then, stop mid-stride and turn. I call to my co-worker. "Hey Sally—"

"Yeah?"

"If I take dining room duty for you, will you do smoke break for me?" I ask.

"Really?" she asks. "You'd do that for me? I hate dining room duty. "

I'd like to take credit for helping her out, but I don't.

"Nope," I say. "You're helping me out. It's my first step to quitting."

"You don't smoke." she says, confusion knitting her eyebrows.

"It's a long story," I say, smiling. "I'll get you the cigarette box. Where's the lunch menu?"

First Child

by Adrienne S Moody

Families were large when and where I grew up. On our block alone there were over one hundred children; I know this as my brother took the time to tally and announce it at dinner one evening. One hundred children. And it wasn't an overly long block either. Being a young girl needing extra money for expensive jeans and a typewriter, I had an abundance of job offers to babysit. It's what girls did. There wasn't any special course to take either. I knew about babies as my youngest sister was born ten years after me and so I was experienced about bottle-feeding and changing diapers. But looking after eight children proved to be a challenge and a life-changing experience.

The Johnston family lived across the street. They had eight kids and they all had names starting with the letter B. I suppose they figured it would make it easier to remember. I recall them lining up (the ones who could stand; three were infants) tallest to shortest for their spoonful of children's tonic. Blaine, Brent, Belinda, Blair and Brenda. Bobby, Bruce and Bryce were in various stages of infancy and required hands on care. I cleaned up the dinner dishes (no dishwasher), bathed a handful of the brood, changed diapers, and settled them into their beds. It was exhausting. I learned what motherhood was all about from this experience. I never saw romance or had any unrealistic notions about child rearing due to my hours of labor across the street.

I decided at a young age that I would be a journalist traveling to exotic countries and would leave motherhood to prissy women whose dream was to push baby strollers and wipe cereal off chins. I saw it as chained to a household where the work never ended and no one seemed to appreciate anything you did. I witnessed Mrs. Johnston arriving home after a Saturday spent shopping in the big city, looking haggard and beyond overwhelmed.

In my 20's my brothers married women who seemed ecstatic about their bulging tummies and beamed at these gurgling, drooling babies. Not for me, I decided and rolled my eyes at the news of another little bundle of trouble about to arrive and make me an Auntie to yet another infant capable of projectile vomiting.

I ignored the biological clock ticking and when it became so loud I couldn't bear it, I bought another animal. At that time, in my late twenties, I had three dogs and three cats. I talked to them like children. I cooked up concoctions for the dogs, feeling very maternal indeed. It pacified me for a while.

What changed my mind? Malcolm did. He was this little devilish cherub born to my eldest brother. He loved my dogs and I loved him. I didn't expect to; it just happened. I decided after he fell asleep on my lap in front of the campfire one summer evening, that I did want one of these. But, only one. And I'd do it only if I could have a boy like Malcolm.

I told my husband that I changed my mind. He was in agreement. And of course, as most women know, just because you decide you want a baby it doesn't mean you're going to be able to have one. We tried for over a year with no happy bouncing result. I was very sad and exasperated. I did everything the books told me to do. I took my temperature waiting for the magic egg to be released. I marked my dates on the calendar. If I was a day late, I went for a pregnancy test only to see that dreaded show of red in the process.

And then I had a dream.

I dreamed that a man in a lab coat motioned for me to come over to this table that looked like a maze. I crouched down beside him and he said to me, 'It's very difficult for the sperm to get through,' and I could see that. Little commas were trying to make it through and kept hitting a barrier. 'It will take a year before one of them does,' he said to me with a smile.

I woke with renewed hope. I put away the thermometer and much to the relief of my very patient husband, our sex life resumed a form of normalcy. I stopped marking red X's on the calendar. I lost track of my cycles. About a year later at my sister's wedding sitting next to my mother, I knew.

"I'm pregnant, Mom," I whispered to her and put my hand to my abdomen.

"What? Are you sure?" she whispered back unable to hide her excitement.

"I'm sure."

"Did you go to the doctor?"

"No. I don't have to. I know."

It was a glow that I felt, a flutter of wings inside of me. I felt life deeply within and there was nothing like it. Of course I went to the doctor and it was confirmed. At six months they wanted an ultrasound and while the technician studied the monitor I asked if she could tell the sex of the baby.

"Yes, I can. Do you want to know?" she asked.

"I already know. It's a boy, isn't it?"

"Yes. It is a boy."

And no, he's nothing at all like Malcolm.

He is as unique as we all are.

And he has taught me all about love as no one else ever has.

Pruning Old Growth
by M Dawn Thacker

The mock orange and lilacs have taken over the side yard. It's been ten years since their last pruning. I'm not diligent. My grandma took clippers to them yearly when she was living. Just after they bloomed, she pocketed her shears and snipped away the old growth. Every five years or so, she'd bring my grandpa into the task. He had the long wooden handled pruners that took extra muscle.

"Way down in there," grandma would say, pointing to the largest in diameter and hardest wood in the middle of the bush , "as close to the ground as you can get. If you don't get rid of that old growth, the new won't have room to mature."

When grandma died, six years to the day after my grandpa, she left behind a yard full of trees, bushes and flowers to carry on her legacy. Even though it was September, she had already mulched the ground under her plants to ensure survival during a bitterly cold winter.

I'll be fifty this year, and I'll bet my grandma never imagined me at this age. I remember when I was younger, thinking in terms of milestones in my life, things to look forward to, graduation from high school, college, marriage, and babies. I didn't think beyond those events because they all seemed so far away, like looking off in the distance where everything is tiny and details blend into the background. Thirty was across the mountain, and fifty was all the way to the next state.

Well, I've almost reached the state line now and I find myself stopping to look over my shoulder. Maybe that's how it's supposed to happen, look forward until you're fifty, then stop suddenly, turn back and search the past for answers. My childhood beckons me for a closer look.

It's not easy going back there. I remember pain, but I had a swing in the maple tree, and a sandbox too. I ate red raspberries, blackberries, and strawberries right off the vine. I played tag with my cousins, laid in the grass making pictures out of clouds, and I wished on shooting stars. Sometimes my wishes came true. I was hugged. I was loved.

So here I am, almost fifty, feeling myself slowly slipping into my grandmother's shoes. I separate the outer branches and reach to the center. I feel it. Little pieces crack, splinter, and break apart. I bring them out, one at a time, and examine the hard, rough exterior that covers the tight rings surrounding my first growth. I back out, work on the outer edges some more, then reach inside again to experience those memories all over again.

I bought my grandmother's house in '86, and live there now. I've been with the same man for thirty years. I've let the bushes in the side yard go too long between prunings. The task is almost overwhelming, but I open my clippers and cut one piece at a time. When my muscles are spent, I call on the man in my life to help me.

"Reach down in there just as far as you can to take out the old growth," I hear myself say. "New growth needs room to mature."

The End

Dearest Reader,

Thank you for reading our second volume. It was a year of stories, but the path does not end. We are only travelers.

Why does a writer write? This is a perplexing question. If only the answer was a simple, clear ideology. There are countless texts on linguistics and language development, books that detail the formation of language, its purpose, and what path we followed to "talk the way we talk". Is there a philosophy that describes our compulsion to pen words and leave them for others to see? Some people just have a propensity to leave a mark. The mere act of living tends to leave many scratches and tracks.

Writers, like wanderers on a beach, can affect by leaving symbols of their travel. Some markings are intended to affect, to record, and our ancestors scribed hieroglyphs and etchings, leaving messages about their habitat and perceptions. Our modern markings end up in books and halls, painted on signs, or tossed and waylaid with duty done, like footprints washing from the sand.

The writer affects using words. The writer can be read, interpreted, or cause an affect. The writer reaches from afar and leaves words for future readers. Plaques and messages are bolted to rockets spewing from earth throughout the galaxy. Pioneer, Pathfinder, Apollo---all carried a message, and they carry a hope to be read as evidence of our existence, our footprints.

In summary, writers write to affect, to be read, and because words fall off them like footprints.

If words are footprints, lead on!

-Readthisplease.com

Volume 2, Editions 7 - 12